WITHDRAWN

HARVARD LIBRARY

WITHDRAWN

AGAINST THE WIND

AGAINST THE WIND
THE MODERATE VOICE IN BAPTIST LIFE

Carl L. Kell

THE UNIVERSITY OF TENNESSEE PRESS / KNOXVILLE

Copyright © 2009 by The University of Tennessee Press / Knoxville.
All Rights Reserved. Manufactured in the United States of America.
First Edition.

The paper in this book meets the requirements of American National Standards Institute / National Information Standards Organization specification Z39.48-1992 (Permanence of Paper). It contains 30 percent post-consumer waste and is certified by the Forest Stewardship Council.

Library of Congress Cataloging-in-Publication Data

Kell, Carl L.
Against the wind: the moderate voice in Baptist life / Carl L. Kell. — 1st ed.
  p. cm.
  Includes bibliographical references and index.
  ISBN 978-1-57233-674-2 (hardcover)
  1. Southern Baptist Convention—History—20th century.
  2. Fundamentalism—United States—History—20th century.
  3. Church controversies—Southern Baptist Convention—History—20th century.
  4. Southern Baptist Convention—History—21st century.
  5. Fundamentalism—United States—History—21st century.
  6. Church controversies—Southern Baptist Convention—History—21st century.
  I. Title.

BX6462.3.K44 2009
286'.13209045—dc22
       2009010597

In memory of

Ralph T. Eubanks
A rhetorical scholar nonpareil, southern gentleman, and mentor

CONTENTS

Foreword I   ix
William E. Hull
Foreword II   xxvii
Bill Leonard

Preface   xxxiii
Acknowledgments   xliii
Author's Notebook   xlvii

Chapter 1. In the Beginning:
Voices of Salvation and Unity   1

Chapter 2. Sons of Thunder:
Voices of Revival and Renewal   15

Chapter 3. The Elliott Controversy and the Broadman
Controversy: Voices of Attack and Defense   27

Chapter 4. The Rise of Fundamentalism:
Voices of Affirmation and Apologia   47

Chapter 5. The Inerrancy Idea:
Voices of Truth and Silence   63

Chapter 6. Serving the Lord in a New World:
Voices of the Moderate Baptist   75

Chapter 7. Why I Am Still a Baptist:
Voices of Hope   81

Postscript: Southern Baptists in the Twenty-first Century   93
Duke K. McCall

Appendix I. Amazing Grace   103
Foy Valentine

Appendix II. Who Are Baptists? A Historical Perspective   111
Loyd Allen

Appendix III. Who Are Southern Baptists?   113
William E. Hull

Appendix IV. Why I Am Baptist: A Personal Perspective   119
Daniel Vestal

Appendix V. On Religious Liberty   125
Bruce Prescott

Appendix VI. Why I Am Still a Baptist:
A Virginia Pastor's Perspective   133
Joe Lewis

Appendix VII. A Summary History of the Conception, Development, and Publication of *The Broadman Bible Commentary*   141
Clifton J. Allen

Appendix VIII. The Story behind "One Song"   165
Pepper Choplin

Notes   177
Contributors   185
Index   189

FOREWORD I

WILLIAM E. HULL

The struggle for control of the Southern Baptist Convention (SBC), which was publicly launched in 1979 and decisively concluded in 1990, marked an unprecedented turning point in the history of the denomination. To reach for an adequate metaphor, this was no fierce storm like the many feuds for which the "Battling Baptists" have long been famous.[1] Rather, it resembled a tsunami caused by the shifting of tectonic plates deep beneath the surface of our common life, resulting in a tidal wave that quietly gained momentum until it crashed into our midst, leaving untold casualties in its wake. In less than a decade, before a new millennium could dawn, everything in the denomination was different: its priorities, its policies, and its personalities. To change the metaphor, a crowd that did not even believe in evolution had engineered a radical mutation in the denominational identity gene.

Moderates have offered many reasons for their banishment from SBC life, most of them based on lessons learned from hand-to-hand combat with their opponents.[2] While these accounts offer valuable insights, I am not sure that they go far enough in explaining why this controversy was so different from the many that the denomination survived without schism. In an effort to broaden an understanding of the dynamics at work in this dispute, I shall mention five factors at play in the wider context that may not have received the attention they deserve as contributors to the conflict.

A NEW MANAGERIAL ELITE

History weaves a seamless robe, but a story has to start somewhere, so let us begin in the mid-1950s. Freed at last from the constraints of World War II and the Korean War, American religion was booming, nowhere more so than in the SBC as symbolized by its "A Million More in Fifty-Four" campaign for Sunday School growth. Suddenly, everything was burgeoning too fast for the traditional denominational infrastructure to handle. Pioneer missionaries were entering new states at home and new nations abroad. Additional agencies were being established and existing programs expanded just as trusted prewar leaders were moving off the scene. Clearly a more adequate support system was needed to manage this runaway expansion.

A blue-ribbon group called the Committee to Study the Total Southern Baptist Program was assembled to address the problem. One of its early moves after being authorized in 1956 was to employ the national consulting firm of Booz, Allen, and Hamilton to provide "professional assistance . . . in the more detailed and technical aspects of the study."[3] By the time the committee submitted its findings in 1958 and the last of its recommendations were approved in 1959, the SBC and its agencies, without fully realizing it, had joined the managerial revolution that was sweeping the corporate culture of America. In a word, the agency heads were "professionalized." Their titles were inflated, usually from executive secretary-treasurer to president and chief executive officer. Their staffs were increased, often from an office secretary to a number of administrative and executive assistants. Their salaries and benefits kept pace with the growing size and elegant furnishings of their office suites.

Here it is important to emphasize than none of these changes were instituted in an effort at self-aggrandizement. Instead, it was simply assumed that the SBC power structure needed to abandon its simplistic homegrown ways in order to manage efficiently an increasingly complex bureaucracy. Far from being a grab for status, the recommendations of the management experts were accepted as a challenge for Southern Baptists to become as sophisticated in administering the Lord's affairs as corporate executives were in guiding their for-profit enterprises. Not only was there a sense of inevitability about the shift, but it was carried out with a minimum of pretentiousness. The more generous emoluments accorded to agency heads did not begin to rival those heaped on their counterparts in the business world. Despite a little grumbling about heavyhandedness as change worked its way through the ranks of agency employees, the SBC managerial revolution was launched with remarkably little opposition.[4] After all, its leaders were known and trusted and their enhanced role was but a tribute to the success that everyone would enjoy.

Worthy motives notwithstanding, one unintended consequence of this professionalizing of SBC agency leadership was to create a managerial elite that gradually lost touch with its grass-roots constituency. The very nature of any professional group is to become inbred and self-policing. Admittance is restricted to those with specialized training who meet prescribed standards. Outsiders who lack their credentials and cannot use their jargon are certainly not qualified to judge their effectiveness. To be sure, professionals remain keenly aware of their constituencies, increasingly seen as customers of the services they render, but the attitudes of the clientele are surveyed utilizing technical methodologies that only a few statistical specialists can understand and interpret. As SBC agencies began to move in this direction, they gradually created a top-down aristocracy of expertise, particularly in some of the seminaries, that became insensitive to the bottom-up democratic impulse lying at the heart of Baptist polity.[5]

It took several years for the new system to become self-perpetuating, but by the 1970s its vulnerabilities were becoming obvious. As the agencies became ever more professional in the way they did their work, many of the churches were moving in the opposite direction, becoming—for lack of a better word—more "populist" in the way they did their work. A few of the tall-steeple First Churches with highly educated clergy tried the professional model, but their strength was steadily waning. The growing churches threw out organizational charts, personnel manuals, and five-year strategic plans, depending more on innovative leadership in an unstructured environment to get the job done. Carefully devised denominational proposals began to be spurned, and soon the once-monolithic "Baptist program" was in tatters. A few agencies tried to make adjustments, but they were trapped by their elaborate internal processes and by the long tenure of their senior executives, which made it difficult for them to keep pace with the latest expectations of their constituencies.

Beyond the quickening pace of innovative changes in the churches lay two stubborn statistics that changed very little. First, most churches were small congregations of fewer than three hundred members located in economically stagnant or declining sections of the Deep South. In 1970, for example, 34,360 churches were affiliated with the SBC, 22,778 of them (66.3 percent) in open country or village settings and only 11,582 (33.7 percent) in cities of over twenty-five hundred population.[6] Even though the managerial elite of the SBC lived modestly compared to their counterparts in the business world, they could not avoid the widening gap between their working conditions and those of small church pastors, many of whom lived on subsistence wages and had no staff except for perhaps a part-time secretary and/or custodian. In professionalizing agency leadership, the SBC thought that it was getting more efficient techniques for administering its programs, but what it actually got was a corporate culture out of step with the dominant culture in the majority of its churches.

Second, the registration rules for voting status at annual sessions of the SBC were heavily weighted in favor of small church representation. Each cooperating church was automatically entitled to one messenger plus one additional messenger for every 250 members or $250 annual contribution up to a maximum of ten.[7] This meant that two or three country churches giving a thousand dollars to the Cooperative Program could outvote a much larger city church giving hundreds of thousands of dollars. When I explained how the system worked to the chairman of our finance committee, an astute accountant, he muttered with evident exasperation, "We don't get to vote our shares!" What I am suggesting here is that the demographics were right for a populist revolt. Which is exactly what Jerry Vines was encouraging when he extolled the mythical Billy Baptist who was confused by the latest theology from Germany and by programs designed using techniques from consulting firms such as Booz, Allen, and Hamilton.

But populist revolts had erupted periodically in SBC life only to subside, so why was this one different? In the past, peace had been restored by strong pastors who were also veteran denominational leaders: George W. Truett, Louie D. Newton, and Herschel H. Hobbs, to name a few. These men had profound rural roots which they retained as they ascended to top churches in Southern Baptist life, never losing the common touch. At the same time, they served for years on various SBC boards, often exerting more influence than the agency head. In 1946, the SBC began a more systematic rotation of board and committee assignments which, when combined with the managerial trends traced above, had the effect of further increasing the internal power of long-serving agency heads. When external trouble arose, however, these executives now found at their side not a highly esteemed pastor who could talk to the grass-roots in language they understood, but a board chairman who had served in that key position for only a year or two and was largely unknown to most Southern Baptists.

A New Climate of Fear

The 1950s were what one historian called "years of confidence."[8] The American dream seemed vindicated by the verdict of World War II. It was an orderly era in which people dressed carefully and went to church in droves. The "greatest generation" was busy launching the "baby boom" as an expression of optimism about the future. However, seeds of discontent were already growing beneath a placid surface of cheerful conformity, but traditional systems of authority were still sufficient to control their explosive potential.[9]

This presumption of continuing progress reached a climax in the Camelot years of the Kennedy presidency (1960–63) but was rudely shattered by a "decade of shocks" stretching from the assassination of John F. Kennedy to the resignation of Richard M. Nixon (1963–74).[10] Suddenly an encroaching chaos became part of everyday life: the slaying of Robert F. Kennedy and Martin Luther King Jr., the collapse of President Lyndon Johnson's Great Society and War on Poverty in the jungles of Vietnam, burning racial ghettos in cities such as Los Angeles and Detroit, civil rights advocates assaulted and arrested in droves, campus riots at elite universities from Berkeley to

Harvard, Cold War stalemate following nuclear confrontation in Cuba, a sexual revolution that undermined the traditional family, and a Watergate burglary that imperiled the U.S. presidency. Suffice it to say that the American dream was in utter disarray. A few avant-garde theologians found religion so impotent to combat these devastating developments that they pronounced God—at least the God we enjoyed so much in the 1950s—to be dead.[11]

The dominant reaction to this massive destabilization that seemed to assault our most cherished values was one of fear, a complex emotion compounded of frustration over unanticipated failures, fretfulness over an uncertain course of action, and foreboding that the worst was yet to come. It was not just the high rate of change that prompted an upsurge of anxiety in the 1960s, but the fact that most of these changes were unexpected, unwelcome, and seemingly uncontrollable. The South, in particular, permitted its fears to be exploited by those seeking to attract political support. This is well illustrated by the 1968 presidential campaign of George C. Wallace, whose strategy remarkably anticipated the dynamics of the SBC takeover.[12]

Running as an independent, the former governor of Alabama spoke to and for "the average man on the street": blue collar workers, small business operators, and farmers—the common people disdained by "all those over-educated ivory-tower folks with pointy heads looking down their noses at us." To those fearful of federal intrusiveness, he promised defiance at the schoolhouse door. To those fuming over Vietnam draft dodgers, he advocated a patriotism of victory at any cost, selecting as his running mate Gen. Curtis LeMay, who famously favored bombing the Communists back to the stone age. Whether it be the upsurge of immorality, the decline of the work ethic, or disrespect for authority, the antidote was the recovery of traditional morality. The Dixie crowds that roared at his rhetoric were predominantly Baptist. They helped Wallace carry the Deep South and forced Nixon to mimic his message to carry the Outer South. The first Southern Baptist vote on elitism versus populism had been cast—and the populists won hands down. Why? Because in a climate of fear most people want a scrappy fighter to defend them, not a sophisticated technocrat to enlighten them.

The most important consequence of this new mood for the SBC was that it reawakened a long-dormant fundamentalism that had been quietly gathering strength in a variety of churches, many of them Baptist. We know from the history of the movement in American Christianity that fundamentalism thrives on the kind of phobias that feed religious resentment. Emerging in the 1890s in response to fears of immigration, industrialization, and urbanization, which threatened a rurally based Protestant hegemony, it reasserted itself in the 1920s in response to fears that Prohibition would be repealed, Darwinian evolution would undermine the Bible, and a Roman Catholic would be elected as U.S. president. Right on schedule it reappeared in the

1960s in response to fears that legalizing abortion would cheapen the sanctity of life, that feminism would undermine the nuclear family, and that secularism would erode the spiritual foundations of the nation.

Resurgent fundamentalism was mediated to SBC life primarily through the ministry of Jerry Falwell,[13] pastor for more than fifty years (1956–2007) of the independent Thomas Road Baptist Church in Lynchburg, Virginia. Daily contact with his growing grass-roots congregation, which eventually came to number half the population of the city, provided abundant opportunities to sense the fears of a typical cross-section of ordinary working-class folk. While SBC agency heads were endlessly itinerating on Sundays to bring a "sugarstick sermon" to strangers then racing back to work at headquarters before there was time to get any reaction to what they had said, Falwell was hammering out a pulpit rhetoric for people who would listen to him week after week for a lifetime.

Because the threats to his congregation were national in scope and political in character, Falwell gradually abandoned his inherited fundamentalist tradition of preaching gospel sermons to the spiritual needs of individuals, especially after the Supreme Court ruling on abortion (*Roe v. Wade*, 1973). In its place he developed a clear, combative message that was explicitly pro-life, profamily, promoral, and pro-American. Three strategies were implemented to spread Falwell's influence far beyond his local church base. First, his ministry purchased a jet plane that permitted him to criss-cross the country speaking at hundreds of "I Love America" rallies. He often traveled 250,000 to 350,000 miles per year. Second, a political action coalition called the Moral Majority was recruited from fundamentalists, evangelicals, conservative Jews, Mormons, and Catholics to agitate for reform by judicial and legislative means. The movement was thought to have raised sixty-nine million dollars from six million people in a decade (1979–89). (3) Liberty University was established in 1971 to offer both residential and distance learning programs that would attract a national and international student body of future civic leaders. With ten thousand alumni and twenty thousand students by the time of his death, Falwell viewed the school as his most enduring legacy.

Because the Thomas Road Baptist Church never formally affiliated with the SBC, the significant role of its pastor in the controversy is seldom appreciated. Falwell was closely connected to every major leader of the insurgency. Jerry Vines was his closest ministerial friend and funeral eulogist. W. A. Criswell delivered the commencement address on three occasions at Liberty University, the only person to do so more than once. Paige Patterson was offered the school's presidency in 1991 when he found himself in difficulty at Criswell College. In the mid-1990s, a fourth of the school's trustees were prominent members of the SBC takeover group, several of whom sent their children to college there. At the time, Bailey Smith claimed that there were "more Southern Baptist ministerial students at Liberty than at any Southern Baptist schools."[14] Despite moderate complaints to the contrary, Falwell insisted that he had never been involved with the internal politics of the SBC, but he really did not need to bother because as long as he maintained a circle of friends such as these, his influence was assured.

Nevertheless, even from a distance, Falwell's contribution to the controversy was enormous. His greatest achievement was to redefine the core agenda of fundamentalism. The movement got its name from the title of twelve booklets published from 1910 to 1915 that emphasized reaching the lost and combating modernism. If SBC fundamentalists had stuck to that twofold agenda, they would not have capsized the Convention, because the laity did not really understand what modernism was all about or how it might subvert soul winning. But when Falwell subsumed those twin concerns under the overarching imperative of "bringing America back to God," he tapped into visceral fears of the laity, who knew exactly what he was talking about. Moreover, he showed pastors how to combine religion and politics in ways that were alien to the Baptist understanding of church-state separation, thereby thrusting them into a civic arena that had heretofore been the preserve of Roman Catholics and northern liberals. To say the least, things would never be the same again.

A New Political Alignment

The fundamentalist formula for reclaiming America that Falwell mediated to his SBC friends required a close partnership between preachers willing to fight in the public square and politicians willing to implement their agenda in government. But where could a mutually beneficial alliance be forged? The Democratic Party was immediately rejected as being in the grip of northern liberals. The conservatism of Barry Goldwater and Richard Nixon was more appealing, but both of these Republican candidates were tone deaf to the concerns of the Religious Right. George Wallace was an attractive alternative, his virulent racism notwithstanding, but as long as he ran as an independent he would be only a political spoiler, and even that role was soon denied him by a would-be assassin's bullet. And so the religious revolutionaries bided their time through the late 1960s and early 1970s, building their countercultural churches and waiting for an opportune moment to strike.

Timing is of the essence in executing a successful strategy, and in the late 1970s two developments that played perfectly into the hands of the Religious Right in general and SBC insurgents in particular coincided. The first was the emergence of Ronald Reagan on the national scene in his strong but unsuccessful bid to wrest the Republican nomination from sitting president

Gerald Ford in 1976. Once Ford lost that election to Jimmy Carter, Reagan quickly became both a frontrunner for the 1980 Republican nomination and a favorite of fundamentalist preachers looking for a political ally.

Once again Falwell was the key to SBC involvement. After Reagan sounded the right notes in addressing a National Religious Broadcasters Association meeting at what was then called Liberty Baptist College, Falwell agreed to meet with several of Reagan's key political operatives in May 1979 at a motel in Lynchburg. Included in the group was Eddie McAteer, national field director of the Conservative Caucus, close friend of Adrian Rogers, and member of Rogers's church in Memphis, who would organize the Religious Roundtable that September designed to involve Southern Baptists in Republican politics on behalf of "national moral issues." Once Reagan secured his party's nomination, the Roundtable sponsored a national affairs briefing on August 21–22, 1980, in Dallas which, as McAteer explained to the eighteen thousand gathered, was intended "not to endorse a political party or candidate, but to pledge allegiance to principles." Surrounded on the platform by W. A. Criswell, Adrian Rogers, Bailey Smith, Jimmy Draper, Paige Patterson, and Charles Stanley, plus Jerry Falwell and Pat Robertson for good measure, Reagan responded by remarking, "I know you can't endorse me because this is a non-partisan meeting . . . but I endorse you." Now the SBC takeover leaders had on their side a soon-to-be president of the United States.

Second, just as Reagan was adding the Religious Right to his political coalition, the South was becoming a competitive two-party region for the first time since the Civil War.[15] In the early 1950s, there was not a single Republican senator from the South (Strom Thurmond of South Carolina becoming the first Republican senator from the south by switching from the Dixiecrat Party in 1964) with only 2 Republican representatives out of 105 in the southern House delegation. Ironically, it was a southern president, Lyndon Johnson, who contributed most to the breakup of the Democratic "Solid South" by signing the Civil Rights Act of 1964 and the Voting Rights Act of 1965, by the liberal social-spending policies of his Great Society programs, and by his inability to win the Vietnam War. Nixon exploited growing Democratic discontent with his "Southern Strategy" in the landslide election of 1972, but it was Reagan who enabled Republicans to displace Democrats as the plurality party among southern white voters.

This historic shift played itself out predictably in SBC life beginning with the 1980 presidential campaign.[16] The challenger was a nominal non-resident member of a Disciples of Christ church whose religious participation was minimal at best, who had long struggled with family problems, and who had gravitated toward a neo-apocalyptic theology that was peripheral to Christian orthodoxy. The incumbent, by contrast, was a quintessential Southern Baptist moderate who actively taught Sunday school as a serious

Bible student, who went on mission trips building houses for the poor, and who faithfully attended church, even in Washington during his presidency. Then why did the Religious Right in general, and Southern Baptists in particular, reject President Carter so decisively almost as soon as he took office? Additionally, he accommodated the more liberal wing of his party led by the formidable Edward M. Kennedy while Reagan purged his party of moderate "Rockefeller Republicans." And finally, because he sought to downplay the Communist threat whereas Reagan later exacerbated it by describing the Soviet Union as an "evil empire." Because he sought input from those with alternative understandings of the family while Reagan championed the traditional view of family values.

By an amazing stroke of good fortune for SBC insurgents, the 1980 presidential election became a referendum on moderate versus militant leadership, Carter and Reagan being ideal to play those roles, and the moderate option was solidly trounced. The denominational militants could not have timed their takeover strategy better to coincide with the moment of greatest political opportunity. Once the needed partnership was sealed in victory, the increasing dominance of militants in the SBC paralleled almost exactly the growing strength of the Republican Party among southern white voters. For example, in 1988, when the SBC controversy had almost been won by the militants, George H. W. Bush got more votes in every southern state than Reagan received in 1980, even though Bush had been identified earlier with the moderate wing of the Republican Party. In 2004, when the denominational takeover was complete, George W. Bush—as quintessential a militant as Carter was a moderate—swept the South so completely that he carried more than 90 percent of the counties where whites are a majority of the population.

For years, at least since George W. Truett and J. M. Dawson, Baptists had tried to keep politics out of the denomination by stressing the doctrine of church-state separation. But, in the 1980s, the takeover leaders redefined the relationship as symbiotic, each sphere reinforcing the other. By deliberate design the takeover leaders worked to make the SBC a core constituency of the Republican Party in exchange for which the party would support the moral concerns of the SBC. The marriage proved so mutually beneficial that both sides continually worked to strengthen it.

To illustrate: Lacking a majority of the voters in its new southern white base, Republicans had to attract a small percentage of black and independent voters to carry the region. A serious problem in reaching either group was the party's poor civil rights record, compounded by the disastrous effects of Goldwater's approach to race relations in the 1964 campaign. The Religious Right understood this dilemma because it had a poor civil rights record of its own to overcome as the nation began to move beyond segregation. So it came up with a new list of urgent national concerns, civil rights and poverty not among them, that permitted the GOP to campaign vigorously for "morality" without ever addressing race. The Democrats had paid dearly to advance civil rights in the South, but this commendable achievement was suddenly made to seem insignificant when compared to the Republican goal of "reversing the tide of godless secularism engulfing America."

Partisan politics proved pivotal in what was billed as a theological controversy for at least two reasons. First, the mass media always ensure that political contention will saturate the American mind, especially as an election campaign nears its climax. For more than a year the presidential candidates are overexposed through endless stump speeches, talk shows, interviews, and formal debates. Hundreds of millions of dollars are spent to bombard voters with seductive advertising designed to secure their commitment to a particular ticket. By contrast, the SBC presidency is decided early in a two-day annual gathering based on a brief nominating speech backed by word-of-mouth campaigning without benefit of budget. It is true that what appears to be an informal process producing a spontaneous result can be manipulated behind the scenes to build support for a candidate among those in attendance, but the great majority of SBC members will have never seen or heard the winner or have any idea what issues were at stake in the outcome. This is only to say that partisan politics is vastly more influential than doctrinal disputes in shaping the Southern Baptist mindset.

The second reason why the secular political process proved so influential is that it was not all that secular. Candidates for public office do not talk about how they would actually govern if elected. Rather, they try to present a compelling case for how they would fulfill the nation's mission, achieve its highest vision, and be true to its core values. Which is exactly the agenda on which the Religious Right agreed with Reagan Republicans in forming their partnership. As a result, beginning in the 1980 presidential campaign, the religious message of the former began to coalesce with the political message of the latter. To put it rhetorically, Adrian Rogers and his successors running for president of the SBC and Ronald Reagan and his successors running for president of the United States learned to talk alike. This gave the SBC takeover group a huge advantage because they were able to ride the coattails—free of charge—of the most powerful decision-making process in American culture.

Politics has been called a barometer of the Zeitgeist; that is, it constantly takes the pulse of the national mood. By 1979, a frustrated United States was ready to consider moving in a completely new direction. The SBC, as the "Established Church of Dixie," a religious expression of the "southern way of life," could not avoid facing the same choice. If Jimmy Carter had convinced southern white voters that his moderate approach to presidential leadership was in their best interests, the denominational decision might have been different, but he was not able to do so. In my first pastorate during the early 1950s, I did not have a single church member who was openly Republican. Everybody was still a "yellow-dog Democrat." In my last pastorate during the late 1970s, I did not have a single church member who was an open supporter of Carter. In theory at least, such a sweeping political shift should have had no effect on the internal life of a religious movement such as the SBC, but those who clung to that theory were soon to be mugged by reality.

A New Loss of Momentum

To this point, we have seen that the 1955–65 decade was a time of growth, confidence, and optimism for the SBC and its primary regional constituency. By contrast, the 1965–75 decade was a time of decline, conflict, and disappointment that saw great expectations go unfulfilled. The pincer-like effect of these countertrends created conditions in 1975–85 that undermined moderate leadership in both political parties as well as in the denomination, opening the way for major changes to be pursued by the Religious Right as well as by Reagan Republicans. Having just surveyed the effect of these developments in the political sphere, let us look now at how those same trends were impacting the life of the churches.

During the 1955–65 decade, Southern Baptists adopted ambitious growth goals that committed them to numerical increase at a higher rate than in the past, such as the Thirty Thousand movement that would have doubled the number of churches and missions between 1956 and 1964. But by the mid-1960s, these goals were proving difficult if not impossible to reach. Regarding numerical increase, the SBC continued to report more members each year, but these gains were not enough to keep up with the growth of the general population. SBC membership as a percentage of southern whites of church-joining age peaked in 1960 and has declined ever since. For example, SBC membership rose from 9,732,000 in 1960 to 15,044,000 in 1990, which looks encouraging, but the percentage of Southern Baptists in the Deep South fell from 36 percent in 1960 to 31 percent in 1990. Regarding the rate of growth, SBC membership increased 34 percent during 1950–59 but only 9.6 percent in 1980–89. Just as Southern Baptists began looking upward in an expansionist mood, all of the trend lines started turning downward.

Translated locally, this meant that many churches were finding it much more difficult to grow. Studies reported that as many as 80 percent of SBC churches were "plateaued," a word used as a euphemism for stagnation. What happened to congregations when the vise of attrition began to tighten? Some churches tried to enlarge the prospect pool by lowering the acceptable age for membership, a few even dipping into the preschool years, but this strategy had obvious limits short of resorting to infant baptism. Others moved in the opposite direction by allowing the median age of the membership to increase, but this graying of the membership raised fears of "what will happen to our church when we are gone?" Either way, the money supply tightened because young children had no resources of their own and senior adults were moving into retirement on fixed income. Many churches that had erected new buildings and added staff in anticipation of rapid growth found themselves hard pressed to meet mortgage payments and payroll when these projections failed to materialize.

With this loss of momentum, church growth soon became the highest priority in congregational life, causing pastors to insist that the SBC furnish leadership in this area. After all, missions and evangelism had always been a dominant purpose of the denomination. Urgency was added to this agenda by the relentless numerical decline of mainline denominations such as Methodists, Presbyterians, and Episcopalians during the late 1960s and 1970s.[17] Unless the SBC did something different, it could share the same fate. In a search for solutions, Southern Baptists began to look outside their ranks for the first time, particularly at three groups that seemed to be successfully bucking the downward trend:

First, were the nonestablishment denominations, exclusivistic rather than ecumenical, that had stood aloof from the liberal trends of the 1950s and early 1960s such as Seventh-day Adventists, Nazarenes, Jehovah's Witnesses, and Mormons. These strict, authoritarian groups offered a simplistic, literalistic, absolutist faith of a kind that conservatives were seeking, and in contrast to their more effete upper crust cousins, they were growing like wildfire.[18]

Next, there were the independent or nondenominational descendants of fundamentalism, most of whom preferred to be called evangelicals. Setting out as an embattled minority in the 1950s and early 1960s, they soon challenged the religious status quo. With Billy Graham as their standard-bearer, Fuller Theological Seminary as their think tank, and the periodical *Christianity Today* as their sounding board, this movement also zoomed in popularity during the late 1960s and 1970s, even as the establishment denominations languished for lack of support.

Finally, the most market conscious of all were the media preachers who spawned a new phenomenon called the Electronic Church. In the early days, most of these celebrities were dismissed as "religious entertainers" until the *Wall Street Journal* took a hard look at their balance sheets and reported a booming industry in which, as far back as 1977, the "take" of the top six superstars was in excess of $250 million and rapidly growing. Those familiar with religious finances immediately recognized that here were corporate empires bigger than whole denominations, all of them solidly ensconced on the ideological Right.

Now for the key insight: Looking both at the decline of the mainline denominations positioned to the Left, and at the growth of freewheeling religious movements positioned to the Right, many Southern Baptists logically concluded that their future lay in following the strategy of the latter rather than the former. Add to this one other related factor: In those years, church growth experts were insisting that "homogeneous" groups grow much faster than heterogeneous groups simply because people like to be with their own kind.[19]

We have now isolated the two fundamental premises that those attempting a takeover of the SBC drew from their analysis of the American religious scene: (1) Success lay in positioning Southern Baptists as the only major denomination on the ideological Right so as to reach a forgotten majority with whom the mainline denominations had lost contact in their drift to the Left, and (2) such positioning would be effective only if all denominational agencies sent out a clear, consistent signal to the multitudes looking for a religion compatible with their ideological conservatism, and this could be done only by ridding the denomination of any employees not sympathetic with this orientation on the Right.

These assumptions were not just theoretical deductions made by observing trends in other denominations, however. The takeover group insisted, with pardonable pride, that their hypotheses had already been tested on the most crucial anvil of all, the local congregation, notably by W. A. Criswell of the First Baptist Church in Dallas, Texas. With unflagging zeal, this intrepid pastor had staked out a position on the far Right, refused to budge for four decades, invited those who differed with him to leave, and in the process grown by far the largest church in the denomination! Criswell became the patriarch of the takeover group because what he did in Dallas provided a microcosm of the changes that they sought throughout the Convention. Nor was Criswell the only exemplar of this strategy, just the most prominent. Advocates of his approach could also point to dramatic growth in churches led by younger pastors such as Adrian Rogers in Memphis, Homer Lindsey Jr. in Jacksonville, and Charles Stanley in Atlanta for confirmation that their strategy had produced the desired results.

A New Pastoral Insecurity

All of the trends sketched to this point converged to impact negatively the morale of many Southern Baptist pastors. The sprawling bureaucracies of SBC agencies seemed increasingly remote to those in smaller churches, causing some of them to refer to the headquarters city of Nashville as "the SBC Vatican." Deeply invested in the lives of their members, they listened every day to fears and frustrations provoked by social disorder that the churches seemed helpless to prevent or to remedy. For a few minutes on Sunday morning they tried to talk sense to a troubled congregation, only to have their words lost in the inflammatory harangues of demagogic politicians who dominated the mass media all week long. Their pulpit message might have had more clout if the church were growing, but the younger generation influenced by beatnik and hippie culture was dropping out of church, and attendance, if anything, was beginning to sag.

Make no mistake: 1965–75 was a tough time to be a successful pastor. You could sense it in shortened pastoral tenure as ministers moved from church to church searching in vain for a happy place to put down roots. Involuntary terminations steadily mounted, many of them exacerbated by racial turmoil not of the minister's making. The situation got so bad that the Baptist state papers began to editorialize on how to mediate internal disputes short of a public firing. Without bishops or judicatories to intervene in times of crisis, several state conventions established a full-time position in church-staff relations to deal with conflict resolution and placement problems. Lacking the protection of legal sanctions or even a mutually agreed upon code of ethics to follow when resolving personnel issues, few employees felt as vocationally vulnerable as pastors and church staff, especially in times of widespread unrest.

This sense of ministerial insecurity provided an excellent opportunity for the takeover group to win a strong following if they could somehow strengthen both the authority and the popularity of clergy in their churches. The support of this group would be invaluable because pastors and staff plus their spouses constituted the largest voting bloc of registered messengers at annual sessions of the SBC. Furthermore, the Southern Baptist Pastors Conference was by far the largest pre-Convention meeting held each year. Begun in 1935 on a strictly nonpartisan basis, its informal organizational structure made it easy to be taken over for political purposes. The program was little more than a preaching marathon, featuring many more fiery sermons than would be delivered at the Convention itself. In every way it provided a perfect staging area to build support for votes taken on the next day. When W. A. Criswell stood at the 1979 Pastors Conference in Houston to say, "We will have a great time here if for no other reason than to elect Adrian Rogers as president of the Southern Baptist Convention," he not only broke the tradition against former SBC presidents endorsing candidates, but also made clear to the eight thousand cheering pastors assembled before him that they were to be a key to that victory. (Rogers won with only 6,129 votes.)

But how did the takeover group secure such enthusiastic support from their fellow pastors? The key to bolstering a stronger sense of authority was to make "inerrancy" the battle cry of the insurgency, a term which they trumpeted to assert that every word of Scripture was "without error doctrinally, historically, scientifically, and philosophically." In other words, to preach the Bible correctly, which they insisted meant to preach it as "literally true," put one's message beyond challenge by grounding it in the eternal truth of God. Because of the prominence of this strategy, it is often supposed that the SBC controversy was essentially theological in nature, that its primary purpose was to establish the validity of biblical inerrancy and to rid the denomination of anyone who did not accept it. A closer look, however, suggests that this may not be the best way to understand the dynamics at work here.

A decade before the controversy erupted, there was a good bit of sound and fury on this subject leading up to the 1970 SBC meeting in Denver. Remembering how divisive the concept of inerrancy had been in the fundamentalist controversies of the 1890s and 1920s, I decided to preach an irenic sermon to our congregation explaining the issues and cautioning against claiming for the Bible what it does not claim for itself. Rather than get into debatable issues of interpretation, I encouraged my listeners to understand biblical inspiration in ways that would not be contradicted by three well-known facts: (1) We do not have any autographs, or original copies of the Bible, that are said to be inerrant and thus must depend upon reputable scholars to reconstruct the best text from existing manuscripts that continue to be discovered; (2) we still have much to learn about the meaning of the ancient Hebrew and Greek languages in which the Bible was written, which is why more accurate translations regularly appear; and (3) even when using a good translation of a good text, contradictory understandings of Scripture will result unless a sound methodology is consistently followed in interpreting its message.

The laypeople who heard the sermon were appreciative of my efforts to build a doctrine of Scripture squarely on the nature of the Bible as we have it. But when the sermon was printed in the official magazine of the SBC Executive Committee that went primarily to pastors, I was rewarded for my efforts with a filing cabinet full of hate mail. Immediately there were demands that I be fired for heresy, even though the contentions summarized above were obviously based, not on my faith but on the facts of the case available to anyone willing to learn them. In working through the outpouring of correspondence, I was amazed to find that no one, not even those who disagreed with me most violently, offered any correctives to the evidence I had presented or countered my position with any evidence of their own. Instead, it was as if they wanted simply to affirm inerrancy in a priori fashion as a self-evident truth and reject me because I did not do the same.

Nothing really changed once the inerrantists seized control of the SBC beginning in 1979. Since they had won what Harold Lindsell called "the battle for the Bible" on their own terms, one might suppose that they would use this mandate to study and settle the infallibility question as a top priority.

The relevant agenda was certainly well known to those on both sides of the debate, but not one item on that agenda ever received any serious attention even though the SBC had six large seminaries qualified to undertake such a task. No search was launched for the original autographs, no examination made of textual variants in the existing manuscripts, no task forces appointed to resolve historical or scientific discrepancies, no seminars convened to deal with theological or hermeneutical issues. Clearly the advocates of inerrancy wanted this complex theological issue decided not by a careful examination of the relevant evidence, but by a series of votes for president of the SBC.

Since those championing inerrancy refused to deal substantively with its meaning, the presidents of the six SBC seminaries decided to sponsor the Conference on Biblical Inerrancy in 1987, when the controversy was still raging and their institutions were under heavy fire. Leading scholars supportive of inerrancy were invited to give major addresses to which those on either side of the SBC debate responded.[20] This was to have been the first of three such conferences, but once the takeover group heard just how complicated and debatable the inerrancy agenda had become, they wanted no more of it and the two remaining conferences were never held. Lying behind that reaction was an increasingly sharp distinction being made by their leaders between scholarly inerrancy and grass-roots inerrancy. True to their populist instincts, they did not want the debate decided by experts—even world-renowned experts on their side—but by the convictions of common folk in the churches.

We are now ready to understand why their approach to inerrancy proved so appealing to many Southern Baptist pastors working under great stress. First, it sidestepped all of the technical questions about ancient manuscripts and languages which neither they nor their members knew enough to understand. Furthermore, it simply ignored troublesome questions of interpretation, such as what the Bible says about polygamy or murderous violence against helpless women and children in the name of God. Instead, inerrancy became a call to preach the Bible with absolute confidence. The syllogism was self-evident: (a) God, by definition, is perfect; (b) the Bible, by definition, is God's word; (c) therefore, the Bible is perfect. That being the case, any message based on the Bible has a divine authority that cannot be challenged. Such an understanding of inerrancy conferred the kind of pulpit clout that harassed preachers in the late 1960s and 1970s wanted to strengthen their ministry, never mind that exactly this same line of reasoning had been used by their forebears to defend slavery and prove that the earth was flat.

One problem with assigning unconditional authority to biblical preaching is that it tempts pastors to become authoritarian, thereby prompting a revolt of the laity. The inerrantists skillfully balanced the scales between pulpit and pew by insisting that grass-roots Christians had the right to determine their own views of the Bible rather than depending on the findings of an intellectual elite with technical expertise. On the SBC Peace Committee, for example, Adrian Rogers was adamant that SBC seminaries should build their professional staffs and faculties from those who clearly reflect whatever dominant convictions and beliefs are held by Southern Baptists at large. In other words, the people rather than the professionals have the final say in what the denomination is to believe. He and Jerry Vines liked to stress the point in extreme fashion by insisting that if Southern Baptists were to believe that pickles have souls, then the seminaries they support should teach just that.

As silly as it may sound, that oft-repeated slogan takes us to the heart of how inerrancy was actually being used in the SBC controversy. More than anything else, it was an effort to wrest control of what the Bible means from a handful of scholars with their endless technical problems to be solved and give it back to the churches where it would be preached passionately and believed on the basis of faith alone. The pastor would strongly influence the congregation by interpreting the Bible with authority, but the congregation would strongly influence the pastor by its response to that interpretation. Tenured scholars have lifetime job security needing only the approval of their peers, but pastors must continually win the lost and build them into a church or they will soon be without a job. The inerrantists wanted the meaning of the Bible and the theology built upon it to emerge, not from the seminar room, but from the dynamic interaction of pastor and people. They also wanted SBC seminaries to teach that understanding to their students.

The five factors we have surveyed were very different, yet they had one thing in common: All encouraged or even demanded systemic change. The times were out of joint. There was a sense of exhaustion with old remedies. Levels of destabilization and alienation were becoming toxic. Discontent had reached a tipping point where clinging to the old was viewed as a greater risk than trying something new. And so presuppositions were challenged, paradigms shifted, and loyalties were renegotiated. Slowly but surely everything began to change, whether it be culture, politics, ideology, or religion. Some even thought that modernity itself, which had characterized western civilization since the Enlightenment, was giving way to an as yet undefined postmodernism. It was simply impossible for a sprawling denomination as diverse and undisciplined as the SBC to escape being engulfed by this enormous ferment.

During the controversy and shortly thereafter, many viewed it only as an intramural conflict, a sort of self-contained family spat. Thus it was said that the takeover succeeded because Paige Patterson and Paul Pressler figured out how to control agency boards through the appointive powers of the SBC president, but hundreds of insiders had known how to do this for years. Or they said it succeeded because the victors bused in their partisans, who registered young children as messengers in order to use their ballots, but voting irregularities were of negligible consequence in determining the outcome of the struggle. Or it succeeded because the SBC had lost its homogeneity since allowing several state conventions in pioneer mission areas to affiliate, but diversity was sweeping the Old South as much or more than the rest of the nation. No, the SBC was going to change in response to pressures beyond its control, and the controversy would be decided by the ways in which the contestants read the signs of the times and negotiated the relentless tides of history that neither side could stay.

That being the case, the issue was never *whether* the SBC would change, but *who* would lead that change. When the crisis came, the moderates were so busy managing things that they were not mastering the wider context, whereas the militants, as outsiders, were forging new alliances with outside groups on the cutting edge of change. The moderates were so entrenched in their positions, as a result of long tenure or of grooming by their predecessors, that they showed little willingness to adapt either their message or their methods to the times, whereas the militants, with nothing to lose, were willing to strike out in bold new directions. Moderate leaders of SBC agencies each had a fiefdom to protect, which tended to make them competitive with one another, whereas the militant leadership was clearly defined and never broke ranks until victory was assured. All in all, it was a textbook case of the perils of incumbency and the passions of insurgency.

In the end, the militants won because militancy was the mood of a majority of the messengers for reasons summarized above. True to its democratic polity, which made no provision for protecting the rights of the minority, the SBC chose to pursue a course that resonated with the mindset of its regional constituency. With a mixture of theological idealism and political realism it decided to start what amounted to a new denomination—which is what it had done in 1845 when caught in the toils of slavery and secession. As Arthur Farnsley put it, "Even within communities of faith, democratic process trumps theology and scripture in time of crisis because the latter are subject to interpretation."[21] Which raises an intriguing question that only the future can answer. Already militant leaders are beginning to experience grass-roots backlash against their entrenched incumbency. As the heroes of the 1979–90 takeover pass from the scene, will their successors be any more flexible than moderate leaders were when the great shaping tides of history begin to run against them?

FOREWORD II

BILL LEONARD

In a sense, it seems unending, the infamous "controversy" that has gripped the Southern Baptist Convention for almost three decades. True enough, the conservatives dominate the Convention and most of the moderates have opted out, investing their energy in new Baptist groups, individual congregations, or entirely different denominations. Conservatives control the national denominational mechanism, the six seminaries, the mission and publishing agencies, and the public pronouncements of the Convention. But as Larry McSwain, professor at Mercer University's McAffee School of Theology, once noted, the controversy remains "unceasingly systemic," continuing to work its way through the old Southern Baptist networks of colleges and universities, state conventions, churches, and even families.

Two moderate-dominated Baptist state conventions—Texas and Virginia—have experienced full-fledged schisms, evident in the formation of a separate conservative-related convention organization in each state. Other state conventions—Georgia, South Carolina, and Florida—are solidly in conservative control, while North Carolina and Kentucky are headed for the conservative camp. Some Baptist-related universities, such as Furman, Wake Forest, Meredith, and Richmond, have ended their official Baptist affiliation, while others, such as Carson-Newman, Belmont, and Shorter College, continue to struggle with issues of doctrine, governance, and control. While some churches are clearly conservative and others decisively moderate, still others continue to divide over denominational funding, program, and identity. Many pastors and professors still walk a thin line between conservative and moderate factions in their churches, schools, and communities. As the controversy continues to work its way through the old SBC system, many of the protagonists seem stuck with one another, not really happy to be together, differing on issues of doctrine and praxis, but bound together by bygone loyalties, traditions, pension funds, giving plans, and institutional commitments that will not let them go.

And then there is the rhetoric. This book completes a three-volume exploration of the nature of rhetoric in the dynamics of SBC life, especially related to the divisions of the last three decades. These volumes are extremely important given the power of speech, particularly homiletics, to raise questions, define differences, motivate constituents, and blend biblical content with contemporary concerns. Rhetoric was at the heart of the conservative success in the early stages of the controversy, and these volumes have documented that reality with clarity and insight. Rhetoric linked biblical authority and biblical inerrancy with southern populism in profound ways that moderates were never really able (or willing) to confront effectively. By casting the controversy as a "takeover" movement rather than a theological dispute, and failing to confront the "slippery slope" of biblical inerrancy (that it actually undermines biblical authority, replaces the text with a theory about the text, and seeks to "domesticate" it), moderates were bound to fail.

During the last few years, however, the obsession with literalism has taken its toll on the rhetoric of Southern Baptist preachers. A new generation of Southern Baptist clergy and laity has grown up with little or no memory of the controversy and the reasons for the upheaval in the denomination. While unashamedly conservative, these young Southern Baptists are divided over Calvinism, the charismatic movement, denominational identity, postmodernism, church growth methods, and the aging leadership of the SBC itself. And while Southern Baptist leaders continue to press old agendas with old rhetoric, new forms of communication have moved beyond them. Old-time preachers, accustomed to awakening the faithful through the pulpit, were not ready for the Internet and its new rhetorical option: blogs. Indeed, conservative bloggers have challenged the leadership of the SBC on issues of denominational control, charismatic gifts, and the nature of the church.

New revelations from SBC leaders suggest that while the denomination remains the largest Protestant tradition in the United States, with more than sixteen million members in over forty thousand churches, baptismal and membership statistics are stagnant if not in an effective decline. Acknowledging disappointment with baptismal and membership growth, Southern Baptist preachers now criticize the denomination's commitments to evangelism and witness activities that once characterized the major work of the churches. The Convention's "culture dominance" in certain areas of the South remains but appears to be in decline.

Why? One reason may involve the nature of Southern Baptist rhetoric as perceived by the general public. As the SBC carried the full measure of its theological "course correction" into the American public square, the Convention continually addressed doctrines, values, politics, and morality beyond its own constituency and increasingly began to identify itself with one political party. These Baptists did not hesitate to speak out against the cultural and religious problems they saw in the larger society as well as in their own ranks. As their national reputation for moral rigor increased, they also confronted the dilemma of any group that engages in public rhetoric. To wit, they have had to learn that what appears to be the rhetoric of conviction in Baptist churches regarding salvation, abortion, women's roles, sexuality, public schools, Disney World, Jews, and the Bible may sound like bigotry or downright meanness when reported in *USA Today* or on CNN. For decades the SBC has reasserted its sectarian response to various issues in American culture, yet Southern Baptists themselves still seem shocked when persons turn away from their compassionate evangelistic efforts and seem hesitant to accept the gospel they proclaim.

This reality was evident as early as 1980, when SBC president and evangelist Bailey Smith declared at the Religious Roundtable that "God Almighty does not hear the prayer of a Jew," a statement still referenced by Jews across the United States when they think of the SBC. Smith had no doubt made that rhetorical declaration multiple times in old-time Baptist revival services across the South, but when it was broadcast on national television, many interpreted it as old-time bigotry and anti-Semitism. I shall never forget the response of my colleague Glenn Hinson, who in "An Open Letter to Bailey Smith" wrote, "Such is the stuff of which holocausts are made." As that rhetoric has continued in the public square for over two decades, many Americans have finally taken Southern Baptists at their word and held them accountable for what they have said about assorted individuals and groups in the culture. Rhetoric created the new SBC and has placed a stamp on it in the minds of many people who have chosen not to go near a denomination whose declarations may seem harsh, bigoted, and without compassion.

And what of the so-called moderates? As the exodus from the SBC accelerated, many clergy and laity faced a serious identity crisis: Can we be Baptist without being Southern Baptist? What makes us Baptists? How will we find ways to work together? The founding of new coalitions or the reconfiguration of older ones offered options that included the Alliance of Baptists, the Cooperative Baptist Fellowship, Baptists Committed, and certain state convention connections such as "Virginia Baptists" or "Texas Baptists." New divinity schools and seminaries were founded to cater to a new generation of ministers, many unfamiliar with the controversy.

Rhetorically, leaders of the moderate movement, many of whom worked hard to "retake" the SBC, were compelled to offer reasons for their departure and their desire to retain a distinctively Baptist identity. This remains a challenge, since many former Southern Baptists fear that the SBC has so "tainted" the name Baptist that it is no longer an option for moderates and liberals. For over a century, Baptist identity was inseparable from the rhetorical and programmatic approaches of the Southern Baptist Convention.

Many churches and individuals are unaccustomed to articulating their own sense of Baptistness other than that passed on to them by the denominationally generated rhetoric and systems. It remains a major challenge for many congregations. In fact, one is still struck by the way in which moderates who have long since jettisoned formal connections with the SBC continue to use its language to define who they are.

Moderate Baptists continue to experience opportunities and challenges related to the increase in women's voices increasingly present in pastoral and other leadership roles as well as in vocations that were in previous eras the almost exclusive domain of men. On one hand, moderate Baptists in the South have been ordaining women to the gospel ministry since the 1960s, and women have served extensively in staff positions in many if not most moderate-related churches. On the other hand, the role of senior pastor remains a predominantly male role in even the most "liberal" congregations. Thus, men and women in moderate Baptist churches continue to celebrate and struggle with a woman's "voice" in the pastoral office. Nonetheless, the importance of that voice impacts Baptist identity in significant ways, offering new models for young women and men, changing the nature of rhetoric in many congregations, and bringing women's ways of articulating the gospel into Baptist pulpits.

As moderates seek to move beyond the SBC, they are also compelled to confront the issue of race. Few if any moderate church-based gatherings are attended by persons of color, whatever their race. Moderate leaders surely know that finding ways to develop cooperative, even connectional, ministries with nonwhite communities of faith represents one of the great challenges and opportunities ahead. This is particularly important where the rhetoric of pulpit and piety are concerned. For example, preachers, young and old, have much to learn from the "African American pulpit" and the role of rhetoric in shaping the identity of African American churches in matters of faith and doctrine, justice and economics. Thus, moderate Baptists might find opportunity to participate in worship services in African American congregations beyond the occasional "pulpit exchange" and token preacher. Face-to-face dialogues on diverse approaches to ministry and spirituality have already begun but have a long way to go. Possibilities raised by the New Baptist Covenant conference, late January, early February 2008 and beyond may open the door to more collective endeavors. One can only hope.

Finally, in a strange way, conservative and moderate Baptists with implicit or explicit ties to the Southern Baptist Convention may discover that twenty-first-century transitions compel them to deal with many of the same ecclesial and global issues, even if they choose not to do it together. Both groups confront the following:

- An aging constituency, especially in some of their most prominent congregations
- A younger constituency with limited interest in denominational identity or old controversies
- Changing visions of the church set by megachurch, media-religion, cell-group, or emerging-church approaches
- Worship practices that are diverse at best, contradictory at worst
- Declining funds beyond the local church programs and the disappearance of "the tithing generation"
- New rhetorical forms that reflect "experimental" preaching, performance-based worship, self-help motivation, or prosperity gospel theology
- Diverse pastoral models, many shifting from the pastor as "sage on the stage" to the pastor as "guide on the side"

Thirty years into the SBC controversy, Baptists on both the Right and Left may be forced to admit that while they were fighting "the takeover" or making "course corrections," religious America set off in directions they had neither anticipated nor with which they can effectively compete.

PREFACE

Against the Wind marks the end of a thirty-year, three-book rhetorical/critical study of the extraordinary changes in the Southern Baptist Convention. At the beginning of the conservative/fundamentalist resurgence in the SBC (1970s), it was clear to me and to my coauthor, Ray Camp (North Carolina State University), that this phenomenon had real cultural and religious stamina, different from any other internal scuffle in this or any other denomination in the twentieth century. How little did we know. . . .

By the early 1980s, we were doing the work of rhetorical critics, examining sermons, texts, SBC literature, and any useful artifact that would provide context and perspective about the developing insurgency in Southern Baptist life. In point of fact, we were studying to become war correspondents. As for my role in the partnership, with a growing number of trips to the SBC Historical Society Library and Archives in Nashville, Tennessee, I was amassing a rich bibliography on an unfolding story. The SBC saga was a developing firestorm of church controversy, swept along by the swirling winds of cultural change. What was happening was a housecleaning of denominational, seminary, and church-agency leadership that would be ten years in the making (1980–90) and another ten years in its denouement (1990–2000).

In the academic marketplace of rhetorical/critical scholarship, particularly concerning the U.S. South, church and state have always shared a common critical spotlight. Far below the radar of national historical scholarship, the story of the SBC's gradual and steady turn to the right continued unabated. Save for 1980–81 SBC President Bailey Smith's claim that "God does not hear the prayer of a Jew," the SBC story was of little national interest. Even among southern historical and cultural critics, the escalating church struggle was dismissed as a "preacher boys' fight" at best and as a subject for occasional coffee talk at worst.

Assisted in the early research phase by the extraordinary talents of Ray Camp, I had a partner who "understood the signs and knew how to read the tea leaves" that appeared in the national sermonic rhetoric of SBC presidents and convention leaders. We correctly perceived the far-reaching implications of a developing national SBC agenda to "clear the temple" of liberals, pro-abortionists, seminary faculty who taught a non-inerrant Bible ("inerrant" means that the Bible is true—literally—word for word), and anyone else who got in their way.

Ray Camp and I wrote *In the Name of the Father: The Rhetoric of the New Southern Baptist Convention* (1999) as the first of three installments chronicling the rhetorical history of the new SBC. Honored with a 2000 National Book of the Year Award and individual awards as Communication Scholars of the Year in our respective states (Kentucky and North Carolina), we set about to prepare the second SBC book, *Exiled: Voices of the Southern Baptist Convention Holy War*. But a serious problem arose.

Ray Camp suffered a major stroke in early January 2000. Life changed overnight for the Camp family and for all of us directly and indirectly connected to an outstanding man and a superior rhetorical scholar. *Exiled* languished for a period of time but was reborn in mid-2000. After another five years (2000–2005), a long list of university press rejections, and a late-in-the-day connection with the University of Tennessee Press, *Exiled* was at last "between the boards" (a bookman's slang for a hardback/cloth edition).

With this book, we came down to the final question: How and from whence cometh the dispersed community of Southern Baptists now called *moderates?* Where are they headed and how will they get there?

It is the thesis of this book that the men and women of the Southern Baptist community who were attacked for their perceived liberality, for their failure to conform to fundamentalists' perspectives, and for their avowed dissent (publicly or privately) to Southern Baptist polity have their denominational roots in post–World War II church culture, particularly in the youth evangelism movement of the late 1940s and 1950s that served to swell the membership of the SBC. In later years, a number of factors led many Southern Baptists away from the denomination of their youth. I argue here that all of these factors serve as the drivers of current and ongoing changes in the denominational drifts of the SBC.

Contrary to current scholarship that suggests that there were no moderates prior to 1979–80, *Against the Wind* takes a different tack into the winds of change in Southern Baptist life. This book argues that there have *always* been "moderates" in Southern Baptist life, but previously there were no reasons to label them as such. These men and women were and will forever remain loyal to the Baptist *ideal* and to the rhetorical themes of freedom—Bible freedom, soul freedom, church freedom, and religious freedom. This book sustains the rhetorical themes of *freedom* in all of its forms as the highest frame of argument for the Southern Baptist moderate community.

Preface

As for the architecture of argument in the SBC, we offer the following graphic perspectives. First, in *In the Name of the Father,* Ray and I established three rhetorics of Southern Baptist life that framed the conservatives' arguments for cleansing the SBC of nonconformist Southern Baptists and for charting the future of the convention.[1]

Theory I: The Rhetoric of Fundamentalism

Rhetorical vision principles
- Jesus Christ is the Son of God
- Priesthood of believers
- Bible is literally true

Theory II: The Rhetoric of Inerrancy

Rhetorical vision principles
- Argument from definition
- "Bully pulpit"
- Bible is literally true

Theory III: The Rhetoric of Exclusion

Rhetorical vision principles
- Attack-expulsion paradigm
- Fear-comfort argument
- Liberal attack

Key Areas of Attack-Defense

Homosexuals
- Attack on fitness for life in Christ
- Denial of membership in SBC
- Expulsion of churches that openly accept them
- Ongoing attempts at salvation of souls and life-styles

Masons
- Attack on men who claim that Masons teach humanism and Christ as guides for life
- Specific attacks on Masonic teachings that diminish the role of the church

Liberals
- Full-scale attacks on any critical review of Scripture that denies a fundamental understanding of the Bible

Women
- Denial of leadership
- Scriptural proof tests
- Defense/denial
- "Repairs" persuasion of their proper place
- Attempts at harmony

Theory IV: Rhetorical vision

A free Southern Baptist can affirm the SBC dictum the "priesthood of the believer" as his or her victory over conservative Southern Baptist policies.

The master counterargument to victimage

is

freedom,

thus

the metaphors of freedom

As a free Southern Baptist, members are considered by the SBC as
- an *enemy*—cast as an *outsider* if they choose to defy SBC guidelines

As a free Southern Baptist, they speak of themselves as
- *grieving*—speaking of themselves as adrift from a familiar SB home that was beneficial and supportive at one time;
- a *war refugee*—speaking of themselves as adrift from a *place* to which they can no longer return; and
- an *expatriate*—speaking of themselves as seeking/finding a new place to worship and serve in a new life as a Southern Baptist outside the constraints of the Southern Baptist Convention.

In *Exiled,* I proposed the fourth of five critical theories, the Rhetoric of the Exiled, to serve as the platform for rhetorical expressions by the diaspora. In their exilic journey, displaced Southern Baptists spent considerable energy in explaining and bemoaning their outcast state, which this theory seeks to explain.[2]

In *Against the Wind,* the exiles' journeys are, in many substantive ways, behind them. The Rhetoric of Freedom, for the moderate Southern Baptist, serves as an architectonic model of persuasion that moves beyond the exilic rhetoric of an earlier time and celebrates the Baptist understanding of freedom—what Deweese calls the key to the Baptist genius. In this book I argue that the fifth rhetorical theory of SBC life is a proactive expression of the believer's security as a free man or woman with a free will—a free Baptist:

The Rhetoric of Freedom: Theory V
A Moderate Southern Baptist Manifesto

The Master Argument for Freedom
Is
All men are created in God's image

Thus:
- All can make personal, private judgments about faith.
- Accordingly, all can stand competent to make personal decisions about their salvation.
- All are free to worship personally and capable of a private interpretation of the Bible.
- All support human rights, gender equity, and equality in the church and the workplace.

Deweese pinpoints ten characteristics that add substance to the theory of the Rhetoric of Freedom as a practical and theological framework for sustaining a moderate's (centrist's, denominational loyalist's) identity as a Southern Baptist:

1. Baptists view Christ as Lord and the Bible as their sole written authority.
2. Baptists defend soul competency, liberty of conscience, the priesthood of all believers, religious freedom, church-state separation, and voluntary and personal confession of faith.
3. Baptists magnify the significance of the individual and of the believer's church.
4. Baptists insist on believer's baptism and a regenerate church membership.
5. Baptists urge that every church member should have a voice; put simply, one vote per Baptist in every business meeting serves as a great equalizer.

6. Baptists stand for noncreedal voluntarism in expressing and living out their faith and insist that such freedom demands moral responsibility.
7. Baptists build checks and balances into their polity by simultaneously exercising freedom, cooperation, and accountability.
8. Baptists emphasize the importance of a trained ministry, congregational worship, Bible-based preaching, Christian education, stewardship, evangelism and missions, and discipleship for all.
9. Baptists, when persecuted, tend to heighten their resolve.
10. Baptists take care of the needs of other Baptists, but they also minister to non-Baptists who both suffer human-rights violations and experience a wide range of other afflictions and disasters.[3]

Beyond the defensiveness of Southern Baptists living after exile, the Rhetoric of Freedom is a natural extension of the good news of the gospel. Embracing the legacy of historical Baptist principles, moderates can begin to move past the scars of the denominational struggle and reclaim their identity as Christians doing good in the world.

It may be argued that exiled Southern Baptists have had to make the difficult journey away from their former home to return to the roots of their Christian experience—freedom from a sinful life to freedom in Christ. So as to capture the nature of their journey, *Against the Wind* is thesis driven, more so than *In the Name* and *Exiled* combined. As a result, arguments and counterarguments are explored in these chapters that will neither please nor persuade all who read the book. Without question, this is the most challenging book of the trilogy. Now, at the end of the road that has lasted for three decades, there are more questions than answers.

Moderate Southern Baptists are a distinctive community of believers coexisting, uneasily, with their more conservative to fundamentalist fellow Southern Baptists. Indeed, moderates often find places of comfort in Methodist and Presbyterian communities, as well as in "new" Southern Baptist churches that have left the Southern Baptist Convention.

Baptist historian Bill Leonard suggests that current trends, both denominational and nondenominational, tend to clear the way for Southern Baptists who choose to leave their denomination:

- A declining identity for many religious denominations
- Denominations increasingly seen as one of many options for church
- Importance of parent body/convention minimized
- Nondenominational and seeker churches increasing[4]

There are many directions moderate Southern Baptists may take, but for one to sit still, pretending the takeover never happened (and if it did, it wasn't much to write home about), is out of the question. When all of the fallout is settled, it is or will be a surprise to all of them to see where they have landed. So, too, will be the answer to the question, What is the future for the moderate Southern Baptist? Time will tell. In the meantime, from whence do they come and whither are they going? These questions drive this study.

Indeed, the so-called moderate Southern Baptist is hard to find, and even more difficult to figure out. Save for the far extremes of the Southern Baptist continuum, moderates can be located, found, or surmised to belong to any number of denominational enterprises within and outside of Southern Baptist life. However, it is reasonable to argue that the easiest places to find moderates would be in the breakaway Southern Baptist organizations spread across the United States.

For example, one such breakaway group is the Cooperative Baptist Fellowship (CBF), headquartered in Atlanta, Georgia, which forms the largest population of moderate Southern Baptists. Performing their work in the manner of a denomination, but without the organizational nomenclature, the CBF is comprised of approximately nineteen hundred churches with approximately 500,000 members. Dwarfed by the Southern Baptist Convention's forty-thousand-plus churches, more than 16.2 million members, and worldwide network dedicated to missions, the CBF is a small alternative enterprise of Southern Baptists doing the work of the Church.

Next, Mainstream Baptist Network, a multistate-focused enterprise connected to Texas Baptist Committed, was funded by Houston food magnate John Baugh (now deceased). Led by David Currie, the San Angelo, Texas–based organization leads a continuing battle against fundamentalists' work in the state conventions, associational networks, and local churches.

Taken together, these two organizations serving the moderate Southern Baptist community account for approximately twenty-five hundred churches, one million church members, and an unknown number of Southern Baptists who financially sustain their state associations and freestanding religious enterprises (charitable local, state, national, and international organizations) that fall both inside and outside of the denominational agencies of the Southern Baptist Convention. There are unnumbered members and congregations throughout the Southern Baptist Convention who chose not to fight the inerrancy question as well as not to deny an individual's right to be silent about all of the matters in this most uncivil of church wars.

Against the Wind is, in many ways, a genealogical, cultural, and numerically difficult search for the communities of Southern Baptists who are labeled, rightly and wrongly, as moderate. No matter their willing or unwilling ownership of the term, Southern Baptists would never accept the archconservative Judge Paul Pressler's definition when he referred to a moderate as "a person who protects the teaching of liberal theology regardless of his or her personal theology."[5] Distancing themselves from conservative/fundamentalists, these moderates (or those unwilling to be labeled at all) would be uncomfortable with affirming the belief that the original text of the Bible was written by God in such a manner as to be free from error or mistakes, especially with the added rhetorical/political holy war's use of these arguments from inerrancy to overthrow the convention governance.

This book is a study of conflicting personal identities, struggles over cultural issues, and fundamental argumentation over who has the upper hand in defining who is a Southern Baptist in the twenty-first century. For many, it is a simple answer—the conservatives were victorious with their recovery/takeback of the Southern Baptist Convention, which was held too long by denominational leaders out of touch with the grass-roots membership. In a ten-year period (1980–90), the largest non-Catholic denomination in the United States was returned to its historic roots of Bible believing and inerrancy preaching, culminating in organizational realignment—a feat unmatched in American church history, as conservatives perceive the process.

For others, the civil/holy war was a bloodbath of broken relationships, destroyed church memberships, failed moderate political campaigns, and ultimate defeat at the hands of an army of accomplished pastor/rhetors at the national SBC meetings. Moderate clergy and laity, in state after state, association after association, and church after church, met the rhetorical champions of the conservative movement in open oratorical combat, losing at every turn of a biblical phrase and in the oratorical thunder of every argument. In point of fact, the battle for the Bible as God's inerrant word was over at the moment it started. Ray Camp, Ken Chafin, and I confirmed victory for the conservatives in *In the Name of the Father*. In *Exiled,* the tattered and battered remnant of Southern Baptists who were on the losing side of the struggle are represented by the thirty-one contributors, whose condition was chronicled by Samuel Hill Jr., the nation's preeminent scholar of southern religious history. In contrast with the essentially political character of the Southern Baptist constituency in the late twentieth century, it is proper to say that Southern Baptists were once "just Southern Baptists"—diverse, different, difficult, often cantankerous, seldom in common agreement, but nearly always hospitable. How times have changed:

Preface

It has been a challenging task to evaluate the rhetorical nature of the Southern Baptist controversy. The many sides of the arguments used to defend, attack, and revisit the conservative resurgence have come and gone for many people. Indeed, there continue to be rumblings and ruminations about where the SBC has been, and how it should or should not maintain its current course heading. In any modern business organization, there are moments in the company's history where a sea change has to occur or the company loses all of its momentum and market share. Often, there is no going back once the slide into mediocrity (or the spike into excellence) begins. Collateral damage is always to be expected and accounted for as part of an organization's overhaul, whether gradual or dramatic. So it is with the current situation in the SBC. For many moderates, the denomination's organizational structure and its company goals, mission, and vision statements have been compromised on every hand by the Convention's conservative/fundamentalist seminaries. Prior to the historic 1979 SBC convention in Houston, Texas, many conservatives thought that students in the Convention's six seminaries were graduating and entering the Baptist church clergy community with far too many real or imagined expansive views of Scripture and social issues. Simply put, many Southern Baptists viewed their friends and family who were seminary graduates as changed for the worse, not the better. In the past and for the present, the majority of small churches in the SBC (which make up approximately 60 percent of all SBC churches) may well prefer a Bible-college-educated pastor rather than a seminary-educated graduate. As one of my college social club (fraternity) brothers, later to become a leading figure in the takeover/takeback movement, said to me over coffee and pie at a 1980s late-night meeting, "You won't believe what the seminaries are teaching our preacher boys. It's scandalous!" I knew then that the battle for the SBC would be a lengthy campaign, and that it would not be pretty.

In the first decade of the twenty-first century, Southern Baptists on all sides are tired of the struggle for definition and the decision making over who they are and whither they are going. Southern Baptists just want to get on with the work of the church, believing that God will bless their efforts regardless of what kind of shingle hangs over the church door.

For all Southern Baptists, they understand that, true to his Deity, he will bless the work of His people. However, he may not be so gracious to the many on the battlefronts of the SBC holy war who have called on him for sanction and unction in His name. If the past three decades have taught me anything (and the work has taught me more than I can share in this book), it is that the Lord's blessings do not fall evenly on those who have used his name to justify course corrections in Convention life while leaving collaterally damaged people and churches in their wake.

Against the Wind is a metaphor for both sides in the SBC controversy—the outsider minority leadership's capture of the Southern Baptist castle as well as the current condition of the people and churches who have left their denominational home for a somewhat uncertain journey and an unclear future. In truth, there are no clear-cut winners in the Southern Baptist Convention holy war. The church and organizational leadership on both sides of the battle, along with their foot soldiers in the pulpits of Southern Baptist life, are set on parallel paths, each doing church in their style "in the name of the Father." The difference between those who live and work at One Lifeway Plaza in Nashville, Tennessee (the headquarters of the Southern Baptist Convention), and those represented by the label *moderate* is paper thin, yet rhetorically it is miles apart. For it is the rhetorical development of scriptural argument in His name that sets those not represented or particularly welcome at One Lifeway Plaza apart from their brothers and sisters in Christ.

It is to them—the displaced, the liberal, the moderate, the different—that this book is dedicated. As Samuel Hill Jr. noted in *Exiled,* "Once a Southern Baptist, always a Southern Baptist." However, like North Carolina's popular writer Thomas Wolfe, they "can't go home again." For in good days or bad, moderates will always be on a journey, far away from home. Listen now for the voices, voices of unity that became voices of diversity, misappropriated voices, voices of the so-called moderate, voices of salvation and support, turned now *Against the Wind.*

ACKNOWLEDGMENTS

Where do I start? Even more, where do I conclude expressing my appreciation to those who helped me study the Southern Baptist Convention? As good a start as any would be to hark back to my master's degree experience at the University of Arkansas in Fayetteville.

My mentor and inspiration, Dr. Ralph T. Eubanks (deceased), for whom I dedicate this volume, led me to appreciate—yea, fall in love with—the study of the American South, its rich history, and especially the rhetorical history of its proud people. From the ongoing rich memories of Eubanks's love of southern rhetoric in his courses to the connective vision of how I might continue his legacy, I was completely hooked on what rhetorical/historical study might seduce my soul.

At the University of Kansas, I majored in rhetoric and public address and American history with a southern exposure when the siren's song struck my ear. There, in a southern history course, I studied William J. Freehling's *Prelude to Civil War: The Nullification Crisis in South Carolina, 1816–1836* and read in its narrative bibliography (I had never seen one of those), "It is a scandal of South Carolina historiography that there is no full-scale study of the fabulous James Hamilton, Jr." I set out in my dissertation to correct such an oversight and connect this South Carolina figure to Eubanks's love for the Old South. My acknowledgment goes to the memory of Ralph Eubanks, who shaped and focused my research agenda on the American South and its orator icons, both historical and contemporary.

As a Southern Baptist and a rhetorical historian, I had always tried to keep these areas of my life separate from each other, as anyone might do with his or her life and occupation. I was not schooled in Baptist polity and practice, even though I had attended a Southern Baptist college (Ouachita Baptist College [now University] in Arkadelphia, Arkansas) and was active in Baptist churches then and now.

Then the 1980 Southern Baptist Convention made national headlines such as no other denominational event had ever done before. For me, "all of the stars aligned" in an instant. Here was a southern enterprise steeped in the arts of oratory now imploding with various types of Baptists in civil strife one with one another. At the center of it all were these master questions: Who is God? What is the Bible? Is the Bible literally true, word for word? The scholar's challenge was too good to be true—the coming civil war in Southern Baptist life was going to be waged in the pulpits of the South. This war had "legs," and "voices." It would be a long struggle for argumentative, theoretical, and religious advantage in which the oral tradition would rule supreme.

Starting in the early 1980s, I began visiting the Southern Baptist Historical Library and Archives in Nashville, Tennessee. There I learned to follow my instincts, especially when my general search began to mesh easily with the archives' videography. I quickly learned to trust the suggestions of Bill Sumners, director; Taffey Hall, archivist; Kathy Sylvest; and Jean Forbis, all valuable staff at the Library and Archives. Over the years, they became friends, confidants, mentors, and guides to the use of those resources. I owe them a debt of gratitude for years of excellent customer service.

I have been fortunate to have many of the important Southern Baptist figures of the twentieth century (and now the twenty-first century) agree to write for me. I remain indebted to these men and women who agreed to tell their stories. From Ken Chafin to Bill Leonard, William E. Hull, Duke K. McCall, James Dunn, Carolyn Crumpler, Cecil Sherman, and Paul Simmons—all luminaries in the pantheon of Southern Baptists—to the people of the pew who told their stories in *Exiled* (Eleanor Williamson, Wayne Bartee, Gladys Lewis, George Steincross, Frank Kendall, Gregory Hancock, W. H. Crouch, Pascal Hovis, and twenty-one other contributors), they have enriched my research beyond all measure. Again, I owe more than a debt of gratitude to these faithful contributors from the pew, the pulpit, and the academy.

Resources and release time, spread over years of research and writing, have been granted so that I might tell the rhetorical/historical story of the takeover (takeback) of the Southern Baptist Convention. My acknowledgment and gratitude go to Dr. Phillip Myers, director of the Office of Sponsored Programs at Western Kentucky University, for his office's continued and substantial financial support. It is not an overstatement to claim that neither *Exiled* nor *Against the Wind* would have been completed were it not for the support of the Office of Sponsored Programs, Western Kentucky University. I owe more than a debt of gratitude for their continuous support spanning a decade.

In the thirty years that I have researched and written about the Southern Baptist question (early on with Ray Camp of North Carolina State University for *In the Name of the Father*), there have been several leaders in the Department of Communication at WKU who have sustained and encouraged my work. Currently, Sally J. Ray, the former department head, has encouraged the process of the last two books in the Southern Baptist series, *Exiled* and *Against the Wind*. I have been enriched by her daily support of my work.

In these times of "show and tell" and "what have you done for me lately?" the second person (after Dr. Ray) whom I have kept updated on the progress of my work has been Dean David Lee of the Potter College of Arts and Letters at WKU. Dean Lee has been, and remains, a boon friend and academic colleague whose support and respect is ever a delight. I thank Dean Lee for his unfailing good spirit and charm.

For someone as dependent on the pen and yellow pad as this writer, it is critical to have qualified typing and word-processing support. I am especially indebted to Laura Wagoner of the Department of Communication at Western Kentucky University for her comprehensive skills at transcribing the written word into the manuscript's earliest drafts.

Beyond the basics, for the editing, polish, deep research, fact checking, and construction of a manuscript, I would be beyond help without the incomparable Zee Evelsizer of the Provost's Office at WKU. For *Exiled,* Zee was an invaluable resource. For *Against the Wind,* Zee is the reason for its acceptability. I accept all of the blame for this book's errors and misjudgments.

Finally, I owe more than can be expressed to my wife, Mary Anne. For all of these years she has provided all the support a husband-writer could possibly need. When words were wrong and ideas wrong-headed, she set thoughts and analysis on the right road. In truth, all of my work is dedicated to her. By acknowledging the aforementioned men and women, I salute them all. By acknowledging Mary Anne, these research entries on the shelves of Southern Baptist history serve as a tribute to her—the woman of my life and the best person I have ever met in my life. Amen.

AUTHOR'S NOTEBOOK

During approximately thirty years of researching and writing about the changes in the Southern Baptist Convention, I have been blessed with essays contributed by the finest scholars, writers, and teachers of Southern Baptist history.

In *In the Name of the Father: The Rhetoric of the New Southern Baptist Convention* (Southern Illinois University Press, 1999), the renowned opponent of fundamentalism Dr. Kenneth Chafin (deceased) wrote an incisive, biting analysis of the takeover of the SBC. His first sentence, "The thesis of this book is true—and it saddens me," foreshadowed a first-person analysis from the battlefield that remains second to none to the present day.

In *Exiled: Voices of the Southern Baptist Convention Holy War* (University of Tennessee Press, 2006), two of Southern Baptists' best and brightest, Carolyn Crumpler and James Dunn, provided lengthy first-person retrospectives on their public and private experiences of exile from the SBC. Additionally, Samuel S. Hill traced the swirling story of Baptists in the South as they mixed and mingled with other Protestant denominations. In the context of continuity and change, Southern Baptists were moving at light speed, leaving the middle-of-the-road Southern Baptist moderates to become strangers in their own home. Life, as Southern Baptists had come to know it, would never be the same again.

In *Against the Wind: The Moderate Voice in Baptist Life,* three additional figures in the pantheon of Southern Baptist scholars lend their voices to the developing story of Southern Baptists. First, William E. Hull (research professor at Samford University in Birmingham, Alabama) leads the reader through an overarching analysis of the business, cultural, theological, social, and personal issues that produced the Southern Baptist controversy.

Second, Bill J. Leonard, former dean of the Divinity School and professor of church history at Wake Forest University in Winston-Salem, North Carolina, offers an analysis of conservatives and moderates as each side squared off in rhetorical warfare. Leonard concludes that each group faces a daunting series of tasks to minister to a twenty-first-century postmodern culture.

Finally, words cannot fully express my appreciation for the third and final contributor's essay that serves as a fitting climax to the numerous voices who have contributed to the rhetorical/historical analysis of the takeover of the Southern Baptist Convention. Duke K. McCall is the most prominent Southern Baptist of the twentieth century. You will find Dr. McCall's clarity of analysis and accuracy of argument as compelling as it is insightful. He looks to Southern Baptists and their collective futures in the twenty-first century as a prelude to an as yet unwritten projection of where Southern Baptist conservatives and moderates will find themselves in the years to come.

For now, we examine the issues at hand—the untold story of the exiles of the Southern Baptist Convention and their loosely connected status as so-called moderates. In the coming chapters, you will read what went wrong and what went right on the road away from the siren songs of Babylon and on the way to Zion.

CHAPTER 1

IN THE BEGINNING
VOICES OF SALVATION AND UNITY

From the beginning of the Southern Baptist Convention (1845) to the present day, there have been divergent views as to what it means to be a Southern Baptist. In terms of preparation for the ministry, Southern Baptists have differed over being "God-called" or being "an educated man of God," more often preferring the former rather than the latter.

Moreover, Southern Baptists in the pew have differed over the nature of Scripture: Is it true, word-for-word inerrant, or is the Bible open to critical evaluation? Finally, there is a continuing search for who and/or what God is, who is Jesus Christ, and who is the Holy Spirit. There are as many perspectives and varied answers to all of these pressing questions as there are groups and subgroups of Southern Baptists. More often than not, the answers to these questions are found in the pulpits of the churches of the Southern Baptist Convention, expounded by seminary/college-trained pastors as well as non-seminary-trained pastors, alike serving as the conduits of knowledge about the nature of the Deity and the holy purposes of the denomination.

It was dissension over these aforementioned issues of faith and practice that led the conservative/fundamentalist silent majority to question the leadership, policies, and practices of the SBC's seminaries to such an extent that worlds collapsed and the nation's largest Protestant denomination was brought to heel by an increasingly vocal minority. As has been well documented and extensively covered from every conceivable angle, the Paige Patterson–Paul Pressler team helped to steer the ship of state—the Southern Baptist Convention—onto a rightward course in 1980 that has a current heading of conservative fundamentalism set on cruise control.

Change of any kind, whether a slight shift or a sea change, doesn't come easily. The dramatic, Convention-altering upheaval generated by the Convention presidents from 1980 to 2006 has resulted in a leaner, organizationally focused, and mature Southern Baptist Convention leadership at the national level. Fueled by the superior oratorical skills of successive presidents during these past twenty-six years and counting, the SBC has solidified its base, consolidated its financial house, and embarked on new and bold initiatives to expand and engage the Kingdom of God for a lost world.

Along the paths taken by conservatives and moderates, there have been untold winners and losers—those who have lost in the battle over who is the real Southern Baptist and on what rhetorical ground they take their stand. In particular, those Southern Baptists who have lost the most (such as those who told their stories in *Exiled*) are the most interesting to study. Southern Baptists who have left the Convention have the greatest rhetorical distance to travel as they explain, excuse, spread blame, or obfuscate the reasons for their defeat, along with their difficult decision to stay in their local church or search for a new church inside or outside the Southern Baptist Convention.

In particular, when Southern Baptists have spoken out or postured against the Southern Baptist Convention, the debate has turned on the nature of the Bible, the objectionable and suspect faculty at the six Southern Baptist Convention theological seminaries, the marriage standard of one man–one woman, and the role of women in the Convention. Now on the outside looking in, moderates in the SBC, losers at every turn to thwart the takeover plan, are scattered all over the national church landscape. It is fair to say that most moderates are as biblically conservative as any fundamentalist. However, moderates appear to be more critically sensitive than conservatives to the variety of ways to understand the Bible. Whatever the nature of their exilic journey away from the Southern Baptist Convention, today's moderate Southern Baptists are no more "moderate" or "middle of the road" than the conservatives/fundamentalists are of one mind and one voice.

Whether moderate or conservative/fundamentalist, the idea of who is the true Southern Baptist has served as a surveyor's plumb line between the suburban/downtown church and the old/new church in small-town America. The Annual Church Profile (ACP) published by LifeWay Christian Resources (of the Southern Baptist Convention) confirms that approximately twenty-six thousand of the SBC's forty-four-thousand-plus churches have an attendance of fewer than 125 people.[1] By implication, the pastors of these churches (many having also another part-time or full-time job) are probably the lone paid staff member. It can be argued that most of these pastors probably have little if any college and/or seminary training, although many may be currently engaged in some form of continuing education.

By extension of the argument from circumstance, it seems reasonable to assume that these churches and their pastors are generally conservative to fundamentalist in matters of church polity and theology. Unfortunately, one of the shortcomings of *Against the Wind* centers on the nearly impossible quantifiability of the public and private theology of these twenty-six thousand small churches and the remaining seventeen thousand larger churches in the Southern Baptist Convention. To somewhat ease the academic uncertainty of who's who in the Southern Baptist census, the scholarly community is fortunate to have a twenty-year-old comprehensive study to use as a stackpole for the demographic/sociological measurement of the Southern Baptist Convention that can help to answer some of these troubling questions.

In 1990, Nancy T. Ammerman's *Baptist Battles: Social Changes and Religious Conflicts in the Southern Baptist Convention* documented the groupings of members in Southern Baptist churches in the mid- to late 1980s. Among the charts and tables that reported the findings of her team, Ammerman estimates that the 1990 membership of Southern Baptist churches breaks down into four groups:

20 percent—Fundamentalists
58 percent—Conservative
21 percent—Moderate
1 percent—Liberal[2]

Figure 1, the same as on Ammerman's figure 1.1, "Beliefs and Identity in the Southern Baptist Convention," displays the generalities and subtleties of the Southern Baptist community.[3]

Ammerman concludes that there are several distinctives in the Southern Baptist Convention (c. 1990) that bear understanding:

- People with fundamentalist beliefs preferred to be called conservative by a two-to-one margin.
- Half of those who rejected fundamentalist beliefs chose to be called conservative. People who chose the conservative label represent the entire theological spectrum of the denomination. The label "conservative" appears to be what is expected of Southern Baptists, no matter one's theology.
- To call oneself "fundamentalist" seems to represent a position in *defiance* of cooperation over purity [emphasis mine].
- To call oneself "moderate" carries political and theological implications.
- Moderates stand as a loosely formed coalition against the fundamentalist direction and leadership in the Convention.

Figure 1.1. Beliefs and Identity in the Southern Baptist Convention

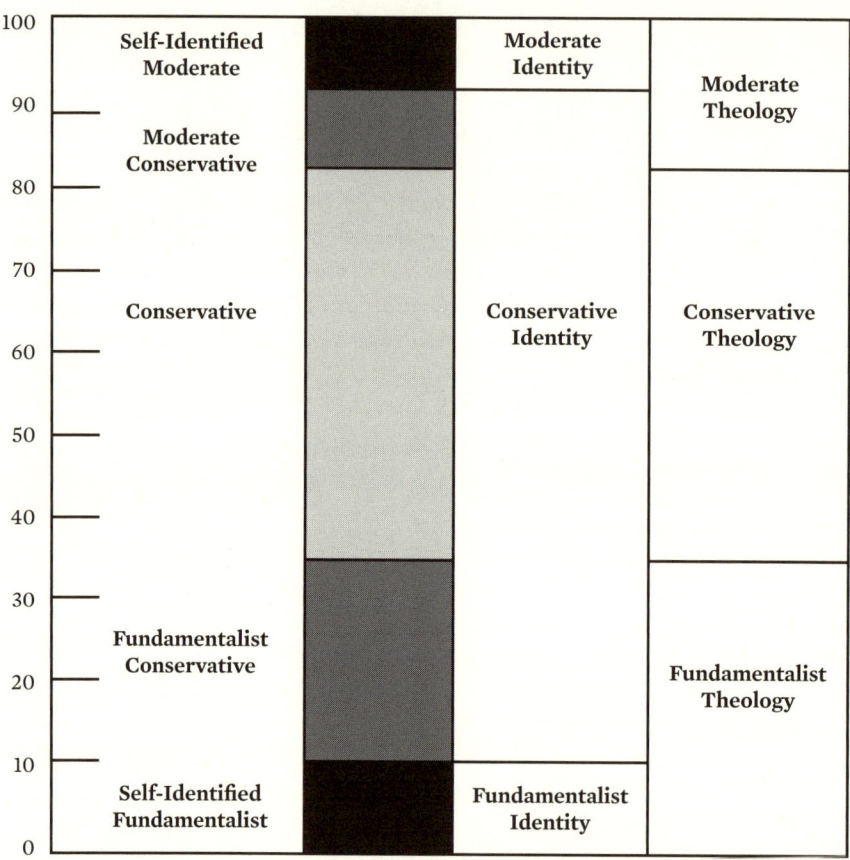

Ammerman's team of researchers outlines the full range of Southern Baptist belief and self-definition in 1990:

> *Self-identified fundamentalists.* Eleven percent held strong fundamentalist beliefs and identified themselves by that term. Super-church pastors, the members of the Baptist Faith and Message Fellowship, and most of the movement leadership belong here, even if they have learned for public relations' sake not to use the term fundamentalist.

Fundamentalist conservatives. Twenty-two percent held strong fundamentalist beliefs, but chose some other term to describe themselves—most often conservative. Men like Richard Jackson and Winfred Moore may belong here. They are inerrantists in theology, but strongly identify with the denomination.

Conservatives. Fifty percent held conservative beliefs and most often choose to call themselves that. Denominational statesman Herschel Hobbs perhaps belongs here. While quite conservative in theology, he is not in full agreement with fundamentalists; and he is fully committed to the conservative denomination he has always known.

Moderate conservatives. Eight percent held moderate beliefs, rejecting most of the fundamentalist way of understanding scripture—but they still chose to call themselves conservative. Much of the denominational establishment could probably be placed in this category. They refused to concede the label "conservative" to people they sometimes saw as "radical" in their departure from Baptist traditions.

Self-identified moderates. Nine percent held moderate beliefs and called themselves moderates. People like (then) Texas pastor Cecil Sherman or (former) Seminary President Roy Honeycutt might be placed in this category. They did not share the fundamentalists' beliefs about the bible, and they did not hesitate to say that they thought the fundamentalist way of doing things was wrong.[4]

Self-identified fundamentalists believe that the Bible contains everything God wants us to know, insisting that Genesis is a "how and when account" of God's return. Self-identified moderates reject, to a high percentage, that one should understand a literal reading of Genesis as well as the extended claim of scriptural inerrancy for the modern versions of the Bible. Moreover, the self-identified fundamentalists preferred the strict constructionist version of the Bible, while the self-identified moderates preferred the Revised Standard or New English versions of the Bible.[5]

In other areas, fundamentalists and moderates differed widely, especially in cultural matters and educational attainment. Again, Ammerman's researchers are instructive:

1. The left wing of the SBC is predominantly middle and upper-middle class, with all that those labels may imply.
2. The right wing of the SBC is constituted of the less privileged in social class.[6]

While such distinctions don't cover everyone in either class, the range of social class issues speaks volumes concerning the differences between Southern Baptist fundamentalists and the Southern Baptist (moderate) ruling class prior to the fateful 1980 SBC presidential election of Adrian Rogers.

As for a seminary education, Ammerman notes that the higher the general level of education, the more likely new and/or large urban churches expected their pastors to be full-time professionals with a "union card"—the Th.D. or Ph.D. from a Southern Baptist seminary. The learned nature of a seminary education—that is, the acquisition of biblical languages and a felicity with various historical/critical methods for studying Scripture—seemed to frame what it meant to be an authentic Baptist. It is no small wonder that seminary graduates tended to favor moderate perspectives on life and Scripture. In sum, people who attended church-related schools (and a seminary) were *twice* as likely to call themselves moderate. What laity and professionals learned in school and/or seminary, respectively, made fundamentalism increasingly unattractive to each group.[7]

Additionally, urbanization serves as another plumb line between moderates and conservatives. Ammerman concludes that people who grew up in the suburbs and small cities were likely to have a moderate theology, while those who grew up in small communities and/or the country tended to be conservative in theology. People who grew up in the city and remained there were likely to identify themselves as moderates. Moreover, siblings who stayed in a city environment maintained a moderate perspective.

In terms of urbanization and its impact in modern times, Ammerman and her team of researchers sustain the argument that people who moved from the farm to the city were most susceptible to fundamentalist rhetoric.[8] As for the rigors of social change, relocation, diverse surroundings, and so on, some Southern Baptists stayed especially "old school" southern in their denominational disposition, while others adapted and adjusted to new ways of doing church Southern Baptist style.

At the end of the day, the voices of middle-class Southern Baptists were to be found in the moderate camp as those who enjoyed the variety of social diversity in their communities while remaining fiercely loyal to the Southern Baptist Convention. The social culture and the church culture for moderate Southern Baptists informed their understanding of how to do church and what they found acceptable sermonic treatments of Scripture. On the matters of theology and education, the scales of denominational leadership tipped in favor of the moderate leadership and laity, who had been educated in Baptist schools and/or seminaries. Moderates were clearly the insiders in the denomination prior to 1980. The same cannot be said in the early twenty-first century.

As for the present day, with the fundamentalist leadership and laity in charge of the Southern Baptist Convention's infrastructure (especially the six seminaries), the theological soup consists of new and different ingredients and radically different proportions. Without question, the world of scholarship regarding the Southern Baptist Convention and all of the non-aligned moderate enterprises begs for a new study along similar lines and the depth of scale of Ammerman's *Baptist Battles*. While we may have a numerical scorecard of who and how many belong to what organization from the 1990 Ammerman study, Southern Baptists remain as divided as ever today on the issues of the Baptist identity. Available scholarship offers no update of the beliefs and identity of Southern Baptists in the 2010s.

In the days of black and white television, a popular show called *What's My Line* arrayed three contestants, all of whom claimed to be a "worm farmer" or some other exotic occupation. A panel of celebrities asked questions to see if they could figure out which one of the three was the real worm farmer. At the end of the allotted time period, each panelist had to make a choice and explain why he or she believed the contestant they chose was the real person. More often than not, the majority of the panelists picked the wrong contestant.

Were all manner of moderates and fundamentalists on a similar television program today, *all* of the contestants would stand when the moderator asked, "Would the *real* Southern Baptist please stand up?" In point of fact, all would have a legitimate claim to the label "Southern Baptist," at least in their own minds.

Of the three imaginary contestants, Southern Baptist scholar Greg Wills might argue that the conservative contestant who stands in response to the moderator's question believes that "the true Baptist tradition consists in maintaining the New Testament faith and practice."[9] (The moderate standing next to him or her would most likely claim the same rhetorical stance). Furthermore, Wills might well argue that the moderate in the threesome would uphold individual freedom as the central Baptist commitment (the progressive and conservative standing on either side of the moderate would say much the same for themselves).[10] Who is to say which Southern Baptist, which true, authentic Southern Baptist, should remain standing with his or her integrity as the only credential while the remaining two contestants reluctantly sit down? In the ongoing debate about who can lay claim to the imprimatur of Southern Baptist, "a lost and dying world" (a phrase often heard from the pulpits of the SBC) moves on unfettered in a society on the go, awash in modern views of life and culture.

Voices of salvation and unity have always dominated the cultural landscape for Southern Baptists. Before there was a so-called holy war over the Bible, culture, and the leadership of the Convention, there was the wooden pulpit, the sacred half-hour (11:30 a.m. to noon), and the decisional nature of the orator-pastor who spoke directly to the educated and the uneducated alike about their soul and God's eternity.

Since 1845, Southern Baptists have not experienced a normative liturgy, nor a hierarchical church structure like that of Methodists, Presbyterians, Episcopalians, and others. Mostly culturally impoverished, Southern Baptists have been biblically simplistic and wanted, even demanded from their pastor, a rhetorical style that "stepped on toes." The persuasive strategy of every Sunday morning service was to deliver a pastor's "experience" that illustrated real-life connections to the Bible. The post–World War II sermonic persuasion was particularly crafted to be decisional—one must renew, rededicate, or convert before he or she left the meeting room. Always focused on delivery, the pastor's "reward" was the catharsis he and the Lord jointly created in the minds of his congregation. The dross of one's life, accumulated from the previous week, was to be purged so each worshiper could start new, fresh, and emptied of self for the week ahead.

The 1950s to 1970s were a period of extraordinary change, growth, and promise for the Southern Baptist Convention. For the first time, new rhetorical themes of interest were catching the attention of the laity, for example, pastoral counseling for newlyweds, established couples, and single adults. With the advent of the 1965 Civil Rights Act, Southern Baptist laity were becoming more aware of a changing world. Southern Baptists were becoming more mobile, moving from place to place and job to job, all the time becoming an omelet of people whose world experience was becoming more complex.

The churches were not immune to the cultural currents affecting American society in general. A number of troubling issues invaded Southern Baptist churches in and around the Vietnam War era, including *Roe v. Wade*; the sexual revolution, epitomized by *Playboy* magazine; and the slow decay of American life (in the eyes of many culture critics).

Well documented in numerous scholarly and popular publications, the over-the-banks floodwaters of popular culture (music, movies, magazines, left-wing radicals, the black power movement, women's liberation and so on) buffeted the church incessantly at every door, window, and foundation. In response, the church offered "fire insurance"—a life saved from the pits of hell. But few churches had sufficient flood insurance to thwart a raging torrent of new cultural ideas.

During these twenty years, a quartet of Southern Baptist pastors flourished as a counterbalance to the richness of the developing popular culture, carving out for themselves a place to deliver God's Word in difficult times. Jerry Vines, Charles Stanley, Ed McAteer, and Adrian Rogers fused the Word of God to the word of the Republic in the Reagan years so as to turn the Democratic Party–vested Southern Baptist Convention and southern states into a Republican-dominated Southern Baptist Convention. What was once a wall of separation between Southern Baptists and the federal government now became a marriage made in Memphis, Tennessee; Atlanta, Georgia; and Washington, D.C. For approximately thirty years, from the late 1950s to the 1980s, the dual themes of salvation and unity were drowned out by a cacophony of voices both outside the church (popular culture) and inside the church (the partnership of God and country) to bind together politics and religion.

By contrast, the moderate-to-liberal voice in Southern Baptist life demonstrated a willingness to listen to and sustain certain persuasive themes in the period leading up to the 1970s–1980s which still remain salient today:

1. A deep commitment to the support of religious freedom. In simple terms, "Keep the Church out of politics, and keep politics out of the Church."
2. An openness and acceptance of any public and/or private spiritual expression. One's expression of faith is his or hers alone; no one should disrespect spiritual behavior.
3. A deep sense of humanism, that is, we are free men and women in God's kingdom who are led to do social good, sustaining support for worthy social issues and social justice.

In sum, the moderate and liberal participants in Southern Baptist life saw themselves as living a life in God's way—a life of doing good and righting wrong.

When contrasted with their conservative/fundamentalist brothers and sisters, the moderates/liberals in Southern Baptist life measured against one another in decidedly different ways. The rhetorical/sermonic core of the conservative and moderate camps sustained three contrasting arguments, each side doing so in proactive, positive language (see Table 3).

While expressive of individual differences, these persuasive theme and countertheme differences between so-called fundamentalists and moderates were just that—themes. Moderate leader Cecil Sherman confirmed that "there was no moderate *movement* prior to 1980" (emphasis added).[11] Sherman should know, for he was among the early architects of the moderate movement. With moderates spread across the Southern Baptist congregational landscape then (pre-1980) and now, it is difficult to decide which side of the aisle to sit on. For conservatives/fundamentalists, the decision is a foregone conclusion. For moderates, they were to find their place in a seat near the back door of the church.

Table 1. Rhetorical Perspectives

Conservative	Moderate
1. Declare the absolute authority of the Bible.	1. The Bible speaks for itself; it can stand intense critical scrutiny.
2. Moderates are "progressives, have few convictions."	2. Moderates sustain their religious freedom.
3. Conservatives are true to Scripture, inerrantists to the core.	3. The liberty of their own conscience with respect to biblical truth is their defense against popular culture and key to their understanding of the Bible.

We have located the moderate Southern Baptist in varying positions along the denominational compass. By contrast, the conservative/fundamentalist Southern Baptists are relatively easy to locate on that compass. The conservative voice is singular and clear. The moderate voice is multifaceted, multilayered, and at times discordant and apologetic. In *Exiled: Voices of the Southern Baptist Convention Holy War,* both well-known and lesser-known Southern Baptists told their stories of an exilic journey. All of these contributors, each in their own voice and in their own way, are or have been members of Southern Baptist churches. Who they are as Southern Baptists may well defy labels and description. What they are against—the fundamentalist theology that drove them and other men and women out of positions of participation and leadership—is clear and nonnegotiable.

The moderate perspective and accompanying voice, argument, and defense of position did not erupt from the late 1970s Paige Patterson/Paul Pressler–directed campaign to win the presidency of the SBC. Rather, a four-generation succession of denominational loyalists who were supporters of their local church; graduates of public, private, and Baptist colleges; and families devoted to the Southern Baptist way of church would gradually come to be known as moderate Southern Baptists.

It may well be said that "once upon a time in America, Southern Baptists were just Southern Baptists." Stretched across the states of the old Confederacy, the post–World War II Baptist churches were peopled by members not so much different from the current communities of Southern Baptists. To be sure, there were cultural and demographic differences between the small churches and their larger counterparts in midtown locations, but all Southern Baptists shared a common litany of faith and practice.

As identified by Ammerman in *Baptist Battles,* both conservative and moderate Southern Baptists would agree to the following imperatives:

1. The sole authority for faith and practice among Baptists is Jesus Christ.
2. Baptists cherish and defend religious liberty.
3. Baptists defend the priesthood of the believer and the individual's soul competency before God.

The 1925, 1963, and 2000 Baptist Faith and Message statements affirmed by the Southern Baptist Convention have progressively outlined, in greater detail, the nature of things scriptural and life as it is to be practiced by Baptist Christians. Most notable is the injunction by the SBC that the "earlier 1925 and 1963 renditions are outdated and obsolete."

For it is in the 2000 Baptist Faith and Message, Section VII, that the committee states that "while both men and women are gifted for service in the church, the office of pastor is limited to men as qualified by Scripture." Kell and Camp offered an extended display of counterarguments in "An Apologetic for Ordaining Women in Ministry" from *In the Name of the Father* that draws from an equally substantive set of Scriptures to defend the contrary position that women *are* qualified for the office of pastor (and deacon).[12]

In the final analysis, it is fair to say that the 1990 Ammerman sociological study provides a predictable picture of so-called moderates and conservatives/fundamentalists in the 2010s. What is even more predictable is that there are an increasing percentage of conservatives who embrace the basic tenets of Southern Baptist fundamentalism.

But what of the moderate community and their perspectives? Speculation may lead one to conclude that the 10 percent moderate and 10 percent conservative/moderate factions of the Ammerman study have slipped in their numbers, whereas the 22 percent fundamentalist-conservatives and 11 percent fundamentalists have increased in their numbers. Indeed, a ruling class tends to draw in marginal participants just because they are in power. The suspected numbers slippage does not mean that moderates have lost some of their voice and argument, nor have they lost their platform. Rather, over time, the rhetorical/architectural structure of the moderate position has solidified and affirmed a rhetorical theory and practice for the Southern Baptist moderate community, no matter the size, demographics, numbers of churches, or the organizational home of their Southern Baptist loyalties.

Moderates in the Southern Baptist Convention were and are part of the membership, before and since 1980. Many of these men and women remain denominational loyalists, committed to Kingdom growth and to church development. They are anxious to learn more about Baptist polity and theology. They are vested in their local church as well as with the possibility of "doing church" that improves their community. But, for untold numbers of Baptists, all of the issues and concerns changed in Houston, Texas, when the 1979 Southern Baptist Convention morphed from a religious gathering into a political arena. Life for many Southern Baptists would never be the same again.

In this book, I define and explain the rhetorical history of the moderate voice in Southern Baptist life. In these chapters, I examine the various origins of the moderate community, the causes they sustain, the persuasive strategies they employ and respond to, and the places where they stand with respect to Southern Baptist life. It is my position that Southern Baptist moderates have always championed a Rhetoric of Freedom as the master argument from which all logical, emotional, and scriptural themes flow, and that they have done so for decades. For moderate Southern Baptists, religious freedom is the sine qua non of their spiritual existence. They just never expected to have to defend their personal liberty—their soul competency—against the ultimate litmus test: "Do you believe the Bible as inerrant and infallible?" For moderates who find themselves on the wrong side of the argument, it never occurred to them that an answer to such a question would/could land them on one side of a debate they never expected to join. For moderates, and for all Southern Baptists for that matter, it was the God-man Jesus Christ to whom they owed allegiance, not the Bible. When Southern Baptist moderates were made to choose one over the other, the Lord Jesus Christ won the argument every time.

The so-called moderate's answer to the above question of the day marks him or her as a liberal—an unthinkable label for an urban, suburban, or country resident in the demographic and geographic South in the early twenty-first century. Stuck with such a mark, current-day moderate Southern Baptists find themselves on the outside looking in, confused, hurt, and abandoned by the denomination that was as dear to them as family. In truth, the SBC *was* family, a cohort that had rejected its own on the grounds of argument by definition: "If you don't accept the Bible as inerrant and infallible, you are not an authentic Southern Baptist."

To state that such an expulsion mattered to all would be inaccurate and misleading. To say that many Southern Baptists were stung deeply would be accurate and alarming. At the end of the day, Southern Baptists who cared little for "the preacher boys' fight," Southern Baptists who were inerrantists but cared little for the national fight for those beliefs, and Southern Baptists who just wanted all of this "mess" to go away—all would be labeled moderates or at least as sympathizers of the idea.

Southern Baptists who felt the sting of the term "moderate" knew that they wanted nothing to do with it, but could not hide the welt after the sting was gone. Saddled with the term, moderate Southern Baptists found themselves stuck with it. They could fight the negativity of the word, champion its varied, proactive potential, pretend that the problem would go away, give up and find a new church home, or locate a friendly Southern Baptist alternative church. Or they could do the unthinkable—move to a new denomination. As one might suspect, many chose to find a compatible Southern Baptist congregation. Whatever their choice of a fresh, new church start, few gave any serious consideration to their undiscovered heritage as moderate Southern Baptists.

Indeed, moderates did not "spring forth whole from Zeus's head." The Southern Baptist community called moderates can trace their heritage from many wellsprings in the confluences of church history. Good and compelling arguments can be brought to bear that explain from whence came the "authentic traditional Southern Baptists" (as moderates now call themselves) of the early twenty-first century. This book affirms a time in recent Southern Baptist history when stakeholders of the past, many still alive and active, became the heroes and martyrs of the Baptist cause. Keepers of the Southern Baptist flame in their developing years, these men and women became the captains of the Baptist ship of state in their adult years. Denominational loyalists all, the first generation of moderate Southern Baptists (a label none would have embraced at the time) came to the throne of grace as youth revivalists and, later, as leaders in SBC life.

It is to their story that we now turn. At Baylor University in Waco, Texas, in the late 1940s, young, untrained college students rode "the wind of God" as the first generation of moderate Southern Baptists of the twentieth century.

CHAPTER 2

SONS OF THUNDER
VOICES OF REVIVAL AND RENEWAL

Some four generations ago, a cadre of young men and women, students at Baylor University in the mid-1940s to early 1950s, began a Youth Revival movement that served, unknowingly and unwittingly, as the forerunner of the present-day moderate Southern Baptist community. Tom Corts, the former president of Samford University in Birmingham, Alabama, hosting a "Revival Revisited" reunion of some of these former Baylor students in 1999, stated that "during the time the youth revival movement swept across the South and the Southwest, it was an instrument for changing lives and destinies. Almost incredible. To this point, incomparable."[1]

Gathering together young men and women who preached, witnessed, led fellowships, and taught the Bible, the Baylor University youth phenomenon spread across the country, igniting a mid-twentieth-century revival spirit that seems now, in the early twenty-first century, all but gone. Former Baylor youth revivalist Bruce McIver's history of the youth revival movement, *Riding the Wind of God,* captures the spirit and rhetorical fury of the young men who ignited revival fires from coast to coast. McIver chronicles the stories of young Baylor men and women who were becoming Southern Baptists, becoming "preacher boys," becoming part of a "new thing," and becoming organizers of a spirited movement such as the country had never before seen.

In the mid-1940s and early 1950s, these sons of thunder at Baylor University preached new life and mercy to young men and women coming home from an awful war "over there." McIver's winsome narrative of these men and women reveals high energy and great expectations, with salvation and rededication by the armful. The youth-led revival period at Baylor was a wonderful rhetorical "Beulah Land" of oratory, hymns, prayer, aftershave, clean suits, spotless shirts, and polished two-tone shoes. Life in Christ's plan was sweet, and the Kingdom was added to daily, from sawdust trail to grassfield revival tents, in local Southern Baptist churches in Texas and throughout the South.

For example, McIver relates how in 1946 in Waco, four thousand people met nightly for days, resulting in five hundred public commitments to Christ.[2] Scores of young men and women, with little or no training in preaching and religious organization, preached salvation and Christian commitment for months that turned into years in the late 1940s to early 1950s.

Every organization, whether business or religious, requires leadership and the acumen to direct a successful enterprise if it is to prosper. A legendary figure in Texas Baptist colleges, W. F. Howard, was just such a man. Howard was director for campus and vocation religious activities for thirty thousand Baptist and Baptist-preference students in Texas Baptist colleges during this time. Howard produced a wide-ranging series of training sessions and print materials to assure the highest standards of uniformity in business practices, church-revival polity, and ethical behavior by the youth revival workers.

The following letter to all Youth Revival workers summarizes the "best practices" of church/clergy/revivalist personnel as presented in 1947:

> Let me think out loud with you for a moment or two. I am jotting down impressions that have come to me. I know you will take them in the usual fine spirit:
>
> 1. You will want to try harder than ever to make every host pastor feel that he is *still the pastor* of the church even though a Youth Revival team has moved in to lead the campaign. If every worker will seek to magnify the pastor in private conferences and in public services, great good will result. I say this even when the pastor seems to be unpopular with his people or when he seems definitely "off the beam" from your point of view. The membership may not be sold on the pastor every time, but they will appreciate your thoughtfulness and Christian ethics. I know you will watch this carefully—along with the many "little things" that mean so much.
> 2. I have been asked by some of you about dating during a revival campaign. I believe you will find it the safest policy to avoid dating boys and girls in the towns where you are working. Perhaps this seems a bit conservative or even extremely cautious, but I am basing my conclusions upon the

reactions of adult leaders in some of the churches where revivals have been held. This certainly does not imply that association with the local young people in fellowship and service is to be avoided. You will be the judge about these matters. I know you will not do anything that will allow hurtful criticism. There is too much a stake.
3. In reporting your travel expense to the local church up to $15.00, include meals and other essential expenses incurred en route. Some have inquired about this.
4. I am grateful for the results reported to date: 157 conversions in 8 revivals. The Lord is blessing your efforts.
5. I am thankful, too, for your spirit because the local folks will remember your spirit long after they forget your songs and sermons.

Your friend,
W. F. Howard[3]

The young men who were instrumental in the movement had no fully developed theology. Personal theologies and denominational careers were to come later in their adult lives. In point of fact, these students at Baylor were somewhat nondenominational in outlook—they were Christ-centered and salvation-preaching. There was virtually no Baptist theology or polity in their sermons, because they had minimal Baptist heritage. As to their denominational linkage to early-twenty-first-century "moderate Southern Baptists," no *direct* tie can be substantiated. Yet as adults, many of these men and women were among the first exiles and martyrs of the fundamentalist takeover, becoming identified as moderates whether they claimed the term or not.

Charles Wellborn, regarded as a leading preacher of the first generation of Baylor revival leaders, argues that the cumulative impact of the movement was in decisions made for special religious vocations. Wellborn estimates that approximately one thousand young people surrendered for the professional church work force, particularly as pastors and missionaries, during these years. Additionally, the number of those who committed later to the clergy are legion and impossible to know.[4] Clearly, any direct influence of the movement on the later SBC controversy can be traced to the impact of the revival leaders in their adult careers.[5] Wellborn divides these men by generations.

First Generation

The first generation had its roots in 1946 in Waco, Texas, with large city meetings and many smaller meetings. The leaders are listed in no particular order.

R. Jackson Robinson—an All-American basketball player and Olympian at Baylor University. The longtime pastor at First Baptist Church in Augusta, Georgia (now pastor emeritus), he was never active as a controversialist or an apologist. His theology was decidedly moderate throughout his career to the present day.

Jess Moody—pastored churches in Kentucky and Florida. He was the longtime pastor of the Church of the Good Shepherd (an early megachurch) and the first president of Palm Beach Atlantic University. Moody was one of the last moderate candidates for president of the SBC.

Foy Valentine—an accomplished leader in Texas Baptist and Southern Baptist Convention life. He was director of the SBC Christian Life Commission (now the Ethics and Religious Liberty Commission).

Bruce McIver—the longtime pastor of Wilshire Baptist Church in Dallas, Texas (now a CBF church), moderate in every sense.

Keith Parks—executive director of the SBC Home Mission Board. Late in life, Parks left to assume a similar position with the CBF.

Howard Butt—a leading Christian layman, founder of Laity Lodge in Kerrville, and author of several books that clearly show his decidedly moderate theology. He was never involved directly in the controversies.

Chester O'Brien (Hardin-Simmons University)—a longtime pastor, the brother of Bill O'Brien, and much involved in the SBC split with Women's Missionary Union.

Ralph Langley—a longtime pastor in Texas and Alabama and moderate in theology and in the controversies.

Warren Hultgren (Hardin-Simmons University)—a longtime pastor of First Baptist Church of Tulsa, Oklahoma, and moderate in theology and in the controversies.

S. L. Harris (Howard Payne University)—a retired pastor, campus minister, and college and university teacher and administrator. He concluded his active ministry as associate pastor of First Baptist Church in Brownwood, Texas.

Howard Bramlette—worked for many years in the SBC Christian Life Commission and then in the Student Department. He was fired by the SBC for unorthodox statements written in the Baptist Student publications.

Jimmy Allen (Howard Payne University)—became president of the SBC.

Ralph Phelps—became president of Ouachita Baptist College in Arkadelphia, Arkansas.

Buckner Fanning—a longtime pastor of Trinity Baptist Church in San Antonio, Texas.

B. O. Baker and *Richard O. Baker*—Dick preached, and B.O. wrote more than three hundred songs and hymns, serving in national and international revival and church venues.

Asa David Couch—an outstanding music director of the first generation at Baylor University.

SECOND GENERATION

Most of the more prominent second-generation leaders were products of, or strongly influenced by, members of the first-generation movement.

John Wood—converted and surrendered to preach in youth revivals. A pastor in Kentucky and Texas and a former president of the Kentucky Baptist Convention, he currently is engaged in international missions initiatives.

Russell Dilday—former president of Southwestern Baptist Theological Seminary in Fort Worth, Texas. A martyr for the moderate cause.

William Duyal—former SBC missionary in Central America. He left mission work to hold important government jobs in Washington, D.C., and a college presidency.

Ross Coggins—worked with Foy Valentine in the Texas Christian Life Commission, served as a missionary in Indonesia, then left mission work to hold positions with various Washington aid organizations. He is a prolific writer who attacked the fundamentalists for their takeover plans.

Richard Brannon—longtime pastor in Kentucky and Virginia. He left the pastorate to become an aide to President Gerald Ford and later headed a church-building foundation in Orlando, Florida.

Davis Cooper—a longtime pastor of University Church in Denver, Colorado.

Cecil Sherman—a well-known pastor in the South, former head of the CBF, a professor at the Baptist Theological Seminary in Richmond, Virginia, and a leading apologist for the moderate Baptist cause during the controversy to the present day.

Bill Sherman—brother to Cecil Sherman and a persistent activist in the moderate cause who pastored for many years at Woodmont Baptist Church in Nashville, Tennessee.

Bill and *Dellanna O'Brien*—Bill and Dellanna served twelve years as missionaries in Indonesia. Later, Bill served as vice president of the SBC Foreign Mission Board. Dellanna became director of the WMU, while Bill became director of the Global Missions Center at Samford University in Birmingham, Alabama.

Justice Anderson—a holder of a bachelor's and master's degree from Baylor University and an M.Div. and Th.D. from Southwestern Baptist Theological Seminary. Anderson reflected on the influence of the "Second Wave" of the

Youth Revival movement (and for that matter, the larger movement of the late 1940s, 1950s, and early 1960s):

> In retrospect, after 9 years as a Texas pastor, 17 years as a foreign missionary professor, and 27 years as a Professor of Missiology at Southwest Baptist Theological Seminary, I find the Youth Revival Movement at Baylor as the most formative period of my life. The healthy balance between the "intellectual-devotional," "evangelistic-discipleship," and "local-world missions" emphases, which have characterized my ministry, were discovered and forged during those years. Thousands of other ministers point to the same period as the seedbed of Baptist ministry and mission.[6]

The full impact of these sons of thunder and the women who supported and sustained the movement in equal roles was documented by the Department of Student Work at Baylor University:

> The Department of Student Work kept careful statistics as youth revival teams were sent out and as revivals were conducted. A capsule of events from 1946 to 1962 is most revealing. During those 17 years, 1,560 revivals were booked through the department. When the invitations were given, 54,916 made public Christian commitments and recorded these on cards made available to them. Of that number, 3,681 committed their lives to some kind of Christian ministry (preaching, youth ministry, music, missionary work, etc.), and 10,024 made first-time professions of faith to follow Christ.
>
> These statistics, of course, do not include hundreds of commitments made in revivals not officially sponsored through the Department of Student Work. There is no way to gather all this data.[7]

However, there *is* a way to appreciate the rhetorical spirit and boyish enthusiasm of the Baylor youth revivals, to sense the power and vitality of the spoken Word of God, and to feel the passion of young voices who would later find new adult voices in their later lives of Baptist Christian service. In 1949, Broadman Press published a compilation of ten sermons by the leading young preachers, rendered just as they were delivered. *Youth Speaks,* compiled by Charles Wellborn, is a testament to the power and outcomes of approximately 250 revivals sponsored by the Texas Baptist Department of Student Work, plus scores of independently produced revivals.[8]

Of the ten sermons in Wellborn's collection, I chose to present "Amazing Grace" by Foy Valentine in this book because not only was Valentine on the short list of martyrs cast aside by the fundamentalists some fifty years after the Baylor Youth Revival movement, but his sermon best represents the excellence of the literally hundreds of sermons delivered in the halcyon days of the period. The entire sermon is reproduced in Appendix I, but the following excerpt hints at the spirit of Valentine's meditation on grace:

> Though I have hunted for a more adequate definition of grace, I have never found one better than that which I learned as a boy: "Grace is the unmerited favor of God." The newness and freshness of this old subject have overwhelmed me. Grace is a wonderful thing. It is magnificent in its import. Grace has become almost an equivalent for Christianity, viewed as the religion of dependence on God through Christ.
>
> God's unmerited favor is a dazzling, marvelous thing, and I like to think of God's matchless grace as it finds expression in the lives of men in the Old Testament days. I like to remember how God in his mercy told Noah to prepare the Ark, and how he spared him and his family when the angry flood waters destroyed the rest of civilization. I like to remember how God's unmerited favor came to bear in the life of Abraham, when he called him up out of Ur of the Chaldees to go into the Land of Promise, to be the father of a great nation through whom the Messiah was to come, and to be the father of a still greater spiritual family. I like to think of God's unmerited favor as it worked itself out in the life of Lot, who, even though he selfishly chose the well-watered plain, compromisingly pitched his tent toward Sodom and, eventually, in shamelessness, dwelt in the wicked city of the Sodomites; who, when God got ready to destroy Sodom with fire and brimstone, was warned by two angels sent at God's merciful direction to flee with his family that they might avoid destruction. I like to think of God's unmerited favor as it spared Moses when he was a baby, and then as it spared him from the unpromising companionship of a herd of sheep and directed him to go down into Egypt and lead God's people out of bondage. I like to think of God's unmerited favor in the life of the whole nation of Israel who, after having feasted on quail and manna, cried out for the fleshpots and the melons and garlic of Egypt; who, time and time again, forsook God, the fountain of living waters, and hewed out for themselves broken

cisterns that could hold no water. And though they turned their backs and not their faces toward God, he loved them and showed them mercy; he was gracious to them.

Even though we glory in these manifestations of God's grace, we hasten to say that they were not his greatest manifestations of grace. His grace has never been so amazing, so dazzling, so divine, nor has it ever reached such stupendous, Damascus-road proportions as in the coming of his only begotten Son, Jesus.

It is in Jesus that we limited, finite, sinful mortals can find ourselves near to the heart of God. And it is because of Jesus that we can receive mercy and not justice from the Father.

Giving an example from his own life (in which he received mercy rather than justice from a police officer who declined to write him a speeding ticket), Valentine examined the idea of "amazing grace" in terms of God's planning love, eager love, and laboring love. The central theme of Valentine's early sermon is a template for today's moderate Southern Baptists. Valentine and dozens of his young colleagues preached a Rhetoric of Freedom in Jesus Christ as their Lord and Savior—the same rhetoric found in today's moderate Baptist oratory. The youth revivals were indeed rhetorics of soul winning, voiced by young men with little or no developed perspectives on epistemology or Christology.

During this same time period, in Nashville, Tennessee, a cohort of dedicated denominational loyalists was leading the SBC. Porter Routh (1951–79) was executive secretary-treasurer of the Executive Committee. James L. Sullivan (1953–75) was president of the Southern Baptist Sunday School Board. It is fair to say that these men and others on their respective staffs were loyal to the SBC, moving the denomination in positive administrative development and in new church starts. Working independently, but in harmony with the Nashville leadership, the young men of Baylor preached a gospel of salvation while the men of Nashville—the SBC leadership—promoted unity among the states of the Convention for overall church growth, program development, and seminary development.

In the late 1940s to early 1950s, there were no persuasive theories, political perspectives, or conservative/fundamentalist rhetorics in the pulpit or in the local church. There was a "rhetoric of togetherness" that extended from the college campus and the seminary classroom to the small church, and to the developing downtown First Baptist Church and what became the "second" Baptist church in most southern cities—Emmanuel Baptist Church.

Around the country, the Southern Baptist Convention's dominant persuasive message was "We need to get to know each other." Through the Baptist Press, the SBC's press agency, Southern Baptists were getting to know their brothers and sisters in California as well as those closer to home. It was the best of times—young men were coming home from war, couples were having children at unprecedented rates, housing starts were at an all-time high, and the calming Eisenhower years were just around the corner. It was a time of expansion and growth on every hand. The SBC was moving forward in giant leaps of faith and program growth.

There would be an eight-year period of Republican political rule and unprecedented SBC expansion, with a "million more in '54" campaign to add men and women to the church rolls of the Convention. All the best-laid plans of the Nashville leadership of the SBC were working. There was no complacency in the well-oiled Southern Baptist machine.

However, there was another event in the making that would knock the Southern Baptist train right off the tracks. While in the academy, the Baylor Youth-led Revival movement was the pride and joy of post–World War II Baptist life, there was a member of the graduate school faculty whose work would turn pride into prejudice: Ralph Elliott and his landmark book, *The Genesis Controversy*. For many, the small worlds of the local Southern Baptist church and the downtown church (peopled respectively by bivocational pastors and college/seminary-trained pastors, for the most part) were to come to loggerheads over two basic questions: Is the Bible literally true and, especially, is the Book of Genesis literally true?

Even sixty years later, this war over the Word rages on: all about the words in the Bible, infallible and inerrant. In dealing with the fallout from Elliott's book, Southern Baptist life found itself on the verge of a new rhetorical battle over old ideas and new realities. As the men and women of the Baylor Youth-led Revival movement matured into college and seminary-educated leaders in Baptist life, there was no sacrifice of their education to their teaching about the Bible. Indeed, reaching a mixed audience of college-educated laymen and everyday, garden-variety, good and honest church people requires somewhat different, unapologetic presentations of the Bible. Common to the Southern Baptist body politic are a wide variety of biblical instructions that range from extraordinary challenges to scriptural interpretation to the simple presentation of a literal Word, clean and unfettered by historical/critical methodologies. There was always an audience for the Bible simply taught. And yet, for some, there was a thirst for a deeper understanding of His Word.

The Baptist youth revivalists of the post–World War II period at Baylor University, were they transplanted to the twenty-first century, would never engage a lost soul or a revival audience with a compelling argument for a literal interpretation of the Bible. Rather, their rhetoric, then and now, would be a persuasive message driven by the desire to bring the lost to a regenerated new life in Jesus Christ. John Wood, former pastor of the First Baptist Church in Waco, Texas, may have said it best: "I was not called to the ministry by the Southern Baptist Convention.... My call to the ministry was a personal call from the Lord. I have no time now to be concerned about the issues now confronting the Southern Baptist Convention."[9]

The Baylor Youth-led Revival movement was a harbinger of the times in the life of Southern Baptists in Texas and throughout the South. Woven into the fabric of SBC life was a spirit of deeply felt fundamentalism that did not believe in peaceful coexistence. A rising tide of anti-intellectualism was coming to the fore through what Martin Marty has described as a "two-party system" in American religion.[10] An anti-intellectual rhetoric, "us" versus "them," was growing its ranks at the same time that a smaller rhetoric of a "larger" Bible was capturing the hearts and minds of many a Southern Baptist. In the democracy of any Southern Baptist church of the mid-twentieth century, there was little if any room for these differing bodies of biblical persuasion to find a resting place in the sermons of the local pastor.

The autonomy of the local Southern Baptist church is the refiner's fire for the educated, God-called pastor as well as the singularly God-called pastor. In their later years of faithful service, these sons of thunder from Baylor would find themselves on the outside of Southern Baptist churches looking in, as the SBC began a decided turn to the far right. Above the growing strife in the Convention, the calling of their youth, the simple rhetoric of their call to soul winning, and an abiding fealty to their Lord would serve them well into their retirement years, albeit now outside the gates of the Southern Baptist Convention.

The magic of the Baylor Baptist Youth–Led revival movement may or may never be seen again in the present day of the conservative takeover (or "resurgence," as labeled by many in the leadership of today's Southern Baptist Convention administration). To be sure, without the continuing discovery of biblical truths, new understandings of the Bible may never be brought to the light of day by modern scholarship. In the next chapter, we see just such a biblical treatise as crafted by the previously noted Ralph Elliott, who was then the first hire of the newly formed Midwestern Baptist Theological Seminary in Kansas City, Missouri.

The young, uneducated men of the Baptist Youth–Led revivals were led to win the youth of Waco, Texas, and later other towns across the South without the benefit of scholarship or a seminary education. Yet, there was a strong tradition of scholarship in Southern Baptist life. As alluded to earlier in this chapter, some ten years later, in 1961, an assistant professor, brilliant by any standard, produced what his peers perceived as a useful compilation of teaching notes and deep historical/critical analysis now turned into a new scholarly treatise on the Book of Genesis. At the height of its impact, *The Message of Genesis* would rock the foundations of the Southern Baptist Convention like nothing before or since.

The next chapter moves this study from a genealogical perspective, connecting the members of the Southern Baptist family then and now, to a critical challenge to the nature of the first book of the Bible. In a decidedly self-imposed, difficult persuasive problem, Southern Baptists were faced with a simple decision, not about the salvation of one's eternal soul, but about the Word—the eternal words of their Bible. Ralph Elliott's *Message of Genesis* went far beyond one's personal decision to accept Jesus Christ as his or her personal Savior. Now the question was can I believe the Bible word for word, true and faithful? *The Message of Genesis,* and later the *Broadman Bible Commentary,* became a brace of litmus tests no one wanted to take. Why and how the publication of these treatises created a firestorm of controversy will be considered in the next chapter.

CHAPTER 3

THE ELLIOTT CONTROVERSY AND THE BROADMAN CONTROVERSY
VOICES OF ATTACK AND DEFENSE

The power of a scholarly idea and the many and varied approaches of the historical/critical method of criticism have served to strip away some long-held viewpoints and bring to the light of day heretofore unknown facts and perspectives about the Bible. When discussing the ins and outs of the Bible, Southern Baptists have always been a quarrelsome collective, from the divisive controversy over slavery to disputes over territory with the Northern Baptists and internal controversies over J. R. Graves and Landmarkism, Crawford H. Toy and gospel missionism, and William H. Whitsitt and Baptist origins.[1] At the end of the nineteenth century, the voices of Southern Baptists were attacking the idea that biological evolution and biblical creation were not in harmony and asking whether the Bible does or does not speak of infallibility in matters of faith as well as in matters of science and history.[2]

Even at the inception of their identity as a denominational organization, Southern Baptists were discussing and fussing about the approach to and interpretation of *who* is God and *what* is the Bible. In the main, there has always been a common voice with regard to the Bible as being the Word of God. In the same breath, however, there have been and always will be differences of opinion concerning any and all interpretations of Scripture. For the entire history of the Convention, Baptists of all persuasions have assumed a biblical position on any given topic in the Scriptures and then chased an assortment of Scriptures and interpretations after their conclusion in order to prove their point(s).

It was J. Frank Norris, the fire-eating fundamentalist pastor of First Baptist Church of Fort Worth, Texas, who started a fight in the 1920s over evolution and the heretical, instructional/historical/critical efforts of denominational leaders, colleges, and seminaries. By any stretch of the imagination, Norris was a rascal of the first order. He was a force, a voice to be reckoned with—but only in Texas. The Norris brand of rigid fundamentalism did not sit well with the national rank and file of Southern Baptists. Some forty years later, the rancor and venom of J. Frank Norris was matched and checkmated with two SBC-wide controversies in the 1960s and 1970s—*The Message of Genesis* by Ralph Elliott (1961) and *The Broadman Commentary*, edited by Henton Davies (1969).

In 1961, Midwestern Baptist Theological Seminary professor Ralph Elliott's book, *The Message of Genesis*, was published by Broadman Press, the publishing arm of the Southern Baptist Convention. Elliott argued that the Book of Genesis probably had multiple authors and that some of the book's accounts containing parables and/or symbolic coverage of events.[3] This book ignited a firestorm of controversy in Southern Baptist life.

While it is argued here that the Youth-led Revival movement at Baylor University can be viewed as foreshadowing the earliest beginnings of the moderate Southern Baptist community, it is Ralph Elliott who becomes the first *exile* of the Southern Baptist controversy, caught up in the takeover movement begun in 1979 at the SBC national convention in Houston, Texas, and continuing in the years to follow.

In a far-reaching 1968 interview in the *Baptist Men's Journal*, Elliott spoke to his history-making book and his exile from Southern Baptist life. The interview captured the pain and fresh beginning for Elliott as his transition from Southern Baptist life to American Baptist life began to bear hope and promise:

> *Q:* Why did you write *The Message of Genesis?*
> *A:* For a long time I had been impressed that we were not allowing the Holy Spirit to really give us this deeper meaning of the Bible. Most of our people had approached the Bible from the sheer literalistic standpoint. I felt we were not getting beneath the surface of words to the real meat of the revelation itself.
>
> *Q:* Which part of your book received the most criticism?
> *A:* My comments about the first 11 chapters of Genesis, in which I suggested we are dealing with theological fact, not day-by-day physical history.
>
> *Q:* What were some of the key questions you raised in your book?
> *A:* The seven days of creation. The most bitter critics felt God created the earth in seven literal twenty-four-hour days. I just cannot buy this. And there was a question of whether Adam was just one man, or if he represents mankind. I raised the possibility the answer was mankind.

Q: How has this dispute affected you personally?

A: There has been much heartache. I was cut off from the people I dearly loved. I did not have then and I still do not have animosity toward those who opposed me. During the first few years, I sometimes felt quite lonely. In some ways I felt like I was living in exile.

Q: Has any personal good come from this experience?

A: The last five years have been very broadening. Baptists in New York State have opened their arms and given me a wonderful opportunity of service. Too, the churches of other denominations in this part of the country have opened their doors in a very warm way. I've discovered some of the finest Christians I've ever known.

Q: Have you benefited spiritually?

A: I think one thing which has happened to me is that through the controversy I have learned something about the deep nature of the Christian faith.

Q: Were there any agonizing moments for your family?

A: Yes. We were faced with two alternatives. We could say there was nothing to Christian faith as a whole because those who claimed they were the most orthodox Christians were the most bitter and ugly in their attitude. Or we could ask ourselves if the Christian faith was really valid. We took the latter position. We came to understand the genuine nature of the redemptive love of Jesus Christ and the Christian community as never before. It's been like being in the Army. It's a great venture, but you hope you never have to go through it again.

Q: How were you treated during the controversy?

A: There were persons who told me they opposed me and others who said they agreed with me. However, my family were the ones who really suffered. We received threatening telephone calls. And once, explosives were thrown on our front porch, damaging the door. For a while, the police had to escort our children home from public school.

Q: Are you more liberal theologically now than when you taught at Midwestern Seminary?

A: Yes. I don't think you can go through an experience like I did without being forced to reflect upon everything you believe. Besides that, the time in which we live calls for more deliberate reflection. I don't like to use the term liberal. I prefer to say I'm far more open-minded. More and more I am coming to believe that the real centrality of the Christian faith, as far as its characteristics are concerned, is wrapped up in the words of Jesus: "By this shall all men know that ye are my disciples, that ye have love one for another." There are things which are not nearly as crucial as the characteristic of love—God's love for man, man's love for God, and man's love for man. Jesus didn't say that man must accept certain dogma to become a Christian. But he must have the spirit of love about him if he is a Christian. This is consistent with what Baptists have always stressed because we have always said that we are not a creedal people.

Q: Are you more open-minded now in your relationships with other faiths?

A: Yes. This has been a real blessing to my life because I've discovered some of the most committed Christians are not Baptists. In the South we are people primarily of one culture. It is primarily a Protestant culture, and in some places basically a Baptist one. One of the values of being forced into another section of the country such as Albany [New York] is that you must face the fact that the Protestant culture is a minority culture. It has forced me into conversation with other Christian groups from sheer practical necessity. If our church did not join in working relationships with other Protestant churches in the area, we would hardly have a Protestant voice. We are in a culture which is 80 percent Catholic. We have discovered that in sharing with other groups we have grown ourselves.

Q: Do you feel Southern Baptist churches have anything to fear at this point?

A: Yes, the loss of many of their laymen. One of the serious losses for any church can become the segment of laymen who have a great deal of perceptivity into the nature of the Scriptures and don't feel their churches are expressing themselves adequately at these points.

Q: Do you think Southern Baptist laymen are mature enough to consider other than the traditional church approaches to this crisis?

A: During the Genesis controversy, I received enough letters to fill two four-drawer file cabinets. Many of the letters were from lay people. Most of them expressed appreciation for helping them to face honestly questions and frustrations they had had most of their lives.

Q: Why didn't they ask their church leaders these questions instead of accepting a take-it or leave-it attitude?

A: They said they feared church leaders would think they were disloyal, not Christians, unworthy, or something of this sort.

Q: What general message did you get from the deluge of letters?

A: That Southern Baptists do not have to protect the laymen. Many of the people who wrote me kept saying, "We must protect the little people." Southern Baptists may lose their most intelligent lay people unless they have more opportunity for honest inquiry into the religious dimension of life.

Q: In all of these crises and problems, what do you see as the mission of the church?

A: The church should free every human being from whatever bondage that enslaves him. It may be social, political, or economic. The church should present a Christian gospel concerned with the totality of life. Now I'm a pastor—a preacher. I like to preach. I feel that I have learned to identify with my people through preaching. However, I feel I still have to earn the right for the gospel which I preach to be heard. The only way the church can earn that right is by identifying with man wherever he is, whatever his needs.[4]

While Elliott came to peace and comity about the matter, *The Message of Genesis* was a critical volley fired over the heads of Southern Baptists, and they have been alternately ducking and recoiling from the book ever since.

Professor Elliott has set his record straight with the recent publication *The Genesis Controversy and Continuity in Southern Baptist Chaos* (Mercer University Press, 2005). It is not the goal or purpose of *Against the Wind* to critique, review, or criticize *The Genesis Controversy*. Elliott speaks eloquently; no more needs to be said about his account, for it is a full and well-documented treatise. What is required here is a rhetorically based perspective on the Elliott story as a prelude to the current Southern Baptist holy war.

As noted earlier, in 1958 Ralph Elliott became the first faculty member of Midwestern Baptist Theological Seminary. As Elliott describes the sequence of events, the editor of Broadman Press, William Fallis, visited Elliott and other members of Southern Seminary (where he was then on the faculty) regarding a prospective series of Bible study books. Hoping to collaborate with his major professor, Clyde Francisco, Elliott began to collect and prepare lecture notes and other materials in hopes of a joint writing project. Such was not to be the case.[5]

While much of the developing manuscript was shaped under Francisco's leadership, Elliott's scholarship was in line with the Old Testament teachers in all Southern Baptist seminaries at the time as he argued that there is a difference of literary style between chapters 1–11 and 12–50 of Genesis.[6] By most standards in the life of the Southern Baptist seminaries of the late 1950s to early 1960s, *The Message of Genesis* was a mild historical/critical treatise concerning Scripture. Elliott's rhetorical problem, among many others perhaps more important at the time, was the book chosen for critical study—Genesis. The first among equals in Holy Writ, the Book of Genesis is the foundational cornerstone of the Bible. To question *this book,* among all books of the Old and New Testament, was to wave a red cape before a charging bull.

The Message of Genesis was published in early July 1961. While clergy and laity alike who read the book during the last half of 1961 began slowly and intermittently to evaluate Elliott's volume, soon enough it became a turning point—a rhetorical artifact that would rock the Baptist community. By some accounts, the backlash against *Genesis* launched the fundamentalist/conservative rhetoric that would, some twenty years later, capture the castle of the Southern Baptist Convention.

K. Owen White, pastor of the First Baptist Church in Houston, Texas, submitted a one-page article first published by the Texas *Baptist Standard* and later appearing in all state Baptist papers. The article was forwarded to Southern Baptist leaders in every sphere of influence and to pastors and major lay leaders for an unprecedented distribution. By Elliott's admission, "White's words exploded like a bombshell.... White was soon included in the Missouri-Oklahoma group as a strategizer and became the group's spokesman at the meeting of the Southern Baptist Convention in San Francisco, California in June of 1962."[7]

In the world of rhetorical artifacts, it is often the comparatively brief public address or written public document that carries the most blunt trauma force of persuasive, emotional, and argumentative appeals. Examples of this phenomenon include Lincoln's Gettysburg Address, King's "I Have a Dream" speech, and Kennedy's inaugural address (with the life-changing phrase "Ask not what your country can do for you"). Although a far lesser known rhetorical event, White's one-page "... Death in the Pot," published January 10, 1962, will be long remembered in the archives of Southern Baptist history, in much the same way as the aforementioned rhetorical events. In many ways, White's article was the "shot heard 'round the world," the first shot of the rhetorical wars to come. White chose to attack any variance on the full reliability and truth of the Bible, especially by what he perceived as a vulgar attack on the Book of Genesis.

Relying on 2 Kings 4:40 as a proof text, White launched the first salvo of the coming war over denominational control and academic freedom, reprinted here in its entirety:

> "Since the parable includes the historical and the non-historical, one can say with Richardson: 'We must learn to think of the stories of Genesis—the creation, the fall, Noah's ark, the tower of Babel—in the same way as we think of the parables of Jesus; they are profoundly symbolical (though not allegorical) stories, which aren't to be taken as literally true (like the words of the textbooks of geology), but which yet bear a meaning that

cannot be paraphrased or stated in any other way without losing something of their quality or existential truth.'"

"'Adam' originally must have meant 'mankind,' not just one person."

"The particular problem of chapter 5 is the longevity of the antediluvians. It is difficult to believe that they actually lived as long as stated. In all probability, the Priestly writer simply exaggerated the ages in order to show the glory of an ancient civilization."

"'God took him' is not necessarily an indication that he disappeared suddenly and was nowhere to be found. It is the Old Testament expression of belief in the ideal of immortality."

"The tower of Babel parable shows the futility and emptiness of human effort divorced from the acknowledgment and service of God. In other words, there are a great many evidences which, while not giving conclusive proof, lend strong credence to the historicity of the patriarchs."

"Quite possibly some of the stories have been heightened and intensified by materials that are not literally historical, for the purpose of the Bible is not merely to give a factual account of events."

"This is not to say that Abraham was a monotheist, but it is to say that he had a concept of God different from that of his pagan neighbors."

"If one cannot be certain of the facts of historicity, what is to be received from the stories?"

"It would appear, then, that in verse 19, Melchizedec was blessing Abraham by the Baal, whom Melchizedec considered to be the highest god of the city-state at Salem."

"Supposedly, during the prophetic period, the narrative was edited in such a way that it was made also to teach a fine lesson about God."

"There developed the tradition that this was what happened to Lot's wife—perhaps not exactly historical. . . ."

"Suddenly, what had been a thought of meditation gripped the inner being of Abraham until he thought he heard it as a clear call from God, 'Go sacrifice Isaac.'"

Does this sound like Boyce, Broadus, Mullins, Robertson, Sampey, Gambrell, Carroll, Scarborough, and other great Southern Baptist leaders? The quotations listed above are from *The Message of Genesis,* written by Dr. Ralph Elliott, now teaching at Midwestern Seminary, Kansas City, Mo.

Being a graduate of Southern Seminary and having served as pastor of Southern Baptist churches for more than 30 years, I love and believe in my denomination and have a burning passion for it to remain true to the Bible as the Word of God. I have a deep concern that our seminaries shall sound a clear, ringing note in their interpretation of the Scriptures and that young preachers shall come from their halls with not an "uncertain sound."

The book from which I have quoted is liberalism, pure and simple! It stems from the rationalistic theology of Wellhausen and his school, which led Germany to become a materialistic godless nation. This is "the wisdom of the world" which seeks to find a "reasonable, acceptable" solution to every problem which involves the supernatural.

Several great denominations in the last generation have drifted from the faith of our fathers, have lost their conviction that the Bible is authoritative and dependable, and now have little evangelistic witness. The drift came from liberalism in their seminaries and their literature.

If the appeal is made for "academic freedom," let it be said that we gladly grant any man the right to believe what he wants to—but, we do not grant him the right to believe and express views in conflict with our historic position concerning the Bible as the Word of God while he is teaching in one of our schools, built and supported by Baptist funds.

The book in question is "poison." This sort of rationalistic criticism can lead only to further confusion, unbelief, deterioration, and ultimate disintegration as a great New Testament denomination. It has happened to other denominations; it can happen to us! Modernism is insidious, dangerous, and destructive.

What can be done?

- Invite men with such views to find a place of service with groups of denominations of like theological inclinations.
- Ask the trustees of our institutions to consider seriously the dangers involved in such theological views and to exercise caution in their approval of faculty members.
- Urge our Sunday School Board to be alert to any trend in the direction of liberalism in our publications.

This is not an incidental matter. It involves the total responsibility of every one of us individually, of our churches and our denomination, in declaring plainly, positively, and unequivocally "the whole counsel of God."

In this brief statement I have made no attempt to review the book. The quotations speak for themselves. I have merely emphasized certain words and phrases in these quotations to shed light upon the particular doctrinal or historical truth in question. The influence of this sort of teaching would substitute intuition for inspiration, reason for revelation, and futility for faith. It is quite true of course that in our study and interpretation of God's Word we are not to forsake common sense, but we also need to remember the words of Isaiah 55:8–9. "For my thoughts are not your thoughts, neither are your ways my ways, saith the Lord. For as the heavens are higher than the earth, so are my ways higher than your ways, and my thoughts than your thoughts."

"There is death in the pot!"[8]

Elliott writes of a meeting in Oklahoma City on March 8–9, 1962, where some fifty leaders met to deal with the developing crisis in the Southern Baptist Convention with regard to *The Message of Genesis*. W. Ross Edwards, pastor of Swope Park Baptist Church, Kansas City, Missouri, delivered a keynote address that served as counterpoint to Elliott's historical/critical analysis of Genesis, that is, the affirmation of a literal and inerrant belief in Scripture and support for the "pastor as autocrat."[9] Edwards's brief speech, heralded as a watershed rhetorical event at the time, may well have served to help launch, unofficially, the Pressler-Patterson political strategy that came to fruition at the 1979 Southern Baptist Convention in Houston, Texas.

Elliott provides a full and eloquent reprise of his story in *The Genesis Controversy*. To paraphrase Elliott's story would be redundant and serve as dilution of his narrative. What is known is that *The Message of Genesis* denied the historicity of Adam and Eve, rejected the Genesis flood as worldwide, asserted that Sodom and Gomorrah were destroyed by natural causes, that there are multiple authors of Genesis, and that the first eleven chapters of Genesis were intended as symbolic rather than a literal history.

In 1962, the Southern Baptist Convention, meeting in San Francisco, California, reaffirmed the infallibility of the Bible, appointed a committee to redraft the SBC's 1925 Baptist Faith and Message, and sent the Elliott issue back to Midwestern Baptist Theological Seminary for resolution. Elliott was subsequently dismissed, not for heresy, but because he would not consent to the seminary request to refrain from securing another publisher for *The Message of Genesis*.

The fallout from the Elliott controversy spread across a variety of denominational landscapes:

1. In 1963, K. Owen White was elected president of the SBC (White was Elliott's prime antagonist at the time).
2. In 1963, the Convention adopted a new Baptist Faith and Message declaring that the Bible is "truth without any mixture of error."

3. In 1963, the Convention declared that a professor is not free to publish, preach, or teach any interpretation of the Bible that is not in harmony with the majoritarian views of the SBC's clergy and laity.
4. It was declared that only the theological views of the majoritarian culture of the Convention may be published in Broadman books and any other publication(s) of the Convention.

Ralph Elliott now has spent more of his professional and denominational life as an American Baptist than as a Southern Baptist. Then, as now, the Baptist reactions to mixing science, historical/critical methods of scholarship, and religion create a heady brew. Although dogged by the accusations about such an alchemy, Elliott enjoyed a rejuvenated career at Crozer Theological Seminary in Rochester, New York, and the pastorate of several churches affiliated with the American Baptist Convention.

Much has been written about Ralph Elliott and the Genesis controversy using epithets too strong to mention here. The Baptist voices of attack have been and remain sharp and clear regarding Elliott's work as a young seminarian and his legacy among Southern Baptists to this day. To be sure, Ralph Elliott is still a welcome guest in a few Southern Baptist circles, while remaining an outcast in many more.

In his own defense, Elliott affirms that the "takeover movement really got underway with the so-called 'Genesis Controversy.'"[10] While declining my suggestion that he was the *first moderate* because of "some cynicism and vitriol in the so-called moderates that I do not share," Elliott may be fairly called the first *exile* of the modern era (as noted earlier)—a close relative of the men and women who would later admit, some reluctantly, to the label "moderate."[11]

While Elliott confides that "in some ways, some of what is written in *Exiled* is foreign to me," he has preached and written about living within the context of the Rhetoric of the Exiled.[12] While pastor of North Shore Baptist Church in Chicago, Illinois, Elliott delivered a sermon on April 26, 1987, titled "The Pilgrimage of an Exile." In *The Genesis Controversy*, he wrote, some eighteen years later, of the same experience (cast nearly identically with the language of the 1987 sermon text) with his current and historic concerns as an exile from the Southern Baptist culture of his youthful and adult memories.

In Elliott's life-altering, extended journey as an exile, several features resonate with the stories of the thirty-one contributors in *Exiled*:

1. Exile is always forced.
2. Exile leads to pilgrimage.
3. Exile is about a journey toward freedom of thought and expression.
4. Exile is often a discovery of new perspectives and self-discovery.
5. Exile is Bible-inspired to force new decisions and clear futures.
6. Exile is a blend of never "going home again" to finding a "new home."
7. Exile is always about being on a journey away from and toward a future always out of reach; hope is about being "number two."

In an extended form, Elliott speaks with the voice of the exiled, in a firm defense of the process and a deepening understanding of separation from the past to the present day of journey and discovery. From the aforementioned 1987 sermon:

> Journey, pilgrimage and exile are among the most important images in all of Biblical tradition. Exile, pilgrimage and journey are among the most important exercises in life's experience. It often is that because one is forced to go into exile that he somehow becomes a pilgrim which causes him to make decisions on a journey which he never would have made before and decisions which he never would have known before, with discoveries of the soul which otherwise never could have come.
>
> Do you remember some of the themes? It was said of those early faith believers—they acknowledge that they were exiles, pilgrims and strangers in the land. To be a pilgrim is to journey to meaning. There are many ways to travel. One can, of course, be a tourist—just traveling around form place to place, with no ultimate goal, no ultimate destiny other than to return to the place from which one came. There are sojourners, of course, who likewise travel in a temporary time to a temporary place with no real interest in either the time, or the place, or the people of that place. But to be a pilgrim is to be on a quest for meaning, looking for a particular purpose. A pilgrim is a person who journeys from the foreign country of the soul, forced to live in a different and strange place, and thereby impelled to make decisions which impact the whole value system of life so that one is never again what one once was before.

I have made a wonderful discovery: one seldom becomes a pilgrim until and unless forced to live in circumstances of exile, where circumstances call for decisions which clarify who we are. Indeed forcing us to discover who we are, and whose we are, and then, praise God, even if we are pushed into exile, we can celebrate the journey.

I really don't have to define the term. Many of you living in this land are exiles from your native homeland. You have come from different times and different places. An exile is anyone separated from his country or his home or his original status, either voluntarily or by the stress of circumstances. It may be physical—when you are caused to migrate from one country to another. It may be cultural—when you are caused to leave a southern clime for another clime. It may be social—when you find yourself in circumstances previously unknown. It may be educational, or intellectual. You are in exile when you recognize that you don't fit. When you hear a different drummer for whatever reason, and you have to make some clarifying choices and grasp some clarifying visions which give a steadying value system to the remainder of life.

Exile was a most important time in the life of Israel. The greatest theological insights came in those days when Israel had no temple. Languishing in a strange land, they were taunted and tormented. But they went through the night of the soul to discover that religion was not a place, but that it's a relationship. A relationship which provides a grace that is greater than any place.

Exile is when you discover and clarify visions which can neither be discovered nor clarified in any other way, and then you thank God for the experience. Exile is when you discover the ownership of some things for yourself. Maybe the things which you had memorized by rote but which never truly became yours until you had the experience of exile.

Job was learned in religion, but it was not until he was caught in the nightmarish exile of the soul that he found it possible to say, "I'd heard of thee with the hearing of my ears, but, ah, now I see you with the seeing of my eye." It is worth any exile to come to the place where you can see things that you could not see before.

I grew up singing about the "Old Time Religion." "Give me the old time religion, give me the old time religion. It was good enough for my father and it's good enough for me." But one day, in a sense not until I was 38 years of age, did I discover, by being exiled from all that was to me at that time held dear, that you cannot have your father's religion. There has to come a time in the night of a soul when it is yours, yours in a way that neither your father nor your mother could have given it you. And then you thank God for the exile.

Do you remember Moses whose mother hid him in the bulrushes—who became the "basket case" who floated into the Egyptian system? And after awhile, lost his identity in that system, severed from the faith roots of Abraham, Isaac and Jacob? Finally one day when he saw his ethnic kind being beat into slavery, he was touched to know who he was, and he fled into exile on the back side of the desert to come to grips with himself and to come to grips with God. Everyone has to do that. And it usually happens in some exile, in some night of the soul.

Exile prepares us to make a contribution even when everyone else cannot see. So it was that Moses went back to lead his people out, and as the Scripture says, initially, even Pharaoh did not know that they were gone. So, when all of the people came out in an exodus of Egypt, and found themselves in an exile of sorts, Moses could help them to see some things that initially they could not see. He saw manna on the ground. Not everyone can see manna on the ground, but thank God for the pilgrimage of the exile which enables us to see.

There are many other exiles in Israel's life. For 40 years they had been roaming around in the wilderness, lost and without direction, and here they are now, having crossed the Jordan, led by Joshua into the initial conquest of the land. Joshua wants to know whether they have learned anything, experienced anything, seen anything, decided anything. But there is nothing magic about exile. It was a mixed mob. For some the rugged years had led to a virility of faith and to a spiritual toughness of mind. But for others it had meant only an unsettledness. They owned the pagan ornaments of the Egyptians and the Canaanites; there was a double mindedness and an unsettledness very much as often we know now. Exile had only meant a capitulation to a temporary thought form with doubts and ugly practices. It is up to you whether you become a pilgrim in the exile.

But standing in sharp contrast was Joshua, for whom the wilderness experience of exile had only polished the diamond of personal faith. His life pattern had been set decades before when, as one of several spies, he went into this promised land. He was one of two who came back believing in the promises and in the hopes of God. It's a classical text. "Choose this day whom you will serve, but as for me, I will serve the Lord." That's what an exile and a wilderness experience forces you to do. It forces you to choose the one whom you will serve for the remainder of your life, and it helps you to declare what that decision means. And it forces you to struggle with something and with someone, and to clarify what is real and what isn't real, even about religion.

Now I know it's dangerous, and one can easily appear self-serving, and it can seem arrogant and egocentric, but I want to make a transition now. A transition to the existential exile of my own life as a Christian. But I would have you remember the title: "The Pilgrimage of an Exile." A pilgrim is one who has not arrived, but is traveling on to a destination not fully achieved, and so, remembering the nature of the pilgrim, put the telling in proper perspective.

I was a hothouse variety Christian. Signing on was no difficult task. For everything about my culture, my family, my setting was geared in a religious direction. It would have been much more difficult for me to say "no" to religion than it was to say "yes." Even in high school I was, so much of the time, the president of the student government, or of the student council, able to set a pattern which allowed me to begin every council meeting with prayer or with one of my great sermonettes, and artificially and oppressively, as I look back upon it, put people into my own mold. Thoughtlessly forcing the Jewish Newman or Lowenstein in that group to surrender their freedoms and to fit my mold.

My first glimpse of exile, forcing me to get beneath the surface of what had been handed to me on a cultural platter, was a period of service in the army. Primarily on duty in the winter's cold of Europe where, for the first time, I saw people die, I watched as men went through hell. I began to recognize that some of the easy shibboleths handed to me were surface deep and would not hold. I made progress during that exile. A progress in spiritual depth. But it was much like Israel's wilderness years, for much was yet unclear.

And then life became easier again and the terrifying struggle was not so necessary. Suddenly, I found myself as a young professor. Sharper than some in my biblical field, easily handing out easy answers to age old questions. One day my answers did not fit and suddenly I was humbled by my arrogance and cut off form my beloved southland, cut off from my professorship, and cut off from those whom I thought to be my friends, and living in exile. I have lived the remainder of my life in religious and physical exile, no longer fitting into the right-wing culture to which I once belonged, never fitting into the cynicism of a liberal theological culture whose surface humanism is often accompanied by cynicism. But I want to bear a testimony to you, that when I was cast out of Jerusalem into exile, I began a struggle, a struggle which has blessed my soul. Initially I wandered, almost in a suicidal setting, I wandered, and I discovered that in a depth far beneath the theological dogmas and forms which I knew so well was a Jesus of experience—often hid by the very religion I was seeking to maintain. And that was when I began to discover, beyond my religious and denominational labels, other ecumenical Christians who had been through the same experience of exile and experience of grace. It was a journeying in the rich exile of the soul that I discovered that there is a spiritual newness which makes the defense of the old fences both unnecessary and undesirable, for God carries me and I do not carry God.

Worry not about exile. Exile is not bad, for exile is when you begin to grow and claim God as your very own and probe beneath the tidy, doctrinal catechism which you may have memorized, in a surface way, as a child. It is because of the exiled experience that I have discovered a value system which holds, which was there all along, which I really was, sometimes, allowing to be hid by the external forms in which it was conveyed.

When I was a young boy, working in the back of my father's store, sorting the pop bottles, there was an old black man who worked for my father named Charlie Price. He would not have known what A was from Z in theology, but I often heard him say, "Yes sir, God is faithful and he will not tempt you above what you are able to bear. Don't you forget that, Mister Ralph." And then he would sing, "He knows, he knows, how much you can bear."

And so, in the exiled times I have discovered that core belief which is much more than easily mouthed shibboleths or conformist creeds, but the bedrock attitudes and relationships that govern all of life and give response to all crises, providing anchor in the storm and compass on the journey. During the exile days, I have discovered the new Christ, the Living Christ, the experiential Christ, the Christ beyond all of the creeds. And while sometimes I miss the old sights and the old sounds of home, I thank God for the growth of exile.

But don't forget the exilic choices. For if you forget to make the choices in exile life can be like a ship without a rudder, like a car without a wheel. And instead of being a pilgrimage, it can be a nightmare. If you, then, would enjoy the pilgrimage of the soul, make the choices and quit straddling the fences, and with choices easily made, one must be willing to exert influences on others instead of being pushed around by the fashions and the fads of life. In picking your way through the wilderness and through the exile, know that there are certain absolutes which

God will share with you in the experience, but you must make some decisions about those absolutes.

A short time ago, Elie Wiesel was awarded the Nobel Peace Prize. As the *Christian Century* said of Wiesel, "His own life is a story of an enforced citizenship in the Kingdom of Night—his name for Auschwitz—and a long, long journey, stretching over decades before any glimmer of a true dawn entered that darkness and gave faint signs of a possible sunrise." He had traveled through one exile, but always pushing back the darkness until now, having traveled through the exile, he could say in accepting the Nobel Peace Prize, "no one is more capable of gratitude than one who has emerged from death's kingdom." Every moment is a gift of grace, our lives are no longer our own. That's what it means to be in the pilgrimage of an exile.[13]

Common to the study of rhetorical subject matter, the historical/critical methodologies are numerous and almost always revealing at some level of critical understanding. Close on the heels of the Elliott controversy, the *Broadman Commentary* controversy would become round two of the late 1960s main events in Baptist life.

In 1970, the Southern Baptist Convention's publishing arm, Broadman Press, published the first volume of the *Broadman Bible Commentary*. From its earliest days, the Baptist Sunday School Board discussed, planned, and executed several modest works that provided assistance in Bible study for the laity. As time and culture moved along at a rapid pace, there was an ongoing conversation in the 1950s about the development of a significant Bible commentary on the New Testament.

After several years of research, writing, and prepublication concerns about the contents of Volumes 1 and 8 of the *Commentary*, the most critical stance was saved for G. Henton Davies, principal of Regent's Park College in Oxford, England. The author of the *Commentary's* treatment of the Book of Genesis, Davies argued for a non-Mosaic authorship and a contrarian perspective on the Abraham-Isaac encounter in Genesis 27.

By action of the 1970 Southern Baptist Convention held in Denver, Colorado, the Baptist Sunday School Board was instructed to withdraw Volume 1 from further sales, and to rewrite that volume with a conservative viewpoint. After the subsequent publication of Volumes 1 and 8, Volumes 7 and 12 were published prior to the 1972 SBC meeting in Philadelphia, Pennsylvania. Volume 1 was withdrawn from publication in 1970 and replaced with a revised volume 1 that same year. The remaining series of commentaries, completing the twelve-volume set, were completed by April 1972. The complete set of Broadman commentaries sold in excess of 330,000 copies, becoming a standard resource for Bible students.[14] (For a detailed, first-person history of the *Broadman Bible Commentary,* see Clifton Allen's coverage of the subject in Appendix VII.)

In *Not a Silent People,* Shurden argues on point that both controversies were stimulated by a study of Genesis.¹⁵ Both controversies were created by heavy fire by conservatives who saw biblical criticism as a liberal affront to doctrines held dear by Southern Baptists nationwide.¹⁶ Led by Ross Edwards, editor of the Missouri state Baptist newspaper *Baptist Word and Way,* and M. O. Owens, a pastor from North Carolina, conservatives "connected the dots" between the Elliott controversy and the *Broadman Commentary.* These men led a chorus of critics and apologists for a decidedly conservative perspective issuing from the Sunday School Board and its publication divisions.

With W. A. Criswell as the Southern Baptist Convention president (1968-69), it didn't take long for conservatives to feel vindicated and moderate-leaning Baptists to feel uncomfortable. With the publication of Criswell's book *Why I Preach the Bible* (in which Criswell affirmed that the Bible is literally true), applause for the book came from many in the SBC, while it generated discomfort for many moderate Baptists.

In the American Civil War, the first salvo arched over Fort Sumter, in Charleston, South Carolina. Yet, in truth, the prelude to Civil War in the American South was not a showering of munitions, but the oratory of South Carolina's John C. Calhoun and his lieutenants who traveled the roads of South Carolina working feverishly against the unfair taxation policies of the North. In parallel fashion, the rhetorical power of Elliott's book and the worrisome biblical criticism of the Broadman commentaries fired warning shots over the bow of the Southern Baptist Convention, with both publications serving as precursors to an impending war over the Bible. Essentially, the ultimate victory of the conservatives/fundamentalists in 1990 was as much about the control of right thinking as it was about the control of the sacred, inerrant, and infallible Bible.

In the mid- to late 1960s, the agencies and enterprises of the Baptist Sunday School Board were under a cloud of suspicion. Could Southern Baptists find comfort in the knowledge that their national offices would sustain their views on Scripture and produce print materials for the proper education of their churches? There was increasing SBC-wide doubt about these expectations.

There was a growing width and depth to the conservatives/fundamentalists' perspectives about the inerrant and infallible Bible. Fueled by the Elliott controversy and the *Broadman Commentary* controversy, Southern Baptists' majoritarian views were becoming less accepting of diverse ideas and more accepting of simplistic understandings of the Bible.

In the early to mid-1970s, the lines were being drawn between Southern Baptists of all persuasions. While many knew they were not in agreement with the conclusions of Elliott's *Message of Genesis,* they were equally unwilling to adhere to the belief systems associated with the concepts of fundamentalism. James M. Wall characterized the variations and subgroups among Southern Baptists at the time in an insightful overview:

IMAGE ONE:
BIBLE BELIEVERS OR INERRANCY DOGMATISTS

At their best, Southern Baptists have unquestionably believed the Bible. According to Wall, others see Southern Baptists as accepting the Bible "not just as a guidebook; it is *the* book." The negative side of this image, Wall said, "is the rigidity of inerrancy," in which Southern Baptist "scholastics are rigidly unbending and intolerant of all who do not accept their exceedingly narrow reading of Scripture."

IMAGE TWO: DILIGENT MISSIONARIES
OR ARROGANT PROSELYTIZERS

Nothing puzzles outsiders about Southern Baptists more than their persistent efforts to persuade others to share their faith. Some see this, Wall said, "as arrogance, self-righteousness, and superiority." Some perceive such witnessing as positive; Southern Baptists perceive it as close to the mainsprings of their faith.

IMAGE THREE: RIGID MORALISTS
OR DEFENDERS OF VALUES

"The perception of the Southern Baptist in this area," Wall said, "is one of defender of values based on religion on the positive side; and a rigid, intolerant defender of narrow moral views, on the negative side." Outsiders see Southern Baptists as concerned with issues of personal morality but less aware of what Wall called "societal evils."

IMAGE FOUR: DEFENDER OF CHURCH-STATE
SEPARATION OR ANTI–ROMAN CATHOLIC

Religious liberty for all, preserved through separation of church and state, remains one of the earliest and most consistent emphases of Baptists. One could argue that this position has led to greater religious freedom for Baptists and non-Baptists alike. However, the public often perceives a less positive role for Baptists, that of intolerant anti-Catholicism. The religious opposition to the election of John F. Kennedy in 1960 was widely perceived, rightly or not, as spearheaded by Baptists. Opposition to an official ambassador to the Vatican, which surfaced again in 1984, though broadly based among American Protestants, was widely perceived as a Baptist phenomenon and in some quarters as a *Southern* Baptist movement. Of more concern to Southern Baptists, perhaps, was evidence that understanding of and commitment to religious liberty might be weakening in their own denomination.

Concluding on a positive note, Wall portrayed Southern Baptists as "a denomination with a passionate commitment and an unwillingness to conform either to the vagueness of the ecumenical movement or the blandness of the no-offense cultural religion. The Southern Baptist Convention represents the mainline body which has most successfully resisted amalgamation into the secular and church mainstream of the United States."[17]

Some twenty years later (1980), Southern Baptists remained divided over who is a Southern Baptist and what central tenets they uphold. There would be voices of affirmation and apologia as the war of words intensified post-1980. As time moved along, denominational leaders, pastors, and laity discovered rhetorical positions and accompanying arguments that sustained differing positions on the Baptist compass. By the 1990s, Baptist rhetors were using Scripture to prove a wide variety of claims and doing so effectively, as documented in *In the Name of the Father*.

The next chapter examines the rank-and-file issues in the controversy from the basic elements of fundamentalism to the less-secure rhetoric of so-called liberals in the Southern Baptist Convention. The gloves were off, the rhetorical civil war was picking up momentum, and Southern Baptists were either choosing sides, turning their backs, retiring to the sidelines to see who would win, or knowing little and caring less about a "preacher boys' fight." In *The Rise of Fundamentalism*, we look at how Southern Baptists arrived at the threshold of the twenty-first century splintered, fussing, going to court, forming parallel Baptist organizations, and contending with a two-message national perception that either "Southern Baptists are nice people" or "Southern Baptists are anti-everything." In chapter 4, we get back to the basics—the fundamentals of how many ways there are to be a Southern Baptist.

CHAPTER 4

THE RISE OF FUNDAMENTALISM
VOICES OF AFFIRMATION AND APOLOGIA

Against the Wind has cast its arguments for the post–World War II origin of the moderate Southern Baptist community in what may be satisfactory or less-than-satisfactory claims, proofs, and inferences. In like fashion, the Rhetoric of Fundamentalism will send one into a certain tailspin of claim and counterclaim. The tenets of fundamentalism and inerrancy, the concept of a Southern Baptist liberal, the implications of the "priesthood of the believer," and the role of the pastor-leader are enough to make many Southern Baptists have second thoughts about their denominational home.

In Appendixes II and III, Baptist scholars Loyd Allen and William E. Hull frame the "Who are Southern Baptists?" question along with the historical perspective of the collective conservative and moderate pasts. For every affirmation of the nature and character of a conservative or a moderate Southern Baptist, there is a countering apologia—a speech or treatise in defense and counterpoint as to who and what may properly serve as the themes and labels of Southern Baptists.

Daniel L. Akin, president of the Southeastern Baptist Theological Seminary in Wake Forest, North Carolina, offered a comparison and contrast of Southern Baptist conservatives/fundamentalists with Southern Baptist moderates that can serve as a template for this book's analysis.[1] At each point of claim-counterclaim, there is an "exception to be taken" by those on each side of the column according to one's individual views of doctrines. The lines of division are clear; the differences are significant.

William Stephens, who is the field representative for the Tennessee Cooperative Baptist Fellowship and formerly the curriculum coordinator of the Discipleship Training Department of LifeWay (the Southern Baptist Convention administrative enterprise, headquartered in Nashville), argues that, beyond all the comparisons and contrasts outlined in tables 2 and 3,

Table 2. SBC Conservatives and Moderates: Theological Differences

Conservatives	Moderates
Theological differences	
Affirm the *inerrancy* of the Bible. Find no errors in the autographs philosophically, theologically, scientifically, or historically.	Affirm the *authority* of the Bible in matters of salvation. Find some errors in areas such as science and history.
The Bible *is* the Word of God.	The Bible *contains/becomes* the Word of God.
Emphasize the necessity of theological *integrity*.	Emphasize the necessity of theological *diversity*.
All are *creationists,* though not all are "young-earthers."	Many are theistic evolutionists.
All affirm soteriological exclusivism (people are saved only through Christ).	Many affirm soteriological inclusivism (some in other religions may be saved).
Affirm Scripture as the foundational source of religious spiritual authority.	Affirm Scripture, along with reason, experience, and tradition, as sources of religious/spiritual authority.
Affirm congregationalism with strong pastoral authority/leadership.	Affirm congregationalism with strong congregational authority and democratic process.
Oppose women as pastors (complementarians in home and church).	Affirm women as pastors (egalitarians in home and church).
View autonomy as a precious check against both hierarchicalism and connectionalism.	View autonomy as the right of every church to do or believe what it wishes and not have its fellowship questioned associationally or denominationally.
Affirm the eternal continuation of both heaven and hell.	Some embrace idea of the annihilation of the wicked.
See the priesthood of all believers as guaranteeing direct access to God for all believers and primarily as a doctrine of responsibility.	See the priesthood of all believers as giving to each the right to believe anything he or she wishes. Often change the term to "priesthood of the believer."
Discover no contradictions or internal inconsistencies in the Bible when it is properly interpreted.	Discover numerous contradictions and internal inconsistencies in the Bible.
Affirm historical-grammatical interpretation.	Affirm historical-critical interpretation.
Find no mythological elements in Scripture.	Are open to mythological elements in Scripture.
Emphasize the transcendent truth of Scripture.	See much of the Bible as culturally conditional.

Table 3. SBC Conservatives and Moderates: Moral, Political, and Denominational Differences

Conservatives	Moderates
Pro-life	Pro-choice
Most favor a voluntary prayer amendment.	Most oppose a voluntary prayer amendment.
All see homosexuality/lesbianism as a sin and a choice of life-style.	Some see homosexuality/lesbianism as an acceptable life-style and a predisposed psychological orientation.
Most are Reagan/Bush Republicans (political right).	Most are Carter/Clinton Democrats (political Left).
Emphasize peacemaking together with a strong military.	Emphasize peacemaking with a much smaller military.
Favor smaller government, lower taxes, state and local rights, greater individual freedom.	Most favor big federal government with multiple social and welfare programs.
Advocate separation of church and state to the extent that government neither establishes religion nor interferes with its practice.	Advocate separation of church and state to the extent that the church makes little attempt to impact community morality through government.
See the other as "moderates," "liberals," or "neo-orthodox."	See the other as "fundamentalists."
View creeds and confessions as important defining documents, though always subject to Scripture.	View creeds and confessions as problematic at best, confining and wrong at worst.
Believe that the institutions and agencies of a denomination should operate with confessional integrity.	Believe that the institutions and agencies of a denomination should operate without confessional restraint.
Are intensely evangelistic and missionary.	Are inclined heavily toward "social ministries."
Are more comfortable in cooperative ventures with evangelical groups such as IVF, Campus Crusade, and Wycliffe Bible Translators.	Are more comfortable in cooperative ventures with groups such as the Cooperative Baptist Fellowship (Atlanta), Baptist Joint Committee on Public Affairs (Washington, D.C.), and other mainline denominations.

Sources: Ammerman, *Baptist Battles;* Thomas Bland Jr., ed., *Servant Songs: Reflections on the History and Mission of Southeastern Baptist Theological Seminary, 1950–1988* (Macon, Ga.: Smyth & Helwys, 1994); Robert U. Ferguson, ed., *Amidst Babel, Speak the Truth: Reflections on the Southern Baptist Convention Struggle* (Macon, Ga.: Smyth & Helwys, 1993); Shurden, *Struggle for the Soul of the SBC.*

fundamentalism's most distinguishing doctrine is *dispensational premillennialism*.[2] Largely based upon a literal interpretation of Revelation 20:1-6, dispensational premillenialism describes Christ's return and subsequent reign at the end of an apocalyptic period. In Christian eschatology, it is believed that Christ will literally reign on earth for a thousand years at His second coming.

Theology for Southern Baptist conservatives/fundamentalists centers on the second coming of Christ. For fundamentalists, the present day is the last church age, the age of apostasy. The ruling perception of fundamentalists is that the SBC was invaded by liberal northern theology at the turn of the twentieth century. And by the 1960s, an important element was added to the developing rhetoric of apostasy—Pentecostalism. Pentecostalism places rhetorical emphasis on interpreting sins and personal transgressions as caused by demonic possession. The concept of demonic activity, coupled with the rhetoric of the last church age, has concocted a powerful rhetorical compound to address the "sickness" caused by a material culture on steroids and the acceptability of many differing perspectives on Scripture (read: liberalism).

Moreover, fundamentalists believe that the rise of the state of Israel is the fulfillment of God's covenant with the Jews. Believing that America can be aided best by an Old Testament governance and by making the country a Christian nation by legislation, fundamentalists tend to believe that by voting Republican one can truly be a Southern Baptist. When the perspectives of Akins and Stephens are considered side by side, one may see the lines clearly drawn between the conservatives/fundamentalists and the moderates.

In sum, fundamentalists' rhetoric argues convincingly that

1. the United States must be rescued from moral decay;
2. as a national mantra, "liberty" has spun out of control and must be brought to heel; and
3. secular humanism has become the nation's civil religion of choice.

In an adaptation of the age-old barnyard argument, Southern Baptists may wonder which came first, fundamentalism or inerrancy? In both cases, the chicken and the church, the answer is universal. First, without the chicken, there is no egg. Second, without the Bible, there is no church, no ownership of the fundamentals, no affirmation of the Word, no call to regeneration and renewal, and thus no real, authentic Southern Baptist.

In her Ph.D. dissertation, "Fundamentalism in the Southern Baptist Convention: The Crystallization of a Millennialist Vision," Helen Turner argues that the millennialist movement grew in response to societal stress and the breakdown of traditional values produced by changes occurring after World War II.³ Turner states that the conservative coalition was rooted in the previously noted millennialist vision—a rhetorically compelling, Scripture-based proclamation of a period of one thousand years during which Satan will be bound and Christ will reign on Earth (Rev. 20:1–6). Only recently have Southern Baptists claimed the label "fundamentalist," Turner says, and that only to describe a militant, conservative-led, and attack-driven clergy and laity. However, past and present leadership in the Southern Baptist Convention believed intently and spoke convincingly that fundamentalism and the people behind the idea were indeed *conservatives*.

Morris Chapman, president and chief executive officer of the SBC Executive Committee, in a report given to the Southern Baptist Convention on June 15, 2004, spoke eloquently of *"the fundamentals of cooperating conservatives"* (emphasis added).⁴ Chapman detailed three concepts at length:

1. Cooperating conservatives are a *convictional people*. Whatever we do, we must remember the roadside of liberalism remains hard against the road of orthodoxy.
2. Cooperating conservatives are a *cooperating people*. We must plant churches on almost every corner of every block in this nation.
3. Cooperating conservatives . . . are a *people of character*. Southern Baptists need to practice what they preach.⁵

The rhetorical frame of the fundamentalist/conservative Southern Baptist lays claim to several argumentative protocols. Wills states that conservatives believe that the true Baptist tradition consists in maintaining New Testament faith and practice.⁶ Wills draws an additional distinction between conservatives and moderates by positing that

> conservatives held that being Baptist meant commitment to right doctrine and scriptural church order as the basis of denominational unity, Baptist identity, and cooperative endeavors. They held that adherence to scriptural faith and practice was a condition of fellowship and denominational leadership. Conservatives held that this was at the center of Baptist identity. It served as a fundamental presupposition of the conservative position.
>
> Moderate leaders argued on the contrary that the Baptist tradition consisted in individual freedom. They expressed it variously as commitment to soul competence, religious freedom,

liberty of conscience, the priesthood of the believer, regenerate church membership, and no creed but the Bible. But at the bottom of each of these expressions, as moderate leaders explained it, was commitment to the sanctity of individual freedom.[7]

Indeed, for Wills, the rhetorical theme of freedom addressed the argument that the moderates' understanding of the Baptist tradition is based solely on one's *individual freedom*.[8] For conservatives, commitment to individual freedom is a legacy of liberalism or modernism, a claim rejected totally by moderates.[9]

A turning point in this book has been reached. At this juncture, there is a chasm that cannot be spanned by either logical or emotional argument. Wills states that because modernism argued for a true Christianity, one must include toleration of divergent interpretations of Scripture to sustain such a view of the Bible. For Wills and others who affirm the conservative/fundamentalist's position on Scripture and the rhetorical premises that flow from this stance, the claims and arguments developed for the moderate's world view are *not* acceptable.

It is not the purpose of this study to parry and thrust with clergy, scholars, or laity who claim the integrity of *either* the conservative or moderate posture on matters of faith and practice. The task undertaken by *Against the Wind* is simply this: to delineate the rhetorical differences between these world views and, in particular, to describe the convictional nature and function of the people known as moderate Southern Baptists.

To be fair, Wills had it right. Southern Baptists who claim the label "moderate" do affirm a rhetoric, that is, a body of persuasive arguments of *freedom* that are unashamedly committed to the principles and accompanying arguments that the most prominent and recognizable group of moderates—the Cooperative Baptist Fellowship—claims as "our unique Baptist heritage and polity." In their printed material, the CBF proudly heralds their "Four Freedoms":

1. *Soul Freedom*—We believe in the priesthood of all believers. We affirm the freedom and responsibility of every person to relate directly to God without the imposition of creed or the control of clergy or government.
2. *Bible Freedom*—We believe in the authority of Scripture. We believe the Bible, under the Lordship of Christ, is central to the life of the individual and the church. We affirm the freedom and right of every Christian to interpret and apply Scripture under the leadership of the Holy Spirit.

3. *Church Freedom*—We believe in the autonomy of every local church. We believe Baptist churches are free, under the Lordship of Christ, to determine their membership and leadership, to order their worship and work, to ordain whomever they perceive as gifted for ministry, and to participate as they deem appropriate in the larger Body of Christ.
4. *Religious Freedom*—We believe in freedom *of* religion, freedom *for* religion, and freedom *from* religion. We support the separation of church and state.[10]

As for the conservative/fundamentalist Southern Baptist leadership and like-minded laity, there is a wide continuum of beliefs that mark their self-identity. On the extreme end of the Baptist idea are moderates who belong to groups such as the Cooperative Baptist Fellowship, Alliance of Baptists, and Mainstream Baptists (all or some of the above), as well as those nonaligned Southern Baptists who would rather switch than fight. Above all, Southern Baptists are trying more or less, each in his or her own way, to be both faithful Christians and Southern Baptists. The task is not an easy one. The differences in theology and rhetorical behavior running through the wide spectrum of acceptable beliefs for conservatives and moderates derive from the *fundamental of all fundamentals of the faith*—the inerrancy of Scripture.

While any number of moderate Southern Baptists may have concerns about wearing the label "evangelical," none will affirm the label "fundamentalist" because of the inerrancy issue. Added to the polar-opposite differences between inerrantists (conservative Southern Baptists) and non-inerrantist evangelicals are differences in attitudes toward social activism and social justice. See, for example, the breakdown of the cultural origins of these two world views of Christian beliefs and behaviors illustrated in table 6.[11]

The separate grouping of fundamentalists and evangelicals may leave some Southern Baptists cold because neither list fully describes *their* belief system or, in the present discussion, defines them as a moderate, "authentic," "goodwill," or "traditional" Southern Baptist. Moderate leader Cecil Sherman unknowingly modeled an appropriate response to all of these issues by developing a set of benchmarks for the concept of a *Baptist*—a two-hundred-year precursor to the denomination called Southern Baptist:

- One who was deeply committed to freedom of the individual to face God, read the Bible and interpret, form a church, call a pastor, do theology without interference from a structured ecclesiastical body or person.

Table 4. Origins of the Two Christian World Views

Views on Faith—by Definition	
The terms "fundamentalist" and "evangelical" are now cultural and political	
Evangelicals	**Fundamentalists**
The Evangelical Theological Society requires members to agree on two points, says president Francis Beckwith:	The Niagara Bible Conference (1878–97) and the General Assembly of the Presbyterian Church in 1910 promoted "five fundamentals" that were published in widely circulated pamphlets:
Inerrancy of Scripture. This is a belief in the truth of the text, but not necessarily the same as a literal belief in each word. Both evangelicals and fundamentalists believe the Bible is necessary and sufficient without any priest, pope, or church tradition.	Inerrancy of the Scriptures (a literal reading of the Bible, not one based on metaphor, poetry, or cultural or historical criticism).
Belief in God the Father, Son, and Holy Spirit as "separate but equal in attributes and glory" and essential for salvation.	The virgin birth and divinity of Jesus.
	The doctrine of substitutionary atonement through God's grace and human faith (there is no other salvation from sin except through Christ, who paid for humanity's sins with his blameless death).
	The bodily resurrection of Jesus.
	The authenticity of Christ's miracles or, alternatively, a specific, controversial view of what will happen in the sequence of events when Christ returns.
Dividing Point	
Church historian David Bebbington of the University of Stirling in Scotland adds "activism" as a key dividing point between fundamentalists, who historically focused on separate, private holiness, and evangelicals, who are called to actively bring their values into the wider society through culture and politics.	

- One who believed the Spirit spoke through all the members of the congregation. Decisions about doctrine and polity could be made by all the members of the congregation under the guidance of the Spirit.
- One who was willing to do the work of interpretation.
- One who never let the pastor grow large. Always the laity was equal to and in constant conversation with the pastor about what God was doing/saying.
- One who never saw the need for more than a confession. A creed was a peril to the Scripture. A creed was always less than the Scripture. So, a Baptist was opposed to a creed.
- One who had suffered from a religion enforced by the state. So, a Baptist was opposed to the state addressing anything about religion. And when Baptists were able to be part of the formation of a state, Baptists designed a state that was neutral on all matters of religion.[12]

Lecturing to a class at Southwestern Seminary in Fort Worth, Texas, on March 9, 1989, Sherman was prophetic when he defined the possibilities for the Southern Baptist of the *future* (read: 2010):

> The Southern Baptist of the future may be a fairly defined person in theology and life style. Our churches may be pretty uniform. Conformity will be the rule if this becomes the case. This conformity will be defined by clergy who instruct both seminaries and publishing houses on what can be taught and what can be printed. The people in the pew will not resent this clergy domination; they will be grateful to be relieved of the responsibility to make hard choices.
>
> We could revert back to form. A good bit of diversity will then be present. We will be harder to define, for we will be following our personal understanding of what is correct doctrine and polity rather than a defined denominational norm.[13]

Sherman's assessment of "a fairly defined person in theology and lifestyle" seems to be borne out in fact decades later. With current SBC leadership pushing hard against abortion rights, homosexuality, and female pastors, the rhetorical character of the message of fundamentalism centers on three themes:

1. The denomination is in trouble because liberal seminary professors doubt/question biblical inerrancy.
2. The denomination can be best served by electing conservative presidents who use their appointive powers (over time) to remove liberals or moderates from seminary boards and all other significant denominational agencies.
3. The denomination requires its loyal membership from all parts of the country to come to the annual national convention and vote for the "takeback" of *their* SBC from the intellectual ruling class in the seminaries and in national leadership.

For all of the aforementioned rhetorical positions taken by the conservatives and the moderates, right or wrong, there was but one question that served as a refiner's fire to burn away the dross that seemed to divide Southern Baptists: You either believe the Bible, or you don't. Bill Leonard spoke for the moderate community when he parried the thrust of that question with "Yes, we believe the Bible, but we've got a checklist about how we believe the Bible."[14]

Southern Baptists are always of at least three opinions whenever two church members are in a discussion. Such a disparity of perspectives in the matter of Southern Baptists and the rise of conservative theology has given rise to "outside-the-box" thinking on the changes in the Southern Baptist Convention. McSwain offers two benchmarks of change that served as harbingers for the new Southern Baptist Convention:

1. The emergence of Mid-American Baptist Theological Seminary in Memphis, Tennessee, adjacent to and conjoined with Bellevue Baptist Church, the mother church of the 1979–80 SBC president Adrian Rogers (deceased). Mid-American Seminary was created to be a conservative-fundamentalist graduate school for the new Right.
2. The growth of the Luther Rice Baptist Seminary and the founding of The W. A. Criswell Center of Biblical Studies (Dallas, Texas), which were developed to provide instruction for the new conservatives.[15]

With the support of Paul Pressler, the architect of the 1979 SBC takeover in Houston, these educational entities developed a social, political, theological, and, finally, masterfully rhetorical movement to win the day and the

Southern Baptist Convention. The objectives of the growing movement were twofold:

1. Resist the emerging historical/critical/theological scholarship within the denomination.
2. Target the most influential pastors in the SBC.[16]

By the mid-1970s, a new pastor-orator had arrived. He was and remains strongly authoritarian, popular in preaching style, Bible-pure in content, and skilled in the developing tools of church growth.[17] Without question, the skilled, biblically trained voices of conservative affirmation were singing one song—biblical inerrancy. McSwain is on target when he couples "the imported ideology of inerrancy" with traditional big-church sources of leadership and the emerging political power of the "new Right" merging into the national Republican Party. The South moved to the right politically and the SBC moved to the right religiously.[18]

Voices of apologia—speaking in defense of oneself or one's organization—were few and far between in the early days of the conflict, but they did not remain so for long. As noted earlier, the leader of the "denominational loyalists" was Cecil Sherman, then (in 1980) pastor of First Baptist Church in Asheville, North Carolina. In a letter, Sherman provided details regarding the now-famous initial meeting of the "Gatlinburg Gang" on September 25, 1980:

> Here is some detail on the Gatlinburg meeting. After the June, 1980 SBC in St. Louis, it was apparent the Fundamentalists were organized and the people who opposed them were not. Their candidate (Bailey Smith) was elected on the first ballot with 51 percent of the vote. We had three people put forward (Jim Pleitz of Dallas, Frank Pollard of Jackson and Richard Jackson of Phoenix). Had there been one candidate from those who opposed Fundamentalism (we were unnamed at that time), we would have come very close. Several of us began talk about getting together and forming some kind of organization. It was just talk.
>
> In the summer of '80, I was at Ridgecrest and Glorieta for the Home Mission Board. More talk. Then in early September, Paul Pressler made his speech in Lynchburg, Virginia (at Old Forrest Road Baptist Church) in which he lined out what Fundamentalists intended to do and how they intended to go about it. It made sense to me. That's when I wrote a letter to

twenty-five pastors. I invited them to Gatlinburg Holiday Inn. We gathered on Thursday, September 25, 1980. The meeting lasted until Saturday noon. Seventeen came:

NC	Frank Campbell of Statesville, FBC
	Carl Bates of Charlotte, FBC
	Henry Crouch of Providence BC, Charlotte
	Cecil Sherman of Asheville, FBC
KY	Ed Perry, pastor of Broadway BC, Louisville
	Carmen Sharp, pastor of Deer Park BC, Louisville
	T. L. McSwain, pastor, I cannot recall the name of his church.
VA	Vernon David, pastor of Alexandria FBC
	Jim Slatton, pastor of River Road BC, Richmond
TN	Earl Davis, pastor, Memphis FBC
	Bill Sherman, pastor of Woodmont BC, Nashville
TX	Clyde Fant, pastor of Richardson FBC
	Kenneth Chafin, pastor of South Main BC, Houston
	Welton Gaddy, pastor of Broadway BC, Fort Worth
GA	Ches Smith, pastor of Tifton FBC
	Bill O'Conner, pastor of Eastman FBC
OK	Lavonn Brown, pastor of Norman FBC

Two women were present: my wife, Dot Sherman, and Myra Bates, wife of Carl Bates. Both sat in the meeting; neither spoke.

Earl Davis opened the meeting with prayer, and I told them why I had asked them to gather. I gave my background with Paul Pressler and Paige Patterson. I told them these men should be taken seriously. I went further and made what sounds like a rash comment. We are going to divide. The important thing is how we divide. I wanted our side to keep the SBC machinery and their side to pull out. Political organization was the only way I saw to effect that happy end of our division.

I told them we did not have long to work. If the other side won for five, six times, it would be hard for us to "break serve." I asked them if they were willing to work as volunteers to defeat the Fundamentalists. They said they would; some would work very hard. Others not at all.

They were strong people; speeches were made by all. Two ideas came up often: We are going to be put out of the house unless we "do something." And great love was spoken for the denomination. Most had been selfless in their service to the SBC. We were to adjourn to our states and begin pulling together a network of political support for an opposition candidate to Bailey Smith in Los Angeles, June '81. We would meet again in February '81 to choose a candidate. That was the meeting.[19]

By this time (1980), the Sherman coalition preferred the label "denominational loyalist" (and those clergy and laity were so called), until years later when the term "moderate" became uncomfortably popular. In recent days, the objectionable term "exile" seems to best mark the clergy and laity who fought at some level of intensity and lost.

In 1980, at the onset of the skirmish that was becoming a civil war, Sherman wrote that the self-described denominational loyalists ("we") were not a self-conscious group. There was within the SBC a group of people who were willing to do two things:

1. We were willing to give a sizeable portion of our church budget to the SBC Cooperative Program.
2. We spoke for the denomination; we gave our time to the SBC. It was a labor of love. A few plums were offered the faithful. . . . They could serve on this committee or that. But in the main they were a selfless bunch. In the main, place in the SBC was earned.

In contrast, the fundamentalists were usually distant from the denomination. They gave a small sum to the SBC. Because their churches gave little, they were usually not on boards or committees. Cite this as discrimination against them. But I asked them if they would put a church member on the board of deacons who gave next to nothing to the church? The SBC needed vested people making policy decisions; this is not discrimination. It is good policy.[20]

McSwain writes that informal state networks did form to get out the vote at the 1981 SBC Los Angeles meeting. But the "gang" label of the "Gatlinburg Gang" cast these pastors as instigators of conflict rather than as point-counterpoint denominational loyalists who wanted their voice to be heard.[21] The mere idea of the word "gang" that existed in the public mind focused on the insider clergy and denominational laity that sent Southern Baptists back to the confines of their local church.

For early 1980s Southern Baptist denominational loyalists, the idea that the concept of inerrancy would serve as the defining nature of their view of Scripture was simply not a consideration. Denominational loyalists saw the developing conservative rhetoric as solely political. What they *did not* understand was that inerrancy was and remains an ideology with its own set of multiple and transformative arguments. All of these conflicting perspectives led to an identity crisis for denominational loyalists who also accepted the label "moderate" to define their position.

With so many terms, definitions, and biased labels for Southern Baptists on both sides of the aisle, are there scholarly methods to portray these communities in meaningful ways? Some would say yes, others would say no. With these reservations in mind, Williams argued that a description of four "camps" in the Southern Baptist Peace Committee (1985) might accurately position all members of the Southern Baptist Convention:

- First, there were the theological and political conservatives. These people understood the Bible as being inerrant, held to traditional orthodox beliefs, and saw a theological problem in the Convention. These conservatives believed that there were dangerous theological aberrations in the Convention institutions and were actively involved in making sure that only those who held the same theological beliefs were appointed as trustees of SBC institutions and agencies.
- Second, there were those who were theologically conservative but rejected the conservative political methodology. These people were generally as conservative theologically as the first group but voted for both sides in order to promote unity. Patterson labeled these as *moderates* [emphasis added].
- Third, there were the denominationalists. These were those who were less concerned about theology and more concerned about the well being of the Convention. These people were for peace at all costs. These may be either theologically conservative or moderate. This group made up the true middle and was generally swayed by logical and rhetorical arguments.
- Fourth, there were those who were theologically moderate. These supported theological diversity and institutional and academic freedom.[22]

The 1985 SBC Peace Committee Report demonstrated that the majority of Southern Baptists are theologically conservative. This self-same majority wants to and will support their institutions and organizations as long as they reflect their theological conservatism. The strong, sustained voices of the conservatives/fundamentalists set forth a series of rhetorical strategies and dictums that serve as the "new fundamentals" in the twenty-first century, for which there are no apologies.

Fundamentalism, and those who adhere to its principles, relies upon one overarching argumentative set of premises: inerrancy ideology. As defined earlier, biblical inerrancy is a deeply seated world view that sustains the actions of a national polity—the Southern Baptist Convention. To challenge the notion of biblical inerrancy on any level or field of argument was to result in being labeled a "liberal." With a rhetorical style reminiscent of a country preacher in the rural South, conservative/fundamentalist leadership and followership drew on argumentative resources that championed alternative answers to societal problems. With the growth of historical-critical scholarship in their seminaries, there needed to be a wholesale change in religious education. The new religious education in Southern Baptist seminaries was to champion theological conservatism at the expense of historical-critical methodologies. The theologically conservative membership of the Southern Baptist Convention was to be armed with a core theology of biblical inerrancy: the complete accuracy and the complete truthfulness of the Bible.

For fundamentalists in the Southern Baptist Convention, the lines were drawn regarding their educational institutions and their local church communities. To battle a society swamped with materialism, there was the yardstick of heavenly principles—the Holy Bible. To battle the encroachment of biblical scholarship questioning an inerrant Bible, there was *the argument from definition*, that is, the Bible is true and faithful, word for word.

In a manner of speaking, the fundamentalists sought to restore the "lost cause" of the Southern Baptist Convention in a way similar to how the people of the South in the Civil War fought to keep their cultural heritage. The lost cause of the Southern Baptist Convention was the Bible, faithful and true, which would not yield to any of the scholarship man could create. Gone is the political party affiliation of the early-twentieth-century Solid South—the Democratic Party (unless things change in the 2008 national elections). Ever present is the Republican Party, the unofficial political party of the Southern Baptist Convention. By contrast, denominational loyalists/moderates fostered progressive views of biblical scholarship, supported the ordination of women, and championed the general rhetorical themes of *freedom*, as noted earlier in this chapter.

The public identity of Southern Baptists in the latter quarter of the twentieth century was divided into two camps. First was the sharply defined conservative majority with clearly delineated values: dogmatic about their adherence to basic beliefs about an inerrant Bible, resistant to the inroads of a modern materialistic culture, and definitely against the "liberal" bent in biblical scholarship. Second was the "moderate" group. Williams argues that

> the moderate agenda involved opening the denomination to a broad range of influences beyond its traditional southern core and thereby questioning many of the cultural elements that had defined being southern and Baptist. Convention leaders had fostered the introduction of historical critical methods of biblical interpretation, had supported the ordination of women, had taken a progressive view of race relations and other social issues, and had not sought to stop the erosion of traditional southern taboos on dancing, card playing, and the like. During the 1960s, these issues had occasionally been addressed directly in SBC programs and periodicals, but almost inevitably a conservative backlash followed. As a result, moderate leaders were reluctant to hit the trail in open support of the agenda that had in fact guided their actions. They were simply convinced that they could not rally majority support for that agenda (and they were probably right). As a result, moderates were reduced to general calls for "freedom" and to responding to the agenda defined by the fundamentalists.[23]

The rhetorical theme of "freedom" became the centerpiece of the moderate's persuasive efforts as they dealt with the takeover of the Southern Baptist Convention. The words of the diaspora should have provided sufficient persuasive munitions to battle the conservative/fundamentalist's heavy artillery. However, the rhetorical strength of the moderates' arguments proved to have too little firepower.

The piercing Word of God proved to be too much for the personal armor of "freedom" to prevent the conservative takeover of the SBC. In the next chapter, we look at the inerrancy idea. As powerful an idea as the "priesthood of the believer" (every follower of Christ has an unfettered access to the Trinity) is to modern Baptist Christians, the nature and character of a perfect Bible is even more powerful. When faced with the ultimate argument, the rhetoric of the moderate Southern Baptist folds like a deck of playing cards in the wind.

It is to this wind—the wind of God in his Word—that we now turn. Moderate Southern Baptists found themselves tacking into and against the wind whether or not they wanted to sail across a sea of modern culture. Such a voyage of the soul was and remains a perilous journey.

CHAPTER 5

THE INERRANCY IDEA
VOICES OF TRUTH AND SILENCE

At its most basic, the concept of biblical inerrancy holds that, in its original form, the Bible is without error. The argument many pastors used is simply this: As God is perfect, so must the Word of God also be perfect. "Inerrancy" and "infallibility" refer to the original texts of the Bible, even though there are many major and minor New Testament texts that vary widely in story and authenticity. In 1978, the Chicago Statement on Biblical Inerrancy was affirmed and supported by a variety of Protestant groups as well as by the Southern Baptist Convention. Acknowledging that there are a variety of literary texts in the Bible, the statement reasserted the authenticity of the Bible as *the* Word of God.[1]

James C. Denison, pastor of Park Cities Baptist Church in Dallas, expanded on the theme of inerrancy by arguing that, in point of fact, "inerrancy" is a term with at least eight definitions:

1. "general" definition of inerrancy—As trustworthy, we can simply trust the Bible in what it teaches and affirms.
2. "formal" inerrancy claims that the Scripture does not contradict itself, but would not necessarily contrast biblical statements with those of scientific and other biblical materials.
3. "material" inerrancy states that Scripture does not lie or deceive or err in any assertion it makes.

4. "soteriological" inerrancy teaches that the Bible speaks without any error when it leads to saving faith, but may or may not contain errors in other areas.
5. "limited" inerrancy suggests that the Bible may or may not contain errors in other areas such as science, geography, and history.
6. "indefectibility" inerrancy says that the unified truth presented in the Bible is inerrant, but not necessarily its individual words or statements.
7. "secondary" inerrancy—the Bible records the quotations and speeches in its passages inerrantly, but does not guarantee the inerrancy of the contents of these speeches.
8. "purposive" inerrancy—the Bible does not intend to be a book of science, history, or geography. The Bible speaks inerrantly to its intended purposes, whatever they may be.[2]

Overall, inerrantists claim the accuracy of documents no one possesses. Thus, inerrancy rests on a tenuous master syllogism:

Major premise: Current Bibles are based on (original) manuscripts we do not possess.
Minor premise: Modern/current Bibles thus can be read as less than true.
Conclusion: Modern/current Bibles are the opposite of what they claim, that is, inerrant.

As a term demanding clarity and focus, "inerrancy" is so widely defined as to be misleading and vapid. To use the word "inerrant" is theoretical at best, untenable at worst. To believe in and trust the veracity of God's Word is in no way challenged by rejecting any definition of the word "inerrancy." And yet, Southern Baptist conservatives took the word and concept of biblical inerrancy and, through the vulnerability of the people to good-to-great preaching, hammered out a bright and shining rhetoric with such persuasive force that an entire denomination was turned on its side to support such an idea.

The inerrancy movement was in full swing in 1969–72 as the redoubtable Judge Paul Pressler of Houston, Texas, and Paige Patterson of Criswell College led a historic campaign to set inerrancy as the litmus test for all Southern Baptists, especially the faculty of its six seminaries. Through the 1979 election of Adrian Rogers of Bellevue Baptist Church in Memphis to lead the SBC, and continuing in a majority of Southern Baptist churches to the present day, both the bully pulpit of the megachurch and the local small

Southern Baptist church set the tone for recovering a national convention gone soft on the Bible and gone tough on rejecting historical/critical methods of analyzing the Bible.[3]

The simple idea that the Bible is literally true from cover to cover seemed so over the top for many Southern Baptists across the Convention at the turn of the 1980 SBC election as to be commonly understood—to go without saying. But for the millions who never had or never would attend a county, state, or national convention, inerrancy was an idea whose time had come; it had always been and would forever be the plumb line for all sinners in the hands of God.

Deep inside the psyche of the Southern Baptist Convention after World War II was a rhetoric familiar to all southerners: "My Bible is true, word for word." In the growth years of Southern Baptist life (1948–58), there was no normative liturgy and no hierarchical structure for the church. Rather, Southern Baptists were biblical purists, responsive to expository preaching that championed a style of oratorical flourish that still thrills the masses to this day. R. G. Lee of Bellevue Baptist in Memphis, Herschel Hobbs of First Baptist in Oklahoma City, and W. A. Criswell of First Baptist in Dallas led an army of preachers in large and small churches to embrace "experiential Biblicism." The Bible was brought to church, it was "handled," it was read aloud, and it led to a genuine *catharsis*.

The Southern Baptist congregations of the 1950s through the present day, despite many changes in culture coming from all manner of people and organizations, are interested in and even demand a powerful rhetoric that "encourages the defeated" and "champions the good in man and the greatness of God through Jesus Christ." Southern Baptist churchgoers have always had a great respect for their preachers and expect to hear powerful sermons. However, when it came to suggesting or even declaring that the "preacher boys" in Southern Baptist seminaries were being taught heretical doctrine, were even being taught that the Bible has errors, and so on—something had to be done.

William E. Hull, then dean of the School of Theology at the Southern Baptist Theological Seminary in Louisville, Kentucky, preached a sermon at Crescent Hill Baptist Church in 1970 that directly addressed the question "Shall we call the Bible infallible?" Hull argued that

> it would be ironic to claim something for the Bible which it does not claim for itself. A check of the concordances will show that Scripture nowhere uses Hebrew or Greek words which would translate as "infallible" or "inerrant"; such terms or their synonyms do not appear in any of our standard English versions (e.g. KJV, RSV). In fact, this type of negative abstract concept

("in-fallible" means "not capable of error") is untypical of biblical thinking, which prefers positive concrete concepts (such as "in-spired," the Greek of which means "God-breathed").

Even the notion of perfection, which appears with some frequency in the Bible (though seldom in relation to Scripture), does not signify the absence of all defects but the presence of a well-rounded wholeness of life—as is seen from the fact that it is applied to quite ordinary men with their share of ignorance and sin.

This lack of any emphasis on infallibility within the Bible itself involves more than an argument from silence. In the New Testament era, Jewish rabbis advocated a highly developed doctrine of inerrancy which viewed every word of Scripture on the same level as the absolute revelation of God.

Jesus and his followers rejected this position by contending that some passages reveal the will of God more clearly than others (cf. Mt. 23:23; Mk. 10:4-9; Jn. 7:22). With bold freedom the early Christians emphasized the prophetic over the ceremonial sections of their Bibles, dropping such prominent features as animal sacrifice, circumcision, and the observance of the Sabbath.

It is impossible to suppose that they viewed the lengthy portions of Scripture which supported these practices as "infallible," i.e. as having absolute validity and binding authority over them. Their sense of freedom did not stem, however, from any lack of respect for the written Words; indeed, they shared the conviction of Jesus that not one letter would pass away "until it be fulfilled" (Mt. 5:18)—which was precisely what he had come to do (Mt. 5:17)!

Hull concluded his sermon with this:

The positive burden of my message is that we need not—and indeed must not—choose between these two positions but should reconcile them. Some have found God in the Bible while others have found man. But both belong together there, inseparably intertwined.

To affirm that only man is there claims too little, while to affirm that only God is there claims too much. Let us move beyond both of these half-truths and unite in the affirmation that the Bible is the meeting place of infallible God and fallible man. In so doing, let us affirm and proclaim the Bible with fresh confidence praying that this same meeting between God and man may take place again in our day.[4]

In the body of Southern Baptist artifacts, Hull's sermon was one of the earliest to challenge the developing popularity of biblical inerrancy and infallibility, delivered nearly ten years prior to the "sea change" at the 1979 national convention in Houston. If the truth of the idea of biblical inerrancy could be called into serious inquiry for the laity, what about the leadership of the SBC? Were its presidents suspect along with the teaching faculty of the six seminaries?

In the process of questioning the ruling class of the Southern Baptist Convention, a leading argument was that moderates controlled the SBC. Conservatives argued that the moderate or liberal presidential leadership had squeezed conservatives out of leadership positions at the highest level of SBC life. However, John Finley, senior minister of First Baptist Church in Savannah, Georgia, argued that the facts lead to quite a different view:

In the thirty years prior to Rogers's election in 1979, the vast majority of presidents were drawn from the ranks of prominent SBC pastors. All were theological conservatives. Two of these, R. G. Lee (1948–51) and Ramsey Pollard (1959–61), actually preceded Rogers as pastor of Bellevue Baptist Church in Memphis. Others included J. D. Grey (1951–53), J. W. Storer (1953–55), C. C. Warren (1955–57), and W. Wayne Dehoney (1964–66).

Herschel H. Hobbs (1961–63) presided over a tumultuous period surrounding the publication of *The Message of Genesis* by Midwestern Baptist Theological Seminary professor Ralph Elliott. Widely respected for his biblical scholarship and denominational loyalty, Hobbs was seen as the perfect choice to lead the special committee of state convention presidents that had been asked to recommend a new confessional statement in 1963.

By contrast, K. Owen White (1963–64) was elected not so much as a denominational insider as for his fundamentalist views. Early in 1962, White had published an article in the Texas state Baptist newspaper that attacked Elliott's book as "poison" and described it as "liberalism, pure and simple." At the annual session of the SBC later that same year, he introduced resolutions affirming "the *entire* Bible as the authoritative, authentic, infallible Word of God" and requesting that denominational trustees rid their institutions of unorthodox views.

W. A. Criswell (1968–69) also was embraced as an ultraconservative candidate. Although he first proposed the creation of the Criswell Center for Biblical Studies just one year after his election as president, Criswell's method for bringing about change relied more on persuasion, eloquence, and prayer than on manipulating the denominational machinery. Duke McCall argues in his memoirs, "I don't think it would ever have occurred to [Criswell] to read the constitution and bylaws of the Convention to see how to change things."

Similarly, Jaroy Webber (1974–76) was considered a very conservative president but apart from the later political strategizing of Paul Pressler and

Paige Patterson. Again, in McCall's words, "I just don't believe Weber would have been party to this. He would have been like R. G. Lee, willing to argue for a more conservative theological posture for agencies, seminaries, colleges, and so on. But trying to change the political power structure of the Convention would have been off limits to him, in my judgment."

Paige Patterson, while president of Southeastern Baptist Theological Seminary in 1994, apparently agreed with such an assessment in a paper titled "Anatomy of Reformation: The Southern Baptist Convention, 1978–1994." In the paper, Patterson argued that previous attempts by fundamentalists/conservatives had failed because they relied on little-known leaders or people who did not understand the political process. "Furthermore," he added, "conservatives generally suffered from a paucity of political acumen and sophistication which made it almost impossible for them to outflank the experienced operatives of the denomination."

Among the thirteen pastors to hold presidential office between 1949 and 1979, three might be fairly characterized as "moderates/progressives." Yet none of the three could accurately be called a theological liberal.

H. Franklin Paschall (1966–68) served during a period of profound social unrest and was instrumental in the SBC adopting the Statement Concerning the Crisis in Our Nation in 1968. Carl E. Bates (1970–72) presided over much of the furor resulting from G. Henton Davies's exposition of Genesis in *The Broadman Bible Commentary*. Jimmy Allen (1977–79), while elected as a popular, evangelistic pastor from Texas, remains the only former president of the SBC to assume a high-profile role with the Cooperative Baptist Fellowship.

During this period, two presidents were laymen and one was a retired denominational executive: Brooks Hays (1957–59), Owen Cooper (1972–74), and James L. Sullivan (1976–77). Cooper was a respected businessman from Yazoo City, Mississippi, while Sullivan had been the revered president of the Baptist Sunday School Board in Nashville. Hays was arguably one of the more "liberal" SBC presidents in modern times, but the label represented his social views more so than his theology. As a member of the U.S. House of Representatives from the fifth district of Arkansas, he opposed Gov. Orval Faubus during the 1958 Little Rock school desegregation crisis and was defeated for reelection by an avowed segregationist. He remained a staunch advocate of civil rights, social justice, and the poor as a special assistant to Presidents John F. Kennedy and Lyndon B. Johnson.

In the three decades preceding the "conservative resurgence," the SBC elected sixteen presidents. Most were pastors of big-city congregations who represented the mainstream of Southern Baptist life; four or five could be described as fundamentalists/conservatives and three or four as true moderates/conservatives. Ironically, it was a layman, not a pastor, who was the most progressive of them all. One is hard pressed to find even one theological liberal in the whole group.[5]

In the inerrancy controversy that shook the SBC from its steeples to its foundations, the dividing rhetorical theme has always centered on two questions: (1) Who is a Baptist? and (2) What does it mean to be a Baptist? There are a finite number of benchmarks that can be said to characterize the moderate voice in Baptist life. To be sure, these marks may well characterize the belief systems of any number of Southern Baptists throughout the Convention, but the following collective themes of a moderate Southern Baptist resonate more uniformly with these Baptists:

1. *A radical support for religious freedom.* It is because moderates feel that their freedoms were damaged beyond institutional repair that they affirm the rhetorical power of religious freedom for themselves as well as for others.
2. *An openness for and acceptance of any private spiritual expression.* At the time of this writing, there are disturbances in the Southern Baptist Convention's missions organizations over one's private prayer or public language, that is, glossolalia. Moderate Baptists are concerned about a larger issue—any public or private expression of spiritual conviction that may appear out of place and/or in bad taste. The rhetorical force of the moderate's acceptance of unusual communication means *any* private or public expression is to be honored.
3. *A deep sense of humanism.* Moderates are free men and women in God's Kingdom called to do social good, to support social issues of humane justice, and to do so because, after the soul's decision to live the Christian life, that is how Jesus Christ lived his life.

Having said this, the issues of separation remain divisional and deep. Pastors and denominational leaders of Convention life have weighed in on every conceivable angle to the growing chasm, veering widely from state to state. In the modern vernacular, many have asked, "What's the problem? Inerrancy? What's that and why does it matter?"

In a plaintive voice, Clifton J. Allen entered the fray with the following:

A presupposition: Nothing of what follows is meant to question the right of any person to embrace and to declare the view of the Bible which makes the Bible most meaningful to him as the Word of God or to imply negative reflection upon his faithfulness or qualification as a servant of the Lord, assuming that he accords to every other person the same right and like confidence as to faithfulness and qualification.

The following questions and comments would seem to call for, if not demand, open and objective discussion, serious and fraternal consideration, and earnest and realistic concern for freedom of expression, diversity of viewpoint, and the avoidance of recrimination and judgmental criticism—all in the context of the current campaign of emphasis on the inerrancy of the Bible by a zealous group in Southern Baptist life:

1. Why should it be considered reprehensible, unorthodox, unchristian, indefensible, or disloyal for one to say, "I do not believe in the inerrancy of Holy Scripture as this is usually understood to connote literal or verbal inspiration or invariable accuracy as to facts and invariable consistency as to meanings"? Rejection of the inerrancy of Scripture in literal verbiage does not mean rejecting or questioning the inspiration of Scripture, even applicable to the original texts of Scripture; nor does it mean rejecting the authority of Scripture or any lack of commitment to Scripture as the guide for faith and practice.

2. What has become of our historic emphasis on the priesthood of believers and the right of every person to responsible freedom under the leadership of the Holy Spirit as to belief about the nature of the Bible, interpretation of its truths, and practice of its teachings? The current emphasis on inerrancy seems to demand embracing one view of inspiration; any deviation from that view is not only wrong, it is not to be allowed.

3. Why must anyone be discredited or disqualified for service to Southern Baptists, in any role of responsible leadership, on the grounds that he or she does not embrace or support the inerrancy of Scripture as it is currently emphasized?

4. Since the view of the inerrancy of Scripture, as held by many persons, is related solely to the original texts of Scripture—which are not known to be extant and are generally not expected ever to be found and established as indisputably authentic—what if they all should be found and proved authentic and should contain errors similar to those in the texts now considered most authentic and trustworthy? Would inspiration be proved a myth? Would the authority of the Bible be discredited? If inerrancy must rest on one hypothetical condition, must not the alternative hypo-

thetical condition be considered viable? One Christian's hypothetical view would seem to be as legitimate as the other's view.

5. If God deemed an absolutely infallible written revelation indispensable to this purpose—that is, absolute accuracy of fact in every detail, absolute consistency in every statement of his purpose and will and attitude, and absolute harmony in every expression of truth related to people—would it not seem imperative that he should have preserved the original texts in full for all generations till the end of time? What holy purpose could the perfect original serve not to be known to the generations of mankind? Indeed, what purpose could the infallible and inerrant original serve in the light of the necessity for translation into thousands of languages, such translations to depend upon fallible persons and the impossibility of transmitting truth perfectly from one language and culture to another language and culture?

6. Does not God's use of fallible persons to receive revelation and to interpret and apply the truth of revelation justify a legitimate question as the necessity for infallible wordage or inerrancy of Scripture in texts no longer available for reference and study?

7. While no question is raised as to the wisdom or goodness of God, the concept of an absolutely inerrant reception of revelation in terms of verbiage with all its concomitants would seem to imply control of the human mind and will out of keeping with the inherent nature of responsible freedom bequeathed to man in creation and raised to the highest level in persons adequately sensitive to the self-disclosure of God and qualified to understand his will and communicate his truth. Such control would almost seem to rob persons of the privilege to respond volitionally and freely to the mind and purpose of God in keeping with their personhood in the image of God.

8. To return to the question at the beginning, why should the integrity of one's belief in the inspiration of Scripture be questioned or discredited if he accepts the Scriptures in the unity of the truth as the word of God, if he accepts the Scriptures as the authority for all matters of faith and practice, if he accepts with unequivocal conviction the New Testament as the one absolutely authentic revelation

of the life and teaching and saving work and eternal lordship of Jesus Christ as the Son of God and the Savior of the world, and if he affirms unreservedly his personal conviction that the Scriptures are given by God to make one wise unto salvation through faith in Jesus Christ and that they are given by God "for teaching, for reproof, for correction, and for training in righteousness, that the man of God may be complete, equipped for every good work"? What more is required for fellowship, for freedom under the Holy Spirit, for faithfulness to Jesus Christ as the living Word of God and the one absolutely perfect and final revelation of God, and for consistency with the principles and beliefs and practices of Baptists throughout their history?[6]

From the pulpit to the pew, the subject of inerrancy was in for a long day of discussion with some churches, with little or no counterargument or concern from the vast majority of SBC churches. For a growing but small community of churches and congregants, the high-minded discussion about biblical inerrancy was little more than a doughnut-and-coffee conversation that touched all of these themes:

- A "preacher boys' fight" (see chapter 6, epigraphy, *In the Name of the Father*).
- SBC, CBF . . . who cares? It is not my concern.
- Who will get the SBC buildings in Nashville, Tennessee, and the money when the dust clears? The lay audience of the SBC that discusses such matters in the "other" sanctuary (i.e., the church parking lot) understands "it's all about the Benjamins!"
- The senior laity of the Southern Baptist Convention (1950s–1980s), who care little for the inerrancy idea, have had their spiritual "ecstasy." Their spiritual fires burn brightly and are properly "backed" with their favorite versions of the Bible.
- Across the Southern Baptist church culture there are Southern Baptists who want their church to be relevant and current for their children and their grandchildren. What is more important than inerrancy is whether "my church" is or isn't attracting new people, whether "my church" is getting their generational young people to stay, and whether new young people are being attracted to reinvigorate their church.

With a full measure of comparison and contrast between Southern Baptists comfortable with the label "conservative/fundamentalist" and Southern Baptists stuck with or at least accepting of the label "moderate," are there unique rhetorical perspectives that separate the two communities? Simply put, yes.

Greg Wills, writing in the *Southern Baptist Journal of Theology* (Spring 2005), summarized the views of moderate Southern Baptist scholarship by noting that for moderates, their view of the "Baptist Idea" is the theme of individual freedom.[7] However, expanding his world view, Wills argued that "being Baptist must also include commitment to certain fundamental doctrines like the inerrancy of the Bible, substitutionary atonement, and salvation only by personal faith in Christ."[8] Of course, every moderate Southern Baptist will agree with Wills's assessment save for the inerrancy benchmark. So we are back where we started, at loggerheads over the "inerrancy idea" and the division created by the argumentative claim made for all Southern Baptists.

In any sporting event, there are first-string players, at times, missing from the starting lineup who could have made the difference between winning and losing. In the Southern Baptist struggle over inerrancy, conservative versus moderate and fundamentalist versus liberal, there will always be a discussion about the missing "voices"—the men who, working together, could have turned the tide in favor of the then-dominant moderates. Indeed, there are many "lost" voices, some belonging to men of circumstance whose stories cannot be told here because of multiple source confidentialities. However, I am not convinced by what I have learned in nearly thirty years of interpersonal, library, and archival research, that taken together, that small, but influential chorus of Southern Baptist pastors whose voices were muted for a variety of reasons *could* have overwhelmed the rhetorical chorus of biblical inerrancy.

With the development of fundamentalism pushing against moderate Baptists, it is imperative to "know when you're whipped." Untold numbers of displaced Southern Baptists have learned that lesson, while others still refuse to believe that there ever was such a fight in 1980, or "a hill on which to die," as penned by SBC takeover leader Paul Pressler. If "serving the Lord" is and remains one's priority as a Southern Baptist—but not as a modern-day Southern Baptist church member—then other venues must be prepared, energized, and supported.

In chapter 6, we look at how moderate Southern Baptists have defined and articulated their new life in Christ in new and varied missional initiatives. More than anything, they tried to discover or create *new* rhetorics to sustain their varied perspectives on "being Baptist." For an expression of faith, a voice of victory to be authentic, moderate Southern Baptists needed a new rhetorical theory to benchmark a new persuasion of doing church. To continue a thirty-year odyssey of rhetorical theory discovery and expression, we look again at the *fifth* rhetorical theory in Southern Baptist life (following the three rhetorical theories explicated in *In the Name of the Father* and a fourth rhetorical theory in *Exiled*).

Voices that were once in retreat are now marching on to Zion in the name of the Father.

CHAPTER 6

SERVING THE LORD IN A NEW WORLD
VOICES OF THE MODERATE BAPTIST

"Are you going to church?" The answer might be for a Southern Baptist—"I'm not going to Sunday School, but I'll be there for the preaching service." For Southern Baptists, preaching is so closely identified with worship that there is no difference.

On either side of the Southern Baptist church aisle, conservative or moderate, there is nothing more important than the weekly sermonic call for personal regeneration or rededication. Rarely will a sermon from any contemporary Southern Baptist pulpit conclude *without* a call to a confessional decision that ranges from a sense of guilt, to a sense of despair, and finally to a sense of deliverance for the congregant. As a historical antecedent, McKibbens affirms the importance of the religion of the heart found in Southern Baptist life, birthed by the historical experiences of the first Great Awakening, the frontier pioneer preachers, the second Great Awakening, and the camp meeting, and continuing down to the modern-day revival.[1]

The rhetorical wellsprings of Southern Baptist preaching, long before the current rift between conservatives and moderates, have always been Bible-centered. With little training in biblical interpretation, the earliest preachers would proclaim the truth of the Scripture with splendid figurative language, especially if they didn't understand what the Bible was really trying to reveal. Again, McKibbens lends support to the impact of sermonic discourse at the turn of the twentieth century when he notes that in studying early sermons in Southern Baptist history, one is struck with the notable absence of sermons *about* the Bible.... Only at the turn of the twentieth century, with the rise of higher criticism and the general spreading of Darwin's theory of evolution, did sermons begin a dramatic shift. No longer were sermons just preached *from* the Bible; sermons began to be preached *about* the Bible. Even as late as 1895, when the semicentennial meeting of the Convention was held in Washington, D.C., not a single sermon at the occasion was preached *about* the Bible; all thirty-three sermons were preached *from* the Bible.[2]

As the early-twentieth-century Southern Baptist church experience waxed and waned, exponentially advanced by the youth-led revivals after World War II, and with the diversity of population expansion and culture growth going on at the same time, there was a concomitant paradigm shift in sermonic discourse in all denominations, especially Southern Baptists. Young men and women were entering colleges, universities, and seminaries at unprecedented rates at the onset of the 1950s. An educated Southern Baptist clergy would, in time, age and develop into the leadership of the Convention. With hearts and minds filled with the Holy Spirit and transcripts laced with courses in biblical languages and historical/critical methodologies, the Southern Baptist denomination's "best and brightest" began to advance a rhetoric of salvation, selfless service, and civic engagement in society. In addition to having a "salvation" experience, newly minted Southern Baptist clergy wanted their congregants to have an experience with being "my brother's keeper."

In *Exiled,* a rhetorical theory was advanced to sustain the various Southern Baptist expressions of loss, grief, and recovery. In a word, the rhetoric of the moderate Baptist was grounded in the joy of their individual freedom in Christ as well as in their sense of the Baptist essence: a world view grounded in the traditional salvation moment extended quickly to a view for the world—the Baptist as missionary. In the Rhetoric of the Exiled, there is an urge to be free of an imposed victimage and free to find a new Baptist life in a new congregation or in a life apart from the Southern Baptist Convention. In short, the Baptist experience is to be about more than salvation; it is about the freedom to serve.[3]

On the other side of the most significant denominational hostile takeover in the twentieth century, now limping into the early twenty-first century, is a *new* rhetorical theory and practice that may or may not bode well for the moderate Southern Baptist community. It was a comparatively easy task to examine an array of sermons and speeches (as Ray Camp and I did in *In the*

Name) and to draw on historical/critical methods in rhetorical criticism for patterns and insights of critical evaluation about the takeover rhetoric of the 1980s to 1990s. It is quite another matter to create a critical paradigm and a set of critical benchmarks in order to draft a rhetorical theory or model for the conservative/moderate debate when there are so many varied reactive, and so few proactive, examples of discourse to draw upon. Whereas the Rhetoric of the Exiled presents a counterargument to fundamentalism's theme of biblical inerrancy, the rhetorical theory presented in *Against the Wind* is grounded in more proactive considerations with accompanying critical rhetorical problems.

CRITICAL RHETORICAL POSITIONS FACING MODERATE BAPTISTS

"Freedom" is a *topoi* (place/discovery/position) of argument with both positive and negative themes. As a *Baptist,* moderates are decidedly and/or are becoming convinced that any return to a denominational model is nothing short of "You can't go home again," as expressed by North Carolina novelist Thomas Wolfe. As all of the dispersed subgroups—Cooperative Baptist Fellowship, Alliance of Baptists, Mainstream Baptists, Texas Baptist Committed, and individual/nonaligned exiles—have said, in one way or another, "We don't want a new denomination." Frankly, each enterprise wants to be solidly independent, each with its own voice, budget, and purpose. For all of these disparate subgroups of Baptists, any form of confederate cooperation or group networking initiative will always be preferred over neo-denominationalism. For now, all moderate Baptists know that the only SBC "look-alike" is the Cooperative Baptist Fellowship. If they so choose, a moderate Baptist can reenter a quasi-denominational life with the CBF without the pain that remains in remission as a former participant in the Southern Baptist Convention. In so doing, moderate Baptists can rejoin a semblance of a denominational model without the baggage of their past SBC experiences:

> 1. As a *Baptist,* moderates can select their mission of choice without regard for what their local church regional or state association or national convention might dictate. Farnsley remarks that "even within communities of faith, democratic process trumps theology and scripture in times of crisis because the latter are subject to interpretation."[4] Free to act as a Baptist with free will, moderates will make funding and service choices in their churches based on personal engagement rather than by serving the unified

budgetary interests of their Southern Baptist church, their state convention, or the Southern Baptist Convention.
2. As a *Baptist,* moderates are free to become whatever is deemed worthy; he or she may participate in a local church community with no obligation to serve national or international interests. In the halcyon days before the great war over liberalism and biblical inerrancy, Southern Baptists were basically united in the Cooperative Program funding initiative to serve state, national, and international needs at all levels of denominational life. Southern Baptists drank deeply from the well of gifted leadership and bold global initiatives. Today, moderate Baptists can choose whatever activity suits their Christian interests, no matter what their denominational interests might have been then and now. However, many Southern Baptists who left voluntarily or were forced to leave the Southern Baptist Convention wish for one voice to trumpet a clarion call to regain the Baptist tradition. It remains to be seen if one voice or enterprise can be found and, if heard, followed and served.
3. Unfortunately, a moderate Baptist community gathered under one banner would mirror a United Nations peace keeping force: armed, but not dangerous. The last thing any conclave of moderate to liberal Baptists wants is to play the role of "reenactors," peace keepers in a land that desires no unification. Their former denominational home—the Southern Baptist Convention—is now in their minds so despoiled (think a Hurricane Katrina or Ike scenario) that there is no way it will ever be inhabitable. For moderate Baptists, the future does not include a return to a quasi-denominational business model. As victims, later exiles, and now sojourners, moderate Baptists have lost any hope for rapprochement with their conservative brothers and sisters. Indeed, it is a brave new world.

These critical issues remain unresolved at the corporate level, although individuals may well have worked out their personal issues as Southern Baptists.

Another unresolved issue, with the potential to shape the future for all Baptists, looms on the horizon. Since the turn of the 1980s, both Southern Baptist Convention members and their moderate Baptist brothers and sisters, in their crusade for national and global soul winning, have flat-lined in their drive to win souls to Jesus Christ. In a word, no Baptist entity (Southern Baptist Convention, Cooperative Baptist Fellowship, or the Alliance of Baptists) has experienced a percentage or numerical *increase* in baptisms in the past three decades and counting. In the Southern Baptist Convention as well as the Cooperative Baptist Fellowship, Baptists are baptizing about the same numbers in 2007 as in 1979. Indeed, the rhetorical problem facing *all* Baptists is personal/corporate evangelism—the "washed in the Blood of the Lamb" rhetorical body of arguments that is the lifeblood of every Southern Baptist church. What we have now in a postdenominational world is, for all Baptist groups, a commitment to missions coupled with *biological* evangelism; that is, the converts in moderate Baptist church life are mainly family. While winning the lost children, siblings, and other family members of current members is an important consideration, the rhetoric of salvation is most often directed to the new, unknown sinner, now tracking away from the organized church in ever-increasing numbers.

There is quicksand beneath the feet of those who argue that the churches represented in the moderate Baptist community are weak on salvation and strong on service and missions. There is little doubt, however, that there is an anti-organizational bias among moderates that may or may not relate to this low baptism statistic. With such a predisposition, it may be supposed that moderate Baptist congregations are populated by recalcitrant Southern Baptists more interested in their defense of bolting their former church "home," their Southern Baptist Convention church, than in participating in personal evangelism in their new church home.

On the other hand, it should be expected that Southern Baptist Convention member churches would have a singular commitment to evangelism. However, neither community, Southern Baptist or moderate Baptist, can point with pride to successes in corporate and church evangelism. In the court of God's justice on the matter, each defendant population, conservative and moderate, is equally guilty of diminished success in soul winning. In the final analysis, conservatives are dead set on soul winning with little to show for it, while moderates have attempted to balance the twin themes of evangelism and service-oriented missions with little evangelistic success to show for their efforts. While weak evangelistic/rhetorical positions on all levels have diminished the moderate Baptist movement, a concomitant crusade to win souls by the conservatives' unified SBC leadership has failed "to move the needle" on winning souls as well.

Indeed, there is plenty of blame to go around regarding evangelism in Baptist life. As for the moderate Baptist laity and the moderate Baptist clergy, the necessity to cope with the theological controversy may well have served to diminish their impact in evangelism. Hensley argues that most moderates suffered emotional anxiety, job or career transitions, and damage to their political or professional influence—so much so as to damage their outreach to a lost world in their respective back yards. Hensley uses the metaphor of exile to describe the fate of moderate Baptists, clergy and laity alike, by noting that "moderates lost their places of leadership, their influence over programs and organizations they had helped create, and their jobs."[5] The inference here is that moderates have been busy, perhaps too busy, at recovery efforts from the marginalization generated by the conservative takeover to be effective at evangelism.

Experiencing some hope in the midst of their exilic journey, moderate Baptists have focused their efforts at honoring the Baptist commitment to a free faith. In their past, as well as for some in their present, moderate Baptists have been exiles in every sense of the word. In their retreat from their pasts, they have avoided the SBC at all costs. At the same time, they have built an enduring connection to the Rhetoric of Freedom. Lastly, they are trying to serve the Lord with a rhetoric of missions outreach that hopefully can lead to soul winning. In their parallel universe, the conservatives' rhetoric is grounded in the rhetoric of evangelism to win the lost, with missions a close second. The battle for souls in both camps continues with different rhetorical/sermonic initiatives, but with nearly similar disappointing results.

It must be asked, Why are moderates still Baptists? If the conservative leadership and followership has seized the day and the SBC, why is it so important to affirm one's Baptist heritage? In chapter 7, we look at why moderates are still Baptist. Moderates sense that a new day is coming. Along with a bright future is an awareness of the past—a loss of denominational identity and a recovery of age-old Baptist standards.

CHAPTER 7

WHY I AM STILL A BAPTIST
VOICES OF HOPE

The work of a rhetorical historian is to examine, chart, critique, and evaluate the persuasive forces of history if, indeed, those forces drive the winds of change. From the outset of the events covered in this book, the power of eloquent pulpiteers was the refiner's fire that spread across the Southern Baptist Convention and changed its history forever. Ammerman argues that

> these leaders were preachers of remarkable ability, able to stir crowds with their words, able to evoke response in their hearers. They had developed a following after years on the revival and Pastors' Conference circuit and were broadly admired as the leading pulpiteers of the day, even by people who later joined the moderate cause against them. Moderate leadership, on the other hand, had developed through the normal denominational channels of training and career, with the best among them moving into institutional roles. There, ironically, their very success under the old system proved a liability in their attempt to persuade Southern Baptists that the fundamentalists should be turned back. The pastors who took up the moderate fight were very good preachers, often with polished literary and rhetorical flair. But a Cecil Sherman was unlikely to move a crowd as an Adrian Rogers could. And Roy Honeycutt's doctrinal expositions could not match the popular appeal of Jimmy Draper's. Many moderates were relatively remote from the majority of Baptists, having left behind the simple small

town life. Both their positions as official denominational leaders and their remoteness from their roots diminished their ability to lead.[1]

The successful rhetorical campaign to recover the Southern Baptist Convention left any number of casualties from both sides on the battlefield. As the chief architect of the conservative takeover, Paige Patterson, admits, "There are regrets. Although conservatives remained true to their word, pledging not to dismiss hundreds from employment (only four have been forced from denominational posts), many—both conservatives and moderates—have suffered hurt, sorrow, and job displacement. Friendships and sometimes family relationships have been marred. . . . No one seriously confessing the name of Jesus can rejoice in these sorrows."[2] In the same breath, Patterson's confession about the costs and benefits of the most significant denominational internecine war in American history is echoed by the question:

> Would I do it again? Before you can say Mephibosheth! I have children and grandchildren. They deserve a chance to be exposed to orthodox theology, to read a Bible they can trust, and to know Jesus who can save them. Furthermore, I cannot relieve my mind of the vision of men and women filing hopelessly across the precipice of eternity and into the chasm of hell. I cannot support, or ultimately leave unchallenged, any doctrine or approach that engenders doubt rather than faith. The potential cost is simply too great!
>
> Public images and portrayals notwithstanding, most conservatives do not enjoy controversy. Like everyone else, they wish to be loved and appreciated by everyone. But our understanding of the history of the impact of the uncritical use of critical methodologies upon the churches and their missions has led us to believe that faithfulness to Christ and to the revelation of God in Scripture is more important than human approval. Without belligerence and in painful awareness of our own inadequacies, we, nonetheless, plant our standard here.[3]

Conservative Southern Baptists have placed their hope in the inerrancy of Scripture as the centerpiece of their success story in reclaiming the Southern Baptist Convention. Without a doubt, the reliability of the Bible was, for many, a hill upon which to die. Clearly, then, the goal was to keep the denomination close to a reliable Bible for the sake of evangelistic and missionary outreach.[4] Still, as noted in the previous chapter, meeting the goals for SBC-wide baptisms has not been achieved.

Writing in 1981 (it could well have been penned in 2009), Bill Leonard argued that

> the SBC has again reached a crossroads in its institutional life due to the growing influence of groups which threaten both unity and diversity. Diversity is threatened because there is little toleration of it in some circles. Both implicitly and explicitly, the pressure for conformity to a particular method of preaching, worship, evangelism, mission, and ministry has already begun. Efforts toward eliminating diversity from boards and agencies are being carefully coordinated. Complete conformity to particular formulas for describing Scripture, church, conversion, and other issues is increasingly demanded. The growing list of doctrinal definitions seems to become more and more minute with each new crisis. Diversity is no longer celebrated among many Southern Baptists—it is condemned.
>
> The unity of Baptist life is likewise threatened. Perhaps the greatest danger is to the preaching of heart religion. While using the language of conversion, some factions within the SBC link faith in Christ to an ever increasing list of doctrines *about* Christ. Personal faith very subtly becomes equated with rational propositions regarding Jesus.
>
> Other evangelical groups have confronted similar problems.... In their zeal to ensure orthodoxy, they unite elaborate doctrinal formulas with simple faith in Christ. With time, succeeding generations are unable to separate saving faith from dogmas about faith, and the very thing the fathers feared the most happens to their children and grandchildren—not because liberalism made them believe too little but because orthodoxy made them believe too much. Faith loses its personal dimension as church members cling to dogmas as a substitute for faith, mistaking doctrines about Jesus for faith in him.[5]

At the outset of the nearly thirty-year war, Leonard accurately framed the onset of an internal conflict among Southern Baptists that has continued to the present day:

> What we are confronting is a "fundamental" change in the basis of denominational unity. The change is from unity grounded in common task—evangelism and mission—to common ideology—fundamentalism, a relatively new and frequently reactionary movement in Christian history. As John Hurt, former editor of the Texas *Baptist Standard,* wrote: "Thumb (through)

the pages of the (SBC) constitution and all those of Southern Baptist history and there is no escaping the fact the convention is functional and not doctrinal. Steer it away from its 'promotion of Christian missions' and you can seat the messengers in a small town bus."

There is a difference in affirming conservative principles within a broad ideological framework, united by common evangelical concerns, and accepting an overarching ideology around which uniformity of doctrine and practice must be established. Will Southern Baptists choose fundamentalism as opposed to evangelical heart religion and mission as their most distinguishing characteristic?[6]

In the first decade of the twenty-first century, the choice has been made, now and for always. To the victor go the spoils—the Southern Baptist Convention.

Why are there so many (or so few, depending on one's perspective) Baptists who want to retain and reaffirm their traditional Baptist heritage? Moderate Baptists are neither more nor less certain of a common set of beliefs than are their more conservative brothers and sisters. Indeed, Baptists of all stripes have always been diverse in their views of biblical matters.

Before there were so-called moderates, there was a leading voice who set a course for those to follow. Delivered while he was President of the North Carolina Baptist Convention, Cecil Sherman's 1980 President's Address was a clarion call foreshadowing the coming specter of war. Speaking on "A Sense of Purpose" (text: John 17:20–23), Sherman, in mid-address, said,

> Sometimes I hear it argued that Baptists are held together by uniformity of belief. I do not think this is so. For instance:
>
> - We do not agree on our interpretation of the Second Coming of Christ.
> - We do not agree on the place of baptism in the local congregation.
> - We do not agree on the doctrine of the Holy Spirit.
> - We do not agree on the way to interpret the first few chapters of Genesis.
> - We do not agree on the way to divide our energies between the doing of ministry and the saying of proclamation.
>
> These are enough. All of these divisions are in this room. Now in these last days there has come another. It is called biblical in-

> errancy. We are not agreed on inerrancy either. *But that which called us together and that which keeps us together is the vision of missions!* You will order the life of your church as your congregation chooses. The members of the First Baptist Church of Asheville will order our priorities as we see fit. But to implement God's great mission task, we will band together with you. Though we do not agree on all matters of doctrine, we agree on most. And on missions we are in hearty agreement. Missions has pulled us together.[7]

The call to missions, from Sherman and others in the moderate movement, today dominates the rhetoric of the moderate Baptist community. Moderate Baptists argue for the voluntary principles of faith and religion: religious liberty, separation of church and state, and voluntary association to carry out the global mission of Christianity. Indeed, it can be argued in all fairness that a constituency sustained by carefully crafted arguments for missions convinces the head; but it may not truly touch the heart.

At the end of the road—a journey of rhetorical evaluation as to how the conservatives claimed the Southern Baptist Convention (see *In the Name of the Father*) and how the diaspora spoke of their exilic journey (see *Exiled*)—we arrive at a crossroads. The essential question is this: Will the moderate Baptist community, with its disparate groups, be able to coalesce around a common voice and a common purpose?

It is my sense that there are many voices and many purposes that could unite the moderate enterprises represented in this work. In the final analysis, however, there is no one or no thing, not even former President Jimmy Carter's New Baptist Covenant meeting held January 30 to February 2, 2008, that can bring all of the parties together at one table to forge a lasting national and international alliance. Bill Wilson, pastor of First Baptist Church in Dalton, Georgia, alludes to these remote possibilities by arguing how

> the plateau we find ourselves on, the waning energy I sense around the moderate world, the concretizing of institutions and methodologies, the devotion to vehicles over vision, has me worried. Too many of us have "married" our young institutions and organizations, to the detriment of being able to envision a new and more expansive future. I believe it is time for us to refocus our attention on *vision* and give less of our attention to *vehicles*.
>
> While the vision of a positive, authentically Baptist alternative to fundamentalism is alive and well, I do not believe we have fully arrived at what God intends us to be or do as we enter the twenty-first century. It is quite possible that the best

vehicle for carrying us down the road of being an authentic Baptist has not been created yet.

I recognize many think that feeling this way and saying this aloud is akin to disloyalty to the Cooperative Baptist Fellowship, but I say this as one who is committed to and grateful for the ministry of CBF. I believe the future vehicle for moderate Baptist life is yet to be revealed and that if it is to be a viable future, we must be pliable and flexible with regard to structures and organizations.

I believe CBF will play a key role in whatever that network or organization is, but that "IT" is still in the incubation stage . . . and probably always will be. I hope and pray that we will be willing to see ourselves as a forerunner of what could be, rather than a finished product . . . even willing to diminish ourselves if something greater emerges.[8]

There is an uncertain future for any global expression of the many moderate Baptist entities. There may never be such a United Nations model for these various state, regional, and national enterprises. After all, these displaced Baptists were expelled from just such an international denominational conglomerate. So, then, who are the voices of moderate Baptists that affirm their continuing loyalty to the Baptist ideal?

To find the diversity of Baptist leadership and laity, I conducted a survey in 2005 to address these varied perspectives. From the latter half of the 1990s to the mid-2000s (a span of approximately ten years), I read and heard a particular expression at every turn of research and conversation. In interviewing, travel, conferences, and convention experiences, I heard the rhetorical posturing of "what it means to be a——[fill in your home state] Baptist." Intrigued by the notion, I mailed a letter of inquiry to every editor of a Baptist state paper. Simply put, I asked the editors of the state papers to fill in the blank for their state and to explain their state's rhetorical position on the SBC issues of the day. From fifty-two surveys sent out, I received thirteen responses. To put it mildly, I got more than I bargained for. Several editors stated that their state's members and churches

1. held firmly to key Southern Baptist Convention policies, but saw themselves as moderate—conservatives;
2. were glad that they were removed from Bible belt political and religious infighting;
3. are "closet" moderates who strongly support freedom of expression, separation of church and state, priesthood of the believer, and soul competency, but remain silent in the

national conclaves for fear of losing resources and power in national Southern Baptist polity; and
4. are divided, particularly in Texas, Virginia, and North Carolina, where there are substantial enterprises dedicated to both the conservative and moderate organizational machines.

The search for a moderate voice at the state level, any voice that would be an alternative to the ruling chorus of present-day Southern Baptist leadership, was an exercise in futility. Yes, there are thousands of Southern Baptists, of all stripes, who will proudly proclaim that they are, for example, a "Kentucky Baptist," but that imprimatur says nothing about the Baptist polity that plants them squarely in one tradition or another.

One editor (whose name and state will remain anonymous) said it best:

> The vast majority of——Baptists want to get on with Kingdom business without divisiveness or disharmony. There is a small percentage on the political and theological left (though still conservative in comparison to many) who identify with the Cooperative Baptist Fellowship. There is another small percentage on the political and theological right who make noise occasionally, yet without gaining significant control. They, too, (like the CBF faction) have some involvement in the state convention and contribute to the Cooperative Program. Those in the high middle are theologically conservative and desire unity as——Baptists work together for evangelism, missions, and ministry.[9]

Scattered voices, located unevenly in every Southern Baptist state, remain silent or only mildly expressive of their differing positions on Baptist polity and Baptist problems. For those who stand and deliver their voice of and for the moderate Baptist community, the message echoes the Rhetoric of Freedom that informs every chapter of *Against the Wind*.

When Ray Camp and I began to build our respective libraries of research and artifacts that sustained the analysis described in *In the Name of the Father*, Ray would often bellow, "We need sermons and plenty of them!" He was right in so many ways, none more so in the need to create a repository of sermons that would be used to build the study of the rhetorical history of the new Southern Baptist Convention. The same consideration holds here for the attempt to document the moderate voice in Baptist life. However, the rhetorical/sermonic artifacts of these pastors are few and far between, a small collection when compared to the rich storehouses of the sermonic discourses used to turn the ship of Southern Baptist state to starboard.

The contemporary moderate voice in Baptist life is, in musical terms, a "Johnny-one-note"—a post-evangelistic, prophetic litany about freedom, particularly all that is entailed in the phrase "religious freedom." At the 2007 Mainstream Baptist Convocation in Dallas, the program theme "Voices of Hope—Why I Am Still a Baptist" was addressed by several prominent moderate Baptists. Most notably representative of participants and other platform speakers were Bruce Prescott of Oklahoma and Joe Lewis of Second Baptist Church in Petersburg, Virginia. (Their sermons appear as Appendix V and Appendix VI, respectively.)

Prescott and Lewis accurately represent today's moderate Baptist voice, doggedly speaking against state-sponsored prayers or religious pledges of allegiance. These two moderate voices rail against faith supported by the public treasury and the current stew of politics and religion. Moreover, Prescott and Lewis provide a rhetorical affirmation regarding the protection and promotion of historic Baptist principles.

Bill Leonard argued prophetically and accurately in his 1981 article in the *Baptist History and Heritage* that "the Southern Baptist Convention, like many American denominations before it, has reached a crossroads in its institutional life."[10] Over a quarter of a century later, spanning the changing of one century to the next, that crossroads now appears in the rearview mirror of Baptist life. With a dominant, conservative rhetoric sustaining the current programs and institutions of Southern Baptist life, the post-evangelistic, post-exilic voices of the Shermans, Prescotts, Lewises, and others in the moderate Baptist community sound to many like sounding brass and tinkling cymbals.

The moderate voices of today's Baptist persuasions are as diverse in their sermons as they are different in spirit and in tone. Sitting in the back pew as a member of any moderate Baptist pastor's community, one will hear a "word from the Lord" that may vary little, if any, in rhetorical distance from that heard by a mainline Southern Baptist pastor's community. As the noon hour approaches, the customary altar call to a new life, a rededicated life, or a moment of shared prayer may not vary one iota, whether heard in a so-called conservative church or a so-called moderate one.

The world view of moderate Baptists centers around the theme of religious freedom rooted in a personal, free decision to accept Jesus Christ as one's personal Savior and God. In spite of that postsalvation education in Baptist polity, there may remain a lingering memory of what it once meant to be a proud Southern Baptist (if he or she was old enough to have experienced the SBC "holy war" first hand). There is still the muscle memory of their exilic journey with its withdrawal pains, and there continues to be the rhetorical/interpersonal problem of explaining "just what kind of Baptist am I?"

In the modern world, speaking of such a disruptive experience elicits a "Come on, get over it" expression that may draw an honest "You can't possibly know what I've been through" retort. The moderate voice in Baptist life is, for the most part, ranged from muted to only mildly bombastic. Will there ever be an international conclave of the approximately eighty-four Baptist entities in the world to trumpet the centrist-to-liberal rhetoric of *Baptists* outside the walls of the Southern Baptist Convention? Time, circumstance, and resources will tell. The brass ring of the Baptist merry-go-round will only be in reach one time. Will those outside the Southern Baptist Convention grab the opportunity? And with that opportunity, the moderate voice in Baptist life will either recede into the background noise of the rhetoric of the new Southern Baptist Convention or resound from the pulpits of Baptist organizations in America and around the world.

In the foreword to *In the Name of the Father,* Kenneth Chafin wrote,

> The thesis of this book is true, and it saddens me. The authors rightly see the inerrancy controversy—the position that holds the Bible is literally true and without error on any subject—in the Southern Baptist Convention (SBC) as the best expression in the twentieth century of the power of the spoken word to change the nature and character of a major Protestant denomination. Their thesis is that it was the fundamentalists' flawless use of rhetoric, in the classical sense, and not their theology or beliefs about the Bible, that allowed them to accomplish their goals.
>
> In the pulpits and on the platforms, fundamentalists have insisted that the whole struggle was for an inerrant, infallible Bible. In the past, the majority of the people were led to believe that it was the real issue, and some naïve souls still think that it is. But if the authors of this book are right, it is rhetoric that has been used to gain power and control, to manipulate people, to mask personal ambition, to cover up personal insecurities, and to hide a fear of the modern world with all its complexities.
>
> In the past, they worked hard to convince people that the controversy was about the Bible. They gathered followers who had been told that they were "shaping a new theology." But, the truth is now evident; the movement was more about a grab for power than the emergence of a new theology. It was more about imposing a "mind-set" than leading more people to experience God's freedom. It was more about excluding all who disagreed with them than finding a basis of unity in Christ. The

proof of this conclusion is evident from what they did once they gained control.[11]

Were Chafin still with us ten years later, I believe that he would have said the same things, that the thesis of *Against the Wind* is true—the moderate voice in Baptist life is grounded in a Rhetoric of Freedom sustained by the author of that freedom, Jesus Christ—except he would have said it even better and with far more passion.

Author's Notebook

The end has come to a historical/critical body of work examining the rhetorical issues at the center of the takeover/takeback of the Southern Baptist Convention. In that time, thousands of miles have been covered, countless yellow and white pads filled with notes, narratives, and chapters, dozens of research trips taken with the help of many friends, hundreds of man-hours spent viewing sermons on videotape and later DVD, and thousands of dollars spent to cover all of the work necessary to produce three books on one subject—the Southern Baptist experience of the past three decades.

In a final accounting of such a research agenda, the author/editor/researcher should take the opportunity to *really* say what he feels as the last chapter of a life's work is presented for public scrutiny. This writer had certainly planned to "speak his mind"—but that has turned out to be a strange twist of fate.

I have always known that in fishing, as in life, the "first fish *I* ever caught I didn't catch; the fish caught *me*." The full measure of the rhetorical study of the Southern Baptist Convention *caught* me, as it caught Ray Camp. We were in the right place at the right time for southern rhetorical historians, waiting for the study—any study—that might become a life's work. Now, a decade removed from my research partner, Ray Camp, I was ready to write *the* conclusion to *our* research project of a lifetime. However, that was not to be. The conclusion I so desperately was waiting to write was "a fish I was not meant to catch." Another fish caught me. It was not a narrative; it was a song.

At a June 2006 choir practice at First Baptist Church in Bowling Green, Kentucky, the minister of music, Richard Suggs, introduced a new piece of choral music—"One Song" by Pepper Choplin. As I "sight read" the song, the words rang true: "When God's people are wounded by holy war, / and brother fights brother in the name of the Lord. . . ."

For the first time in my experience, here was a song that addressed the SBC controversy. In a word, I was stunned . . . and I remain so to this day. I stopped singing, read ahead, and knew in an instant that Pepper's "One

Song" would serve as my last word on the subject. You will find the sheet music, Pepper's story behind the music, his web site, and a link to a choral rendering of "One Song" in Appendix VIII. I could not, nor will I try, to say it any better. However, Ray Camp does have one last comment, one last word, to conclude our three-volume study.

In chapter 9 of *In the Name of the Father*, Ray wrote, *"In the Name of the Father* is an unfinished story." And I can still hear him say, "If you think differently, you underestimate the power and communication artistry of the new Southern Baptist Convention."[12]

POSTSCRIPT

SOUTHERN BAPTISTS IN THE TWENTY-FIRST CENTURY

DUKE K. MCCALL

My predictions of the future of Baptists in this century are based on living ninety-three years. I am emboldened by the fact that I will not be around to have to defend the prophecies that miss the mark. I would, however, like to know how Southern Baptists impact the future and how the future impacts us. Perhaps that is important enough for me to hear the echoes in heaven. What happens among Southern Baptists is that important.

When a great chorale sings Handel's *Messiah,* it assumes that history is HIS story. Then the future is defined by the chorus: "The kingdoms of this world shall become the Kingdom of our Lord and of His Christ and He shall reign forever and forever." While this has been the correct view down the ages, it does not discuss what next week will be like, nor what the next century will be like.

Through the prophet Isaiah, God said that his ways are not our ways and his thoughts are not our thoughts (Isaiah 55:8–9). Alas, what the sovereign God desires for Southern Baptists probably will be modified in the future as in the past by our disobedience. Therefore, this attempt to project Southern Baptists through the twenty-first century is not a biblical view of what ought to be but an extension of past responses to the impact of the systems within which we live.

The poet told us what our own experience has taught us about the erosion of time on our ways: "New occasions teach new duties. / Time makes ancient good uncouth." Southern Baptists will be changed by time as the concerns and values of society swing. Not the pendulum, but the corkscrew, will symbolize the shift. The future will not return exactly to the past, but human nature will respond in the future to similar circumstances just as it did in the past.

I grew up in Memphis at the western edge of Tennessee. The Landmark movement developed in West Tennessee and colored Baptist thought with the idea that only a local Baptist church could be a true New Testament church. Only members of a local church were automatically invited to the Lord's Supper. Valid baptism had to be performed in a Baptist church by its pastor. Other clergymen, including visiting Baptists, were often shunned and barred from officiating in a Baptist worship service. This provincial stance fitted the spirit of the times.

In similar fashion, the United States in the twentieth century before World War II sought to live in isolation from the rest of the world. Then Hitler and Japan jerked us into the middle of the world conflict. Millions of Americans served all over the globe. Attitudes and values changed. After the war the United Nations was established, its headquarters in New York City. The World Council of Churches was formed in 1948. Southern Baptists rejected that organization but welcomed the Baptist World Alliance headquarters office to Washington from London and moved into leadership and support of the BWA. Presidential candidate Wendell Willkie verbalized the dominant new idea of that time with the phrase "One World."

Alas, by the end of the twentieth century the trend toward unity had turned again toward isolation. Southern Baptists withdrew from membership in the Baptist World Alliance. The political leadership of the United States essentially ignored the United Nations as it moved into war with Iraq.

The point here is not to judge these shifts but to recognize how powerful they are and to observe that they had similar effects on the political and religious communities. Whether the corkscrew as a symbol of the recurrence of circumstances points up or down, or maybe sideways, does not matter. Humans will disagree at the time over whether the world is improving or retrogressing. Only the historian will have the perspective to judge.

Religion is a major element in an unstable and complex world. Geography can be visualized by a globe with all the nations in different colors. Also needed on that palette are symbols for layers in the systems of society: political, economic, social, educational, religious, and more. Each layer is defined only by its observer. Layers overlap and intrude upon each other; they cannot be pulled apart and dealt with one at a time. This is the systems view of the world from which I am trying to describe Baptists in the century ahead.

A collection of things becomes a system when any one element can alter the performance of the whole. That means that the future of Baptists will turn on whether the decision makers are conscious of Jesus' teaching that Christians are "in" the world but not "of" the world (John 15:18). Religion is a part of the world system, so Southern Baptists will be both cause and effect. Hopefully they will change the world, but inevitably the world will have an impact on them. This "systems analysis" way of thinking avoids a common mistake, which is to deal with one subsystem in isolation, as if it does not connect with anything else. Such an approach almost always backfires as other subsystems respond in unanticipated ways and modify what was intended. Southern Baptists are one of the subsystems of society.

The place to begin is to project what we know about people into the future. People are the common denominator of governments and churches. Will there be more or less of them in the century ahead? We have been accustomed to thinking about "the population explosion." Now we read that the birth rate in North America, Europe, and Japan is dropping. In Europe, as an alternative to immigration, Italy offers one thousand euros to a family who has a second child. Sweden offers substantial benefits for having children; Scotland is preparing similar measures. Japan grows increasingly concerned at the prospect of a 30 percent decline in its population by mid-century.

Despite a similar birth rate decline, the United States population will likely keep growing because of immigration. The country's economy will continue to be a magnet drawing great numbers of individuals to the United States despite great risks and great costs. Those risks and costs will continue whether the immigration is legal or illegal. Immigration has been slowed in the past only by legal restrictions in the 1920s and economic collapse in the 1930s. The political furor over Hispanic immigration to the United States will have little effect on future census figures. No official explanation has been offered for the inability of the government to stop the flow of illegal immigrants from south of the U.S. border. It is evident that farms and industry want cheap labor. Greed appears to be at the base of the problem.

Alas, greed is prompted by power as well as money. Both the Republican and Democratic parties are jockeying to enlist as voters into their ranks the twelve million Hispanics already within the United States. The two political parties also have an eye on the flood of potential voters yet to come. The political system is acting without concern for the religious system. However, both are acting on the same premises. The Roman Catholic Church welcomes these predominantly Catholic immigrants from the far south as much as either political party. This immigration will tend to accelerate the shift away from Protestant or evangelical influence in the United States. Not only immigration but also the Hispanic birth rate will speed this change in the culture and political climate of America.

The South and West, as they have since World War II and the end of segregation, will have the largest flood of immigrants and explosion of cultural diversity. It was about 1970 when, contrary to expectations, birth rates of World War II boomers plummeted and immigration from Latin America and Asia surged.

All this is creating a historic change in the people systems within which Southern Baptists live and work. Interracial progress begun in the last century will continue to alter the system in which Southern Baptists have been most comfortable. Fortunately, they have responded to prophetic leadership to begin adapting to a population mixed in race, culture, and financial resources. This prompts the evangelistic outreach and mission programs of each state convention to vary in terms of the state population, which, for example, in the year 2000 was Florida (sixteen million), Texas (twenty-one million), and California (thirty-four million). These state conventions have a larger mission field on their doorsteps than the eighteen states of the Southern Baptist Convention had at the beginning of the last century.

For a century it has been customary to ignore the district associations as appendages of the state conventions. These local associations came from England to the United States three hundred years ago in 1707. They were the original expression of the instinct for cooperation between churches. History has marginalized them as too small for a vision of changing the world. However, in the twenty-first century they are transforming themselves with new programs of social service (a cup of cold water in Jesus' name) and mission outreach to subgroups of the population (e.g., employees at the race track). They are inventing new organizing structures to link churches that are not held together by geography. This could be an alternative to the megachurch movement.

The logistics related to the size of some of the state conventions is leaving room for renewal of the local association. Indeed, some are no longer local. They are casting a wide geographical net with projects that appeal to churches that are not next-door neighbors. The twenty-first century is already watching a number of district associations experimenting with new roles and relations based on church "size, demographics, culture, theology or mission philosophy." Communication technology and ease of travel make this networking possible.

Until recently, Southern Baptists have networked as a proudly Caucasian body. But Caucasians are a shrinking portion of the U.S. population. The Southern Baptist Convention must become more interracial in its programs and leadership as well as its membership or become a niche denomination.

From Pioneer days through the twentieth century, Southern Baptists have found a field "ripe unto harvest" in the rural countryside and "blue-collar" urban communities. This has been the focus of the denomination's "home missions" and evangelism. Will that outreach shift to these new immigrants who are filling the tough jobs in the cities and farms? An affirmative answer is contradicted by modest efforts and success in the past. A nationwide outreach by churches, schools, district associations, and state conventions to immigrants is overdue. These new fields will fit the biblical meaning of "ripe unto harvest," for that will be where the unreached crowds can be found. The dispersal of Hispanics across the entire nation will provide a massive challenge to the churches in cities, towns, and countryside.

The role of women in SBC churches will be pulled toward the role of women in the United States. It was the explosion of new freedom for self-determination of females in the last quarter of the twentieth century that coincided with and frightened conservatives who had taken over the SBC. The changes intruded into economics, politics, marriage, and social life, but at the Southern Baptist church door the sign said, "This change shall not pass!"

In the New Testament the Apostle Paul is ambidextrous. He affirms both the old and new evaluation of the role of male and female:

Galatians 3:28: "There is neither Jew nor Greek, slave nor free, male nor female, for you are all one in Christ Jesus." (NIV)

1 Timothy 2:11–12: "A woman should learn in quietness and full submission. I do not permit a woman to teach or to have authority over a man; she must be silent."

I suggest that we read these verses as literally true. In that case the subject of the last sentence is Paul and not God. ("I do not permit a woman. . . .") The Galatians verse enunciates the controlling principle—"one in Christ Jesus"—but Paul tells Timothy how he handled a contemporary situation—"she must be silent." This example will not change the SBC, but it will show how someone who believes the Bible is true can update his sexist prejudices.

In the 1950s as president of the Southern Baptist Theological Seminary, I recommended a higher salary scale that provided for women two-thirds of the pay for men. By 1960 there was only one salary scale for all. Only the Music School in Southern Seminary at the mid-twentieth century had female students. Carver School (WMU-owned) women students were allowed to take any seminary class, and student wives could audit them. In time I accepted the faculty recommendation that Molly Marshall be elected as a professor of theology. If I, a theological seminary president, can learn and change, anybody can do it.

With a woman and a black male competing to run for president of the United States in 2008, the vestige of my prejudices is requiring examination. Thus it is personal experience that prompts the prophecy that after the middle of the twenty-first-century Southern Baptists will add sexist prejudice to racial prejudice as a sin of the church fathers on the repentance debris pile.

The year 2006 will prove to be the nadir of contempt in the United States for the opinions of the rest of the world. Good will and respect are like a bank account. They are accumulated to be spent. By 2006 the United States had little left in its account except fear of its military might. Most citizens resented that, so "they threw the rascals out" in the congressional election. Alas, they did not put statesmen into office to restore respect and world leadership by an act of Congress.

Like the United States, Southern Baptists have been traveling alone in the world. Respect and affection have been eroding. They need to return to the Good Samaritan role they played well at the close of World War II. They need links to other Christians around the world. The World Council of Churches is not a growing option. If the SBC and the Baptist World Alliance cannot forget the power struggle between individual denominational power brokers at the turn of the century, the choices are few. Early efforts by the SBC leaders to create their own world organization have been given the cold shoulder by other Baptist "conventions." Only a change in the SBC hierarchy can open the door for a dignified return of the Southern Baptist Convention to leadership in the Baptist World Alliance fold. By the mid-twenty-first century that should take place.

That is an optimist's view. A pessimist would think about the aging of the population in the United States. This trend is well known because of its feared effect on Social Security. If Social Security is significantly altered, the elderly will not retire but continue to work or seek work. That in turn will significantly affect businesses, which will not have jobs for younger career starters.

Unfortunately, churches and their institutions face the same problem of finding room for younger leaders. That will mean little change in church programs or values in the first third of this twenty-first century for Baptist lay leadership. Assuming a good economy, business retirees will have time and energy to give to churches. Retirees with a longer life span will not only seek employment but also cherish voluntary positions of leadership and service in both churches and communities. Church leadership will age and tend to look backward instead of welcoming the future. An antidote would be a good system of rotation for board membership designed to introduce new, inexperienced members. The common practice of reelecting old board members after one year off the board should be modified to introduce members of a younger generation.

These people system changes will tend to minimize if not eliminate the North American Mission Board. The missteps of that agency's leadership before 2006 add to its vulnerability. It has already provided the major Southern

Baptist scandals of both the twentieth and the twenty-first centuries. On the other hand, its successes have provided growth of state conventions across the nation

These state conventions are a better alternative for domestic missions than a central organization. This has been obvious for at least fifty years in that most of the Cooperative Program funds sent to Atlanta for the North American Mission Board have actually been spent by the state conventions through various kinds of "partnership" programs. This wasteful funding mechanism has served as a pressure device to keep the state conventions in line with Southern Baptist Convention programs. Thus the North American Mission Board continues to appeal to SBC leaders despite its clear obsolescence.

A few changes in the Cooperative Program would improve efficiency and greatly strengthen the Baptist state conventions. Indeed, a major overhaul of the program is overdue. Like the nation's budget, it has been the victim of political changes until it reflects political power more than fiscal rationality or denominational strategy. Votes in the 2006 session of the Southern Baptist Convention signaled grave concern over the Cooperative Program. A shift in SBC leadership points to an oncoming revision of the program's strategy. It looms in the near future, but the political stars are not yet in alignment.

An educated guess as to when it could happen most effectively is about 2015, after at least three "new breed" theologically conservative SBC presidents have served their allotted two-year terms and have appointed the Convention's Committee on Boards. An effort at an earlier date would come from impatience and result in little change, because the mindset at the end of the last century will still be in office. The SBC Executive Committee and the boards of the agencies will not quickly adjust to the 2006 change in the vision of the new power brokers. The term "power brokers" is intended only to describe, not to denigrate, good men who must use the power given to them by the Convention. A target date for a renewal of the Cooperative Program is its centennial in 2025.

Renewing the Cooperative Program with the new vision and emphases of the new generation of leaders will shape the life of Southern Baptists for the twenty-first century. This will be comparable to the birth of the Cooperative Program in 1925. It will not alter the theological focus, but it will determine whether Southern Baptists major on evangelism and missions (and how), or on theological education (which will affect theology), or on social work (which will maintain the present alliance with national politics).

The purpose that drove Southern Baptists from the 1920s through the 1980s was the Great Commission. Almost every decision in every Baptist communion from the local church to the national convention was shaded by its effect on "winning the world to Christ." The revolution in the last quarter of the century to change the leaders of the SBC (which was overdue) was driven by theological orthodoxy with the slogan: "The Bible is literally true." W. A. Criswell, the godfather of the revolt, when asked if he believed the Bible to be "literally true" responded, "Yes, provided you do not take the word 'literally' literally!" As a biblical scholar, he knew that neither Hebrew nor Greek nor Aramaic nor the English language works that way. Language by its nature is symbolic, but it can deliver truth to its reader or listener without the need for creedal summary. According to the Bible, the Holy Spirit guides believers, not just scholars or clergymen, into the truth. Promoting Bible study and relying on the Holy Spirit to maintain orthodoxy would open anew the opportunity for Southern Baptists to focus on the purpose Jesus gave his followers: "Go therefore and make disciples of all the nations, baptizing them in the name of the Father and the Son and the Holy Spirit, teaching them to observe all that I commanded you; and lo, I am with you to the end of the age" (Matt. 28:19–20).

The birth rate and the materialistic nature of society suggest there will be fewer ministers in the twenty-first century, but God may have other plans. That has been true for Southern Baptists for a century. Population changes already in progress will have a debilitating effect on the supply of ministers. In the past, the ablest ministers came from the less-sophisticated states because the church members there told the talented youth, "You should be a preacher." In the sophisticated states the talented youth were told they should be lawyers or doctors. The issue is not God's call, but the ability to hear it when the churches are not "calling out the called."

Population aging will not be a major factor for the six Southern Baptist seminaries. Having already played the numbers game and maintained enrolment statistics past the 1980 conservative revolution, they will continue to be the largest theological institutions in the world. The education and attitude of students entering the SBC seminaries has been refocused since 1980, when, for example, Southern Seminary had students enrolled from 803 different colleges and universities. The present use of seminary-operated Bible schools as the source of seminarians creates homogeneity and provincialism on seminary campuses. The birth of a dozen new Baptist theological schools since the 1980s will continue to have little if any effect on the six SBC seminaries. Their challenge will be the rising educational level of the people in the pew and the type of education dispensed by Baptist and other universities. This will alter the expectations congregations have for their pastors and other church staff.

The distaste for religious organizations which has developed in the United States because of religious controversy magnified by church leaders becoming involved in political controversy means that conservative seminaries will continue to face hostile news media and some ridicule. They have turned that into a public relations asset by claiming their opponents are against orthodox religion. This will continue to work well through the twenty-first century as it has in the past.

Societal factors, which are producing negative responses to organizations including denominations and churches, will provide an environment for Southern Baptists to return to the original Baptist focus on the individual. This will revive the emphasis on the priesthood of the believer. That, in turn, will interrupt the current evolution toward Roman Catholic structures and theology.

A mixture of Bible and human nature and enough centuries would develop even Baptists into an infallible papacy. It took the Roman church 1,875 years to do it, but Baptists are more efficient and are moving faster. Alas, momentum in that direction has been stunning: use of the Baptist Faith and Message as if it were a creed, the concentration of political power so a self-appointed College of Cardinals could name the next SBC president (until 2006), and the transformation of the role of pastor from the church servant to the ruler. This was not the intention of denominational leaders who were "defending the Bible." They were looking the other way while following the trajectory of human nature.

Long ago the great pulpiteer Charles Haddon Spurgeon advocated turning the Bible loose rather than defending it. Like a lion, it will defend itself, he said, for God's Word will not return unto him void (Isa. 55:11). Baptist executives have not lost faith in the Bible or God. It is the common man whom they no longer trust to act on divine direction, either individually or in the community of the church. Thus a return to the "priesthood of believers" is blocked. The Bible is interpreted by the self-chosen rather than the congregation. The Holy Spirit is subordinated to the human intellect. Reason is deemed more trustworthy than human experience, where the Holy Spirit links earth and heaven by guiding ordinary individuals and/or geniuses, as Jesus promised in John 16:13: "He [the Holy Spirit] will guide you into all the truth."

A cultural shift to support individuality will support a fresh Baptist commitment to "the priesthood of believers," but it will not be enough. One or many new theologians (lay or ordained) must look through the lens of Baptist history at the role of the individual Christian in God's plan. Then leadership must give way from hierarchy to democracy. Theologically the foundation must be not "the voice of the people" but "the priesthood of the believers," whether or not this wording is used. It is the believers guided by the Holy Spirit to know and do the will of God who must make the decisions within the fellowship.

At the same time, faith in the church as the instrument of God must veer away from linking church and state. A human organization (which the church is not) can profit from sharing political power even while politicians for their or their party's benefit are using it. As a community with a divine purpose, the church best serves society when it is God's instrument working to change human nature into the people of God. That requires miracles.

A century ago Southern Baptists were trying to change the popular meaning of the word "church" from the building to the congregation. Good intentions did not keep that effort from overshooting the landing strip. In the twenty-first century the definition of "church" in the minds of most people is an organization or institution. For example, local churches are building blocks that make up the Southern Baptist Convention. Or a church is a body of Christians led by a pastor. Or it is a membership list that pays for certain programs.

Strangely, it is the megachurches that focus on "fellowship," which is the New Testament word for the church community. There is evidence that this is the explanation of their growth to mega numbers. Without disparaging orthodoxy (which is the current SBC stack pole), it is time for denominational leadership to define goals and implement programs to enhance "unity of the Spirit in the bond of peace" (see Eph. 4). When loneliness is the most prevalent emotion of the time, the church of Lord Christ should be the refuge for all.

In a world of war, terrorists, and religious jihad, followers of the Prince of Peace, which clearly include Southern Baptists, must avoid controversy and exhibit the love required by the two great commandments:

> Jesus said unto him, "'Thou shall love the Lord thy God with all thy heart, with all thy soul, and with all thy mind.' This is the first and greatest commandment. And the second is like unto it, 'Thou shall love thy neighbor as thyself.'" (Matt. 22:37–39)

APPENDIX I

AMAZING GRACE
FOY VALENTINE

> And the Word was made flesh, and dwelt among us, (and we beheld his glory, the glory as of the only begotten of the Father,) full of grace and truth. John bare witness of him, and cried, saying, This was he of whom I spake, He that cometh after me is preferred before me: for he was before me. And of his fullness have all we received, and grace for grace.
> —JOHN 1:14–17

> For as by one man's disobedience many were made sinners, so by the obedience of one shall many be made righteous. Moreover the law entered, that the offence might abound. But where sin abounded, grace did much more abound: that as sin hath reigned unto death, even so might grace reign through righteousness unto eternal life by Jesus Christ our Lord.
> —ROMANS 5:19–21

Sermon reprinted from Charles Wellborn, comp., *Youth Speaks: A Collection of Youth Revival Sermons* (Nashville: Broadman Press, 1949). Reprinted by permission, Southern Baptist Historical Library and Archives, Nashville.

Appendix I

> But God, who is rich in mercy, for his great love wherewith he loved us, even when we were dead in sins, hath quickened us together with Christ, (by grace ye are saved;) and hath raised us up together, and made us sit together in heavenly places in Christ Jesus: that in the ages to come he might shew the exceeding riches of his grace in his kindness toward us through Christ Jesus. For by grace are ye saved through faith; and that not of yourselves: it is the gift of God: not of works, lest any man should boast.
> —EPHESIANS 2:4–9

Though I have hunted for a more adequate definition of grace, I have never found one better than that which I learned as a boy: "Grace is the unmerited favor of God." The newness and freshness of this old subject have overwhelmed me. Grace is a wonderful thing. It is magnificent in its import. Grace has become almost an equivalent for Christianity, viewed as the religion of dependence on God through Christ.

God's unmerited favor is a dazzling, marvelous thing, and I like to think of God's matchless grace as it finds expression in the lives of men in the Old Testament days. I like to remember how God in his mercy told Noah to prepare the Ark, and how he spared him and his family when the angry flood waters destroyed the rest of civilization. I like to remember how God's unmerited favor came to bear in the life of Abraham, when he called him up out of Ur of the Chaldees to go into the Land of Promise, to be the father of a great nation through whom the Messiah was to come, and to be the father of a still greater spiritual family. I like to think of God's unmerited favor as it worked itself out in the life of Lot, who, even though he selfishly chose the well-watered plain, compromisingly pitched his tent toward Sodom and, eventually, in shamelessness, dwelt in the wicked city of the Sodomites; who, when God got ready to destroy Sodom with fire and brimstone, was warned by two angels sent at God's merciful direction to flee with his family that they might avoid destruction. I like to think of God's unmerited favor as it spared Moses when he was a baby, and then as it spared him from the unpromising companionship of a herd of sheep and directed him to go down into Egypt and lead God's people out of bondage. I like to think of God's unmerited favor in the life of the whole nation of Israel who, after having feasted on quail and manna, cried out for the fleshpots and the melons and garlic of Egypt; who, time and time again, forsook God, the fountain of living waters, and hewed out for themselves broken cisterns that could hold no water. And though they turned their backs and not their faces toward God, he loved them and showed them mercy; he was gracious to them.

Even though we glory in these manifestations of God's grace, we hasten to say that they were not his greatest manifestations of grace. His grace has never been so amazing, so dazzling, so divine, nor has it ever reached such stupendous, Damascus-road proportions as in the coming of his only begotten Son, Jesus.

It is in Jesus that we limited, finite, sinful mortals can find ourselves near to the heart of God. And it is because of Jesus that we can receive mercy and not justice from the Father.

Last April, my friend, Joel Fergeson, and I drove up from Fort Worth to Nashville for the Southwide Conference of Baptist Theological Students which was being held at the American Baptist Theological Seminary. To get there in time we had to drive all Wednesday night. And after the very profitable and enjoyable conference was over Friday afternoon, we decided that we had better start back to Texas and drive all night again in order to get to our church fields on time. While, Joel drove, I got in the back seat, stretched out as best I could, and went to sleep. When we had been on the road an hour or two, I suddenly found myself rudely awakened as Joel shook me by the knee. "Wake up," he said, "wake up; the cops have got us!" I rubbed my eyes and looked sadly up ahead to see the officer getting out of his car. "What's the matter, Doc? Did you run a red light?" I asked. "No, I couldn't have run a light." "Well, were you speeding?" "No; I don't see how I could have been going too fast." By this time the officer was at our window. "What's the hurry, boys?" he queried. "You were going 55 when you came into the city limits; and you were kind enough to slow down to 45 downtown." (We detected a note of sarcasm in his voice.) "Seems to me that's still a little too fast." We agreed with him that we thought it was, too. "You look like good boys. Where've you been?" We told him. "Where are you going?" We told him. "What do you do?" We told him. "Well, I don't see how I can keep from giving you a ticket," he said. We didn't either; but we certainly hated to see him do it. He paused a few moments, bent down and looked us over again, and finally said again, "You look like good boys." (I guess he was trying to convince himself.) There was another long pause. "I tell you what I'm going to do," he said, "I'm going to let you go!" And we were, at that moment, without question, the happiest people in Tennessee! Why? We had received not justice but mercy. And we knew it. And we were glad.

Thank God that it is through his amazing grace in Jesus that we receive mercy and not justice.

In trying to comprehend something more of the meaning of "grace," I found, among others, the following three connotations: planning love, eager love, and laboring love. In an examination of the idea of grace, these three thoughts are worthy of our most prayerful consideration.

1. Planning Love. God's unmerited favor expresses itself in planning love. When he saw the disobedience of Adam and Eve in the Garden of Eden, his love discerned man's need. He perceived that sin abounded and that it would

Appendix I

continue to abound. And so it was that his love prompted remedial action. To prepare for the coming of the Messiah, he chose a son of Terah and from him built a nation, gave the Decalogue, inspired prophets, and breathed into the hearts of men the breath of spiritual life. And through the Old Testament days we see the minute preparation for God's shining hour. Finally, when the fullness of time was come, his love embodied itself in the Lamb slain.

In Jesus, God's planning love reaches its magnificent climax. No wonder the author of Hebrews spoke of him in Hebrews 5:11 and said, "Of whom we have many things to say, and hard to be uttered." They are hard to be uttered not only because men are hard of hearing from sin, but also because our vocabularies are inadequate and altogether too limited to describe him. He is the Prince of Peace. He is the Rose of Sharon. He is the Lily of the Valley. He is the Lamb of God. He is the Lion of the tribe of Judah. He is the jeweled Jesus. He is the incomparable Christ. He is the matchless Messiah. He is the satisfying Saviour. He is the life-giving Lord. He is Intercessor. He is Friend of friends. He is risen, though crucified. He is living, though dead.

No wonder Isaiah said of him: "His name shall be called Wonderful, Counselor, The mighty God, The everlasting Father, The Prince of Peace." I think if Isaiah had hunted for a hundred years for a better word to describe Jesus, he would never have found a better one than this first term: Wonderful. He is truly wonderful in birth, for never was man born as Jesus was born. For Him the stars changed their courses and men changed their calendars. Wise men traveled hundreds of miles that they might see him. A king came down from his throne that he might find him. And even the angels sang in chorus heralding his advent. No wonder the poet said of him:

> That night when in the Judean skies
> The mystic star dispensed its light,
> A blind man moved in his sleep—
> And dreamed that he had sight!
> That night when shepherds heard the song
> Of hosts angelic choiring near,
> A deaf man stirred in slumber's spell—
> And dreamed that he could hear!
> That night when in the cattle stall
> Slept child and mother cheek by jowl,
> A cripple turned his twisted limbs—
> And dreamed that he was whole!
> That night when o'er the newborn babe
> The tender Mary rose to lean,
> A loathsome leper smiled in sleep—
> And dreamed that he was clean!
> That night when to the mother's breast

> The little King was held secure,
> A harlot slept a happy sleep
> And dreamed that she was pure!
> That night when in the manger lay
> The sanctified who came to save,
> A man moved in the sleep of death—
> And dreamed there was no grave!

And though Jesus was wonderful in birth, he was more wonderful in life, for certainly never man lived as this man lived. He "was in all points tempted like as we are, yet without sin." His was the perfect life, perfect in love, perfect in service, perfect in humility, and perfect in work.

And though Jesus is wonderful in birth and more wonderful in life, he is most wonderful in death, for never man died as this man died. Charles Wells has said: "Jesus never had a desk, or a budget, or an executive committee; but there is something wrong when there is no cross." If we are to believe the gospel at all, we are to believe that Jesus came into the world to die. As some men count victory, he was born to lose. His glory was in his shame. His victory was in his defeat. His success was in his failure. His joy was in his sorrow. His crown was in his cross. It is through this Christ of the cross that we today have both the promise of eternal life and the abundant life here and now.

This is his planning love, an expression of God's amazing grace.

2. Eager Love. Eager love is a connotation contained, too, in the New Testament idea of grace. God does not just work out a plan of salvation, set it upon a shelf, and stand back and say, "Here it is. If you want it, come and get it." He is eager in his love for man.

I think I would still be single if, after having fallen in love with the woman who is now my wife, I had said, "Now, Mary Louise, if you ever decide you want to marry me, you may reach me by telephone at the Southwestern Baptist Theological Seminary in Fort Worth, or you can just drop me a card at Box 6057, Seminary Hill Station, Fort Worth, Texas." If I had not been more eager in my love for her than that, I feel sure she would not be Mrs. Valentine today. It took many a long trip to Houston, many hours of diligent persuasion, many phone calls, many ardently written letters, before my eager love found success.

In his love for mankind, God must be infinitely more eager than any man could ever be in his finite love for any woman. Of course, Jesus came into the world in order that men and God might have fellowship together. But his primary purpose under God, in coming into the world, was to seek and to save that which was lost. He was willing, then, to go to any ends, even to the cross, that man might be redeemed. And he is as willing and as eager in his love today as he was then.

When Jesus said, "Come unto me, all ye that labour and are heavy laden, and I will give you rest," he expressed a magnificent eagerness. The verb literally means "here; after me; come here to this place; come now." The word translated "come" always intends the imperative. Though kindly, it is an altogether imperial command. This eagerness did not stop with the earthly life of Jesus. It continues until now, and is a part of the very heart and nature of God himself.

We saw his planning love. Here we have seen briefly his eager love, which is also an expression of God's amazing grace.

3. Laboring Love. Still another connotation involved in God's amazing grace is his laboring love. I am told that when one of our now prominent Southern Baptist Theological Seminary professors was in college, he was about to have to drop out of school because of financial difficulties. In fact, he had come to the place where he had no other alternative. Sadly he went home to break the unhappy news to his family.

When he reached home, he found them about ready to eat the evening meal. He took his place with the rest of the family around the old dining table. The plates were turned bottom side up, as was the custom. After the blessing was asked, the young man, upon turning his plate over, was amazed to see under it two ten-dollar bills. Those were days when $20.00 meant a great deal more than they do now. He had no idea where so much money could have come from, until he noticed his mother's hands, stained almost black. Then it was that he came to find out that, with her own hands, she had picked out a large quantity of black walnuts, had taken them into town and sold them, and had brought all the money ($20.00) back to him that he might stay in school. It. was mother's laboring love that encouraged him and enabled him to go back to college. And it was her laboring love that is partly responsible for his testimony and position of great influence today.

If a mother's laboring love expresses itself so, how much more does God's laboring love come to the surface as an expression of his amazing grace.

The Jesus I know was a working Jesus; he labored with his hands, and was not ashamed to do it. The carpenter's trade and the manual labor connected with it were not things to be ashamed of. Jesus labored with his head, for it was by concentration of all his mental powers that he taught the unlettered fishermen to build his kingdom. This must have been a colossal task; and to accomplish it, I know he must have labored long and hard with his mind. And he labored with his heart. Here he is praying that he might not fall prey to temptation. There he is praying that. a blind man's sight might be restored. Here he is again praying that the disciples may not fall into the hands of the devil. And there he is again in the Garden praying that the Father's will may be done. He is laboring with his heart. He has his emotions, his innermost desires, his mind, his will laboring for men. His was a laboring love; and his is a laboring love. For Jesus continues to work the works of him that sent him; and today by his Spirit he labors in his love for us with soul cries that cannot be uttered. And Jesus himself is at the Father's side in intercessory labor for us.

This is God's laboring love, a marvelous expression of his amazing grace.

In view of such amazing grace, which expresses itself in such planning love, in such eager love, and in such laboring love, how can any man refrain from giving him the pre-eminence? Our hope, indeed our prayer, is that in all things he might have the pre-eminence in your life.

Young man, with worlds yet unconquered before you; young woman, with the flower of life yet unopened in your hand, I beseech you to plan your life for him as a bride planning her wedding. I beseech you to be eager in your love for him as a little boy or a little girl about to start on a high adventure. I beseech you to labor as strong men who have heard the Master say, "The harvest truly is great, but the labourers are few."

> Were the whole realm of nature mine,
> That were a present far too small;
> Love so amazing, so divine,
> Demands my soul, my life, my all.

APPENDIX II

WHO ARE BAPTISTS?
A HISTORICAL PERSPECTIVE

LOYD ALLEN

I am reminded of the cartoon character reading a final exam question: "Describe the history of Western Civilization; use both sides of the paper, if necessary."

No Christian tradition spends more energy categorizing and debating its "distinctives" than Baptists. Sorting out what makes a Baptist Baptist is a cottage industry among Baptist historians, myself included.

Baptists are descendants of Anglican Puritan Separatists. Anglicans separated from papal authority at the Reformation (1500s); Puritans were Anglicans seeking to purify their church of vestiges of Roman Catholicism; and Separate Puritans were those who separated from the Anglican Church, believing it was unreformable.

The original Baptists were Separatist Puritans who, in contact with Anabaptists, did church in the early seventeenth century in a way that came to be known as Baptist. Some of these original congregations held a Calvinist theology. Some did not. All were Baptist. Through the following centuries, other groups in other places who accepted or developed the Baptist way also took the Baptist name.

The earliest Baptists and their legitimate heirs stand within the Christian, Western, Protestant lineage of Christian faith, along with Quakers, Congregationalists, Presbyterians and others.

Copyright 2002–7 EthicsDaily.com. EthicsDaily.com is an imprint of the Baptist Center for Ethics. Reprinted with permission. www.ethicsdaily.com.

Appendix II

Baptists confess a Trinitarian faith; they believe the Bible is the ultimate authority for faith and practice; and they affirm equal access to God for all persons. Such traits help define Baptists as Christians and Protestants, but they do little to reveal what makes them Baptists.

Baptists are "definitionally challenged" and diverse partly because no supreme leader, no hierarchical or representative institution, and no written document is the final judge of authentic Baptist identity. To say, "All Baptists believe . . ." is to step on thin ice.

No one speaks for all Baptists. As the proliferation of Baptist confessions attest, Baptists value statements of faith, but Baptists also historically reject any ONE statement of faith as the criterion for authenticity for other Baptists.

The means used overshadow the conclusions reached in the Baptist world. Within the limits of the larger Christian tradition, Baptists are distinguished more by the process of their theologizing than by its product, whether Calvinist or Liberation or some other.

The original Baptist process rests on freedom to obey Christ directly. Embattled dissenters, believing authentic faith to be a voluntary matter between the believer and God, claimed liberty to follow Christ apart from crown, bishop and majority opinion. Baptists, then and now, are Christians resolutely determined to remain free to form Christian communities of voluntary believers who obey God without outside interference. Therefore,

1. Baptists support religious liberty for all, so that each may accept Christ willingly and without coercion.
2. Baptists support the separation of church and state, lest the state mediate the terms for acceptable faith.
3. Baptists keep church governance local in nature, so each congregation remains free to pursue its particular mission and ministry, steering its own course in cooperating with other organizations, secular and ecclesiastical.
4. Baptists govern their congregations by democratic methods in order to preserve the freedom of each member of the body to speak on equal terms with other members as they corporately seek God's guidance.
5. Baptists baptize only those capable of personal accountability in their faith commitment, ruling out infant baptism.

A Christian congregation is Baptist to extent it demonstrates these distinctive traits. Who are Baptists? Baptists are those who seek freedom to obey God directly and form their structures and processes accordingly.

APPENDIX III

WHO ARE SOUTHERN BAPTISTS?

WILLIAM E. HULL

During most of our history, Southern Baptists suffered obscurity as the neglected stepchild, or even the unwanted black sheep, of the American religious establishment. But more recent years have found us blinking from the unaccustomed glare of national publicity as our heartland, the once-blighted Sunbelt, became a pivotal region both economically and politically; as one of our preachers, Billy Graham, became the most famous evangelist in the world; as one of our laymen, Jimmy Carter, became President of the United States; and as our ranks swelled to make us the largest evangelical denomination in the country.

Suddenly, everybody wanted to know who Southern Baptists really were. Our annual sessions began to be covered by the mass media, our leaders began to be interviewed for feature stories, even our controversies began to be analyzed in an effort to detect religious trends. As we moved from the shadows into the spotlight, what answers regarding our identity did we have to offer a curious public?

The most deliberate effort at self-definition for this image-conscious age came at our 1978 meeting in Atlanta when, for the first time, we adopted "a symbol for the Southern Baptist Convention."[1] This now-familiar design depicted the Bible and the world held together by the cross. These three components were selected to identify the cardinal convictions which lie at

---

Reprinted by permission of William E. Hull. Dr. Hull was pastor of First Baptist Church, Shreveport, Louisiana, when this sermon was given on June 16, 1982.

the heart of our common life. Therefore, let us use this official denominational logo to clarify afresh, both for ourselves and for all who would inquire, something of what it means to be a Southern Baptist.

I. Our Message: The Bible

That open book at the base of the SBC symbol represents Holy Scripture as the foundation of all that we seek to do. Baptists are, first and foremost, a People of the Word. The Bible is given pride of place in our confessions of faith because it serves as a singular source of religious authority. We have no creeds or canon law or ecclesiastical hierarchy to compete with the Bible as our sole rule of faith and order. It is the fountainhead of all our preaching, the textbook of all our teaching, and the inspiration of all our devotions.

But why should we accord Scripture an utterly unique place at the very core of our collective being? Because it provides the only access to our Lord Jesus Christ! Negatively, I invite you to ransack every ancient source outside the Bible—whether Jewish, Greek, Roman, or Christian—in quest of authentic information and insight on the saving ministry of the Messiah. You will find that the results of such a search can be put on the proverbial pinhead. It is simply a fact that, apart from the Bible, we know nothing really important or trustworthy about that Life which is the sum and substance of our faith.

Positively, however, when we open the Bible we find an inexhaustible source for understanding the revelation of God in Christ. The Old Testament prepares us to grasp every facet of his person, whether as Mosaic Prophet, Davidic King, Isaianic Servant, or Danielic Son of Man. The Gospels provide a four-dimensional portrait of his incarnate life from the Womb to the Tomb. The epistles add an apostolic perspective on his enduring significance for the believer, the church, and ultimately the entire universe. Anyone seeking to discover the meaning of Christ has nowhere else to turn but to the Bible.

Because the Bible is our ultimate source for a God-given understanding of Christ, its significance is inseparable from the significance of its Lord. The Bible is unique because Christ is unique! It has no rivals because Christ has no rivals. When we call the Bible "authoritative," it is because all authority has been given unto Christ in heaven and earth (Matthew 28:18). When we call the Bible "the Word of God," it is because Christ is that Word-made-flesh who, from all eternity, was with God and was God (John 1:1). When we call the Bible "infallible" or "inerrant," it is because Christ never fails to lead us unerringly to the Father (John 14:5–7).

Not only is the Bible the only book that enables us to interpret Christ correctly; it is, for that reason, the only book that Christ sends his Spirit to help us interpret correctly. The promise of the Upper Room, that the Paraclete will guide us into all truth by taking what is Christ's and declaring it to us

(John 16:13–15), is a guarantee that our understanding of Scripture is meant to grow. That is why John Robinson said to the Pilgrim Fathers as they set forth on the *Mayflower* in 1620, "The Lord has more light and trust yet to break forth out of His holy Word."[2] Like the widow's jar of meal and cruse of oil in the hands of Elijah (I Kings 17:16), or the lad's five loaves and two fish in the hands of Jesus (John 6:11), the Bible in the hands of the Holy Spirit becomes an inexhaustible treasure of spiritual riches for all who seek them.

Symbolized, then by the open book, is our one and only message. We honor no other book because we have no other Savior. We preach the Bible because, as Paul put it, "we preach not ourselves but Jesus Christ as Lord" (II Corinthians 4:5). We search the Scriptures, whether in Sunday School or in seminary, because they bear witness to Christ (John 5:39). It is our bedrock conviction that the Bible will not fail because Christ never fails! It will not lie because Christ never lies! It will not disappoint because Christ never disappoints! Its words will ever be on our lips because they are "wonderful words of life."[3]

II. Our Mission: The World

We turn now to the second component in our SBC symbol, a globe looming just above the open book. This design implies that the Bible exists not only for ourselves but for the world. It suggests that the gospel declared in Scripture is for every person on the face of the earth. Our logo announces for all to see that, if the Bible is our message, the world is our mission.

The original Charter of the Southern Baptist Convention, adopted in 1845, declared in its preamble that our purpose was "the propagation of the gospel." This founding vision has been given fresh impetus in our day by the adoption of Bold Mission Thrust as the central imperative of our denominational life.[4] Launched in 1978, this massive enterprise commits us to share the gospel with every person in the world by the year 2000. It challenges *every* church and *every* agency to do *every* thing possible to win *every* person to Christ before the second millennium of the Christian era has run its course.

There is, however, a profound mystery to this all-embracing definition of mission. Our history is not inclusivist. Baptists began as a small, persecuted remnant, and have never been an established church with close ties to world leaders. Our organization is not universalist, as in the Roman Catholic Church with its international headquarters and worldwide leadership structure. By contrast, we are a highly decentralized body emphasizing the autonomy of local congregations, most of them quite small. Our people are not internationalist in their loyalties. Most of us are rather provincial, little traveled, poorly read on world affairs, not deeply involved in such global organizations as the United Nations.

Then why this overriding desire to win the world for Christ? Not because we are prepared for it either historically, organizationally, or temperamentally, but because we are commanded to do it Biblically. We are like those frightened first-century peasants who had never been a hundred miles from Palestine but who heard the risen Lord say, "Go ye into all the world" (Mark 16:15), and who took him at his word! Like the shoe-cobbler, William Carey, who confounded his contemporaries with the audacious notion of a worldwide witness, we have decided that the Great Commission means exactly what it says!

Bold Mission Thrust, therefore, is not an expression of denominational imperialism; rather, it is a determined effort to insure that the word which God has entrusted to us will not return unto him void (Isaiah 55:11). If Bold Mission Thrust succeeds, it will be a divine miracle, not a human achievement. Humanly, the great majority of us are Southern-white-middle-class-conservative-evangelicals, and, like most groups in our polarized society, we would prefer to stick with our own kind. But the Great Commission did not say, "Go ye into all of Dixie and make disciples of every Southerner" (cf. Matthew 28:19-20). Jesus did not say, "I, if I be lifted up, will draw all conservative evangelicals unto myself" (cf. John 12:32). Paul did not say, "I am ready to preach the gospel to all middle class whites" (cf. Romans 1:14-15). In place of these grotesque perversions, we define our mission as extending to the ends of the earth. In defiance of inherited prejudices that would bind us with cultural strictures; in defiance of staggering costs that would postpone our goal to a more prosperous era; in defiance of escalating political tensions that would counsel compromise in the name of sober realism, we cry with John Wesley, "The world is our parish."[5] In so doing, we determine to embrace not only the rich diversity of American life but also the planetary pluralism that, without a new reconciling center, threatens Armageddon in this generation. We resolve to penetrate every geographical region, every ethnic group, every socio-economic class, and every ideological persuasion with the good news of a universal Savior who transcends all of these cleavages and thus can unite our incredible differences.

It is difficult for outside observers to grasp the radical universality of our mission. Media pundits tends to positionize us in the religious marketplace with 19 percent of the American population that likes to view itself as "evangelical," or with 47 percent that prefers to call itself "conservative."[6] While there is nothing wrong with recognizing these historical and sociological affinities, any effort to restrict our influence only to certain groups in society overlooks the mandate of Bold Mission Thrust to identify with 100 percent of the human spectrum because Christ died for us all! We witness to people, not because they are conservative or moderate or liberal, but because they are lost! We welcome them, not because they are white or Southern or middle class, but because they believe! It is not our task to lead the Gallup Poll sweepstakes by appealing to some favored group in society, but to empty hell of its prospective tenants!

III. Our Motive: The Cross

Turn for a final time to our SBC symbol and you will see that its third component is a cross superimposed upon the book and the globe, holding them together. This is a graphic way of saying that conflict arises when the Word of God confronts the world of man. So it was with Jesus. He was killed, not for teaching on the hillside, "Behold the lilies, how they grow" (Matthew 7:28), but for crying in the Temple, "Behold the thieves, how they steal" (Mark 11:17). For him the cross was that Gethsemane spirit of obedience in the face of utter jeopardy which prayed, "Not my will but Thine be done" (Mark 14:36). For us, the cross means that no price is too great, no sacrifice too costly, no suffering too painful to accomplish our mission of proclaiming the whole Word to the whole world.

But why should a hideous instrument of death come to occupy so central a place in our SBC logo? Because Calvary reminds us that entrenched evil will not give up without a fight. Baptists first learned that truth when they were born on a cross. Persecuted for daring to apply the New Testament to their own lives, hounded into jail for refusing to bow to religious conformity, their pilgrimage through history has indeed left a "trail of blood."[7] Nor have we, after all these centuries, ceased to run the gauntlet of Christ's enemies. Bill Wallace was martyred in China because he embodied spiritual commitments that were intolerable to his Communist oppressors.[8] All over the world Baptists have dared to pick a fight because, like Thomas Jefferson, we have "sworn upon the altar of God eternal hostility against every form of tyranny over the mind of man."[9]

We are not called, however, to fight God's battles with the Devil's weapons. Instead, the cross further reminds us that we are to meet the furies of hell with a costly compassion:

> For not with swords' loud clashing,
> Or roll of stirring drums;
> With deeds of love and mercy
> The heav'nly kingdom comes.[10]

Lest anyone misunderstand, let it be said that Southern Baptists are not a political action movement, or a religious lobby, or a single-issue pressure group, or an ideological voting block. We do not intend to coerce, intimidate, or manipulate the world to do our bidding. Instead, we have but one motive: to love the world into a saving relationship with Jesus Christ. For our friends, we have only gratitude; for our enemies, we have only forgiveness. If that be weakness, then, with Paul, we are persuaded that it is "the weakness of God which is stronger than man" (I Corinthians 1:25).

In that great battle between the Word and the world, why do we fight "'neath the banner of the cross?"[11] Because courageous love, offered in obedience to God's will, changes human hearts as nothing else can. In the first century, Caesar had unlimited power to coerce but none whatsoever to convert. He bludgeoned the entire civilized world into submission but left it a spiritual wasteland. By contrast, Christ commanded no armies, but his helpless love melted hearts of stone that gladly served him long after Caesar was forgotten. Today, a mean spirit of religious intolerance and fanaticism is sweeping the globe, from Ireland to Iran, which threatens to engulf our land as well. Against this rising tide of frustration and hatred we lift, not a sword, but a cross. As our badge of identity testifies, we have taken our stand with the Crucified who will win with his wounds or not win at all!

Over and over again we have confirmed the paradox of his cross in our own experience. When we are brash and arrogant, God does not bless; but, when we are broken and helpless, he comes to our rescue. It is the lesson Paul learned: "When I am weak (in my own strength!), then I am strong (in God's strength!)" (II Corinthians 12:10). To be sure, we yearn to share Christ's victory over the forces of evil. But we remember that God vindicated Jesus because he was first willing to die. As an individual and as a cause he was first willing to die. As individuals and as a denomination, we will never know the power of Christ's resurrection until we also share the fellowship of his sufferings, "becoming like him in his death" (Philippians 3:10).

How hard it is to understand Southern Baptists! For years now we have been told that the central drama of our destiny was to wage a fight to the finish between two warring factions, one called "liberal" and the other called "conservative." But a look at our logo says that this scenario is not so. Deeper than all of our surface skirmishes, which are but symptomatic of these troubled times, lies an identity shaped, not by politics or ideology, but by an open book, a lost world, and a suffering Savior. This identify calls us, not to be "liberal," but to be loving; not to be "conservative," but to be crucified! A broken world will not be won by any of the code words or catch phrases over which we sometimes squabble, but only by the gospel of our Lord Jesus Christ proclaimed and preserved in Scripture.

Our symbol says it well, but the time has come to translate that symbol into reality. Therefore, let us stand united: with an open Bible in our hands, with a lost world in our eyes, and with a cross of love in our hearts, saying to one another and to all who watch, "This is who we are! This is what it means to be a Southern Baptist!"

APPENDIX IV

WHY I AM BAPTIST: A PERSONAL PERSPECTIVE

DANIEL VESTAL

I want to be careful in defining myself as a Baptist simply by involvement in a denominational-type of organization. When I say I am a Baptist, I'm not saying I'm a *Convention Baptist*. Will Campbell once wrote, "The SBC is more Southern than it is Baptist and it is more Baptist than it is Christian."

I must confess there was a time when I thought that to be a Baptist and to be a Southern Baptist were the same thing. I no longer feel that way. Also, when I say I am a Baptist, I am not saying I'm a *cultural Baptist*. I know some folks who say, "I am a Texas Baptist," meaning they identify with the culture of the frontier, espouse rugged individualism, have a "bigger is better" mentality, like great institutions, large churches with large programs and large budgets. That's a wonderful culture, but don't equate that culture with being Baptist. Likewise, I know some folks who love to say, "I am a Virginia Baptist," meaning that they identify with a genteel culture or a treasured tradition with education that produces a gentleman pastor and more formal liturgy in worship. Again, that's a wonderful culture, but don't equate it with being Baptist. I know some other folks who call themselves Bible-believing Baptists, and by that they mean they "don't drink, don't chew and don't go with girls who do." It is a culture of negativism, rules and strict behavioral patterns. Don't equate that culture with being Baptist.

From a pamphlet published by the Cooperative Baptist Fellowship. Reprinted by permission.

Instead, I have come to identify myself as a *convictional Baptist,* a Christian who expresses faith and lives life compelled and convicted by certain principles that Baptists have championed. These biblical ideas have captured me. I am passionate about them. I am surely not the first person to be passionate about them. In fact, one of the benefits of studying history is to see how individuals before me in very different circumstances came to these convictions, how they loved them, expressed them and, in some instances, died for them.

Also, one of the benefits of traveling is to discover how individuals around the world have come to convictions about these values and, in very different cultures and circumstances, seek to live by them. The Baptist movement is a global one. If one studies its rich history, one discovers a movement that has resulted in the starting of thousands of churches, the founding of hundreds of colleges, the sending of missionaries, and the support of all kinds of benevolent ministries.

I am a Baptist because I believe in a non-hierarchical approach to doing church.

Just a few months ago, I was in Europe for the Jubilee Celebration of the European Baptist Federation. EBF is made up of fifty Baptist unions in Europe, many of them very small and struggling under a state church. One afternoon, I was visiting with Malkhaz Songulashvili, the general secretary of the Baptist Union in Georgia and pastor of the largest Baptist church in that country. Out of a population of five million, there are five thousand Baptists. This young Baptist is a brilliant linguist, a studied theologian and an ardent missionary. He began to talk about the difference between an Orthodox Christian in Georgia and a Baptist Christian. He expressed deep appreciation and indebtedness toward Orthodoxy for its development of trinitarian theology, Christological confessions, and a sense of mystery in worship. But then he said, with his eyes flashing, "It is in the doctrine of the church and the life of the ordinary Christian that the Baptist witness is so important."

In Orthodoxy, the hierarchical character of the church diminishes personal faith and individual responsibility. There is a vertical structure with authority and status from top to bottom:

Patriarch
Metropolitan
Archbishop
Bishop
Archmandrit
Protopresbyter
Dean

Priest
Archdeacon
Deacon
Reader
Member

In contrast, Baptists have championed the idea that every person is a priest before God. The church is not where the bishops gather, but where two or three gather in the name of Jesus. There are no intermediaries between God and the individual. Every person can open Scripture and listen to the voice of the Spirit.

Now, this idea may seem "old hat" to us in the United States, but I can tell you that this idea is radical in Tbilisi, Georgia, Eastern Europe. The oppression of Baptists by the Orthodox Church is a result of this radical ecclesiology. This view of the church that says every member is a minister, every Christian is a priest, every believer can be a Bible student and every church is free is a radical view. I am a Baptist because I believe in a non-hierarchical approach to church.

I am a Baptist because I believe in a non-creedal approach to faith.

The difference between a confession and a creed is that, in a confession, we declare what we believe. We declare it freely and without coercion. In a creed, we declare what we must believe, or, more specifically, what others must believe. Baptists have always been confessional, but they have resisted creeds. They have always believed no creed but Christ, no statement about the Bible, but only the Bible itself as their authority.

This non-creedal approach to faith has caused some to accuse Baptists of not believing anything, or failing to set theological or doctrinal parameters. Others have rightly noted the stream of anti-intellectualism that runs deep within the Baptist family.

There is the story of the Baptist preacher who was against education because he believed it interfered with the Second Coming. He used as his proof-text that verse where Jesus said, "In the hour that you think not, the Son of Man cometh." But for every one of these kind of folks, there are many others who have believed deeply in loving God with the mind as well as the heart.

Baptists have been passionate about doctrine and theological education, both at the lay and clergy level. But we have been non-creedal in our commitment to doctrinal integrity and theological inquiry. We have championed the freedom of every individual to interpret Scripture, to discern God's will and to act out of conscience.

I am a Baptist because I believe in freedom.

I love the kind of house that freedom builds. It's a big house that has space for differing and sometimes even competing ideas. We are better for those broader perspectives. Baptists create a house where differing perspectives are not only tolerated but encouraged. So, in the Baptist house, you have a Jerry Falwell and a James Dunn; a Jesse Helms and a Jesse Jackson; a Billy Graham and a Martin Luther King, Jr.; a Bill Clinton and a Trent Lott. It is true that freedom not only creates a large family, but at times a fussing family. In the Baptist family, we will disagree.

Everybody has heard the story that where there are two Baptists there are three opinions. We're not like the creedal folk. At Wheaton College, every student signs a creed, every faculty member signs a creed, and every administrator signs a creed. Now, Wheaton is a fine institution and I commend it; but it's not Baptist. In a Baptist university or a Baptist church or a Baptist institution there will be diversity, differences, and even difficulty. But that tension is intrinsic to what it means to be Baptist. Freedom creates diversity. Baptists are neither faint of heart nor weak of constitution, leading to stories like that of the woman who said, "I'd like to be a Baptist, but I'm not constitutionally able."

One is a Christian by grace and a Baptist by conviction. But, in all this freedom, is there any center, is there a unifying vision or foundational principle that binds us Baptists together? That question leads to one last reason that I'm a Baptist.

I am a Baptist because I believe that a personal experience of God's grace revealed in Jesus Christ is what binds us together.

More than 100 years ago, Walter Rauschenbusch, a Baptist pastor in Rochester, New York, and sometimes called the founder of the "social gospel," wrote a series of articles published in the Rochester Baptist Journal entitled "Why I Am a Baptist." In the first of those articles he writes,

> The Christian faith as Baptists hold it, sets spiritual experience boldly to the front as the one great thing in religion. It aims at experiential religion. We are an evangelistic body. We summon all men to conscious repentance from sin, to conscious prayer for forgiveness. We ask a man: "Have you put your faith in Christ? Have you submitted your will to His will? Have you received the inward assurance that your sins are forgiven and that you are at peace with God?" If anyone desires to enter our churches we ask for evidence of such experience and we ask for nothing else. We do not ask him to recite a creed or catechism. The more simple and heartfelt the testimony is, the better we like it. If it is glib and wordy, we distrust it. Experience

is our sole requisite for receiving baptism; it is fundamental in our church life.

We apply the same test to our ministry. The first thing we ask a candidate is about his conversion and Christian experience. The next thing we ask him is if he is conscious of being personally called to the work of the ministry; that also probes for experience with God. Finally we ask him for his view of doctrine, but there, too, we discourage any mere recitation of what is orthodox, and are best pleased if all his intellectual beliefs are plainly born of inward conviction and experience.

In this direct insistence on conscious personal experience a true Baptist Church is about as clear-cut and untrammeled as any religious body can well be.

When we Baptists insist on personal experience as the only essential thing in religion, we are hewing our way back to original Christianity. (Emphasis added.)

The language of Baptists in trying to get at personal experience is sometimes confusing to folks. We talk about "being washed in the blood." We ask people "Have you been to the cross?" or "Are you saved?" "Have you been born again?" "Have you accepted Jesus as your Savior?" But, though we fumble with words and say it poorly sometimes, we know deep down that the one great thing in religion is personal experience with God's grace revealed in Jesus Christ. This is the center. This is the common tie that binds us together.

I know Baptists who are Calvinists and Baptists who are Armenians. I know Baptists who are charismatic and Baptists who are not charismatic. I know Baptists who are liberal and others who are fundamentalists. Some are "high church," and some are "low church." Some are Republicans and some are Democrats. But the central reality of life in the Baptist witness is personal experience of God's grace revealed in Christ.

So I'm glad to be a Baptist kind of Christian. Aren't you?

APPENDIX V

ON RELIGIOUS LIBERTY

BRUCE PRESCOTT

In the current issue of the MBN [Mainstream Baptist Network] Newsletter is an article I wrote on "Passing the Torch for Religious Liberty." I would like to build on that article and talk about how the torch was passed to me. I would like to say that I caught the torch in Sunday School or in Training Union or from a series of sermons that I heard my pastor preach. But that was not the case. With a few exceptions, from the time that I was a teenager, Baptists have done a poor job of conveying our heritage. The truth is, I learned about our Baptist legacy as champions for religious liberty from my mother.

I grew up in New Mexico, and my mother encouraged me to study Baptist history after she saw my seventh grade textbook on New Mexico state history. A great part of the history of New Mexico is the history of Spanish Conquistadores and Catholic priests. She was afraid that my public school textbook had so sanitized the missionary methods of the Conquistadores that I would become unduly impressed with the piety and virtues of Catholicism. She knew something about the Spanish Inquisition and she knew that Baptists had been persecuted by both Catholics and Protestants. So, she decided that it was high time for her son to learn about what it means to be a Baptist. She handed me a booklet that she had studied years earlier in a Training Union class. It was a little red pamphlet, about fifty pages long,

---

Reprinted by permission of Bruce Prescott. From a presentation at the National Mainstream Baptist Convocation held in Dallas, Texas, February 23–24, 2007.

that was entitled *The Trail of Blood*, and it had a chart in the back that traced the history of the Baptist church all the way back to John the Baptist at the Jordan River.

As a thirteen-year-old boy I was very impressed with *The Trail of Blood*, but even before I graduated from high school I had discovered that most Baptist preachers make lousy historians. The idea that Baptists can trace their lineage back to Jerusalem is an old Landmark Baptist myth; it's not history. I learned that while I was in high school working on a project for my history class.

When I began reading some real church history books—books from church historians of all denominations and theological perspectives—I discovered, to my great surprise, that Monatists and Donatists and Albigenses and Waldenses were not really Baptists. They were persecuted mercilessly for their faith by other Christians, but they were not Baptists. What J. M. Carroll really did in his pamphlet was to trace the history of religious intolerance, and then he claimed that everyone who was ever persecuted for their faith was a Baptist.

Any schoolboy who did a little research for himself could learn that J. M. Carroll was wrong. And frankly, it has been a long time since I have heard someone pushing the old Landmark myth of Baptist successionism. That myth has been replaced by a new myth today. And the new myth is far worse than the old myth. The old myth was harmless. The new myth is dangerous. Those who believed the old myth merely filled their minds with a false sense of pride. Those who believe the new myth have taken it upon themselves to fill high elective offices and positions of political power throughout our country.

The new myth has been promoted by the Christian Coalition, Focus on the Family, the Southern Baptist Convention and a host of other "Religious Right" organizations for more than a quarter of a century. Their myth is every bit as much a fable and a fairy tale as was the old Landmark myth about Baptist successionism. Any schoolboy or schoolgirl who takes the time to do a little research for themselves can learn that it is wrong. But, people have been listening to TV preachers weave fairy tales about the United States being a "Christian Nation" for so long that they assume it must be true and they won't bother to do the research. Today, for more than half of the Christians in America, it is an article of faith that the United States was a "Christian Nation" until 1962. In their minds, some liberal, secular humanist judges on the Supreme Court kicked God out of the public schools in 1962 and American culture has been on the decline ever since.

Baptists should know better.

The one thing that was true in the old Baptist myth in *The Trail of Blood* was that the history of Western Civilization has been a bloody trail of religious persecution. It was a bloody trail because Christians united church and state and evangelized by birth and by force of law instead of by the persuasion of preaching. In those "good old days," people became citizens of the state and were baptized into the church on the same day—the day of their natural birth.

Before Baptists founded the colony of Rhode Island, every nation that had ever existed on the face of the earth believed that separating religion and government would create divisions and disrupt the peace and tranquility of society. Freedom of thought and liberty of conscience were the equivalent of treason in those "good old days"—and nothing disturbed the peace like people thinking that faith was a personal decision and that only believers should be baptized. That is why the Christian magistrates of Europe drowned Anabaptists and burned them at the stake. That is why the Christian magistrates in Colonial America banished, whipped and imprisoned Baptists and Quakers. And, after bearing the brunt of those persecutions, that is why the Baptists who fought in the Revolutionary War refused to adopt a constitution that lacked an explicit guarantee that church and state would be separate.

Those eighteenth-century Baptists did something that no people had ever done before them—they created a society that guaranteed both freedom *of* religion and freedom *from* religion. They insisted that minorities should be protected from the tyranny of the majority in matters of faith and conscience. They created a society that guaranteed freedom of conscience to *every* citizen. They did that by making it possible, as colonial Baptist evangelist John Leland put it, for "a Pagan, Turk, Jew or Christian" to be eligible to serve in any post of the government—today I'm sure he would add "Mormon" to his list. Leland and his fellow Baptists refused to ratify a constitution until an amendment separating church and state was added. When all is said and done, the first amendment to the constitution of the United States is the single greatest contribution that Baptist people have made to the history of western civilization.

Baptists were doggedly relentless in pursuing religious liberty for everyone—even for the atheist who, as Anabaptist Balthasar Hubmaier surmised, "wished to do nothing more than to forsake God." We were relentless about religious liberty because it is essential to our understanding of the way that God relates to humanity.

God did not send his son to die for principalities and powers. God sent his son to die for people. Jesus was not concerned with earthly kingdoms and nation states. God's kingdom has always been a spiritual kingdom—a kingdom of love and grace.

The spiritual nature of God's relation to man was revealed from the very beginning. God was not making androids and robots. He was making human beings—in the image and likeness of a loving, personal God. That means that

Appendix V

we were created to live in loving personal relationship with God and with others.

Genuine love springs up voluntarily, from a willing heart. You cannot force someone to love you. Love cannot be coerced. It's a matter of trust and commitment.

God desires that everyone love him and trust him and his Spirit is continually calling us to live in relationship with him. But, if love is a free response of trust and faith, then the freedom to reject God and his love must also be a possibility.

The truth is, at one time or another, we have all sinned, and turned away from the glory of God's love. Every sinner—that's every human being—has personal experience with this aspect of the freedom that God gave us.

If God leaves us free in matters of faith and religion, what right do men have to try and force it upon people?

God never commanded us to force the children of people who hold vastly divergent faiths and beliefs to say generic prayers in public schools. In fact, Jesus discouraged public praying. He said don't stand on the street corner and blow trumpets when you are praying. He told us to go to our closets and do our praying in secret.

Christ never commanded us to force atheists and Buddhists and agnostics to acknowledge God in pledges of allegiance to some earthly authority. Jesus separated church and state. He said, "My kingdom is not of this world" and he advised us to "Render unto Caesar the things that are Caesar's and render unto God the things that are God's."

For nearly a generation, TV evangelists and Southern Baptist preachers have been standing in their pulpits and raising their authoritative voices with loud conviction preaching exactly the opposite of what Jesus said. They are preaching from the false gospel of civil religion—not the gospel of Jesus Christ. There is no authority from the Bible for state-sponsored prayers or for religious pledges of allegiance. Neither the Spirit nor the words of Christ condone their civil religion.

What kind of anemic, watered-down religiosity thinks that a little "ceremonial deism," a handful of Ten Commandments monuments, and a few public displays of piety could have anything at all to do with Christ's command to proclaim the gospel to the people of all nations?

I'm certain of this. Our Baptist ancestors would have scoffed at the idea that nationality had anything to do with being a Christian. Nations can't be Christian. Only people can be Christian. People don't become Christians by being born into a "Christian Nation," people become Christians by being "born again."

Real Baptists don't believe in faith by proxy. Faith is not a birthright and real faith is not passed down like an heirloom from one generation to the next. Real faith has always been a matter of the heart and conscience. That is why Christ gave each person direct access to the throne of grace. Each person must come to faith by personal conviction and individual commitment.

We don't believe that saints or priests or preachers or parents serve as our mediators. There's only one mediator between mankind and God—the man Christ Jesus—and every one of us is called to be his priest and commissioned to be his ambassador.

Real Baptists believe that the gospel is "good news" and we firmly believe that every one of us—not just the preacher—has a responsibility to share it. To share it we have to be open to genuine dialogue and honest discussion with everyone that we meet—especially with our unbelieving friends and acquaintances.

The early Baptists were always discussing their faith with people who had different convictions. That was because very few people shared their beliefs and convictions. Like the Apostle Paul who preached in the marketplaces and amphitheaters of a pagan world, they were confident that the gospel of Christ has nothing to lose and everything to gain from a thoughtful comparison of beliefs and convictions. They were convinced that those who cut off discussion and persecuted people of different convictions had a weak faith that could not bear honest scrutiny and thoughtful examination. Those who used force of law and government to defend their religious culture and heritage were merely striving to preserve a dying faith.

Those early Baptists had a lot of first hand experience with dead and dying belief systems—the kind that relied on the force of government to preserve their hold over minds and hearts. That's why the early Baptists were never in favor of uniting church and state. All they asked was to live in a society that practices the Golden Rule—"Do unto others as you would have them do unto you." We wanted to live in a society where people would extend to us the same courtesy and respect that they asked for themselves. We pledged to extend to all others the same courtesy and respect that we asked for ourselves. For Baptists an ideal society is one where each person respects the right of every other person to live according to the dictates of their own conscience in matters of faith and religion.

In political life, nothing was more important to us than securing and preserving respect for liberty of conscience. In a society that granted liberty of conscience, every person would be assured the right to hear a thoughtful, sensitive presentation of the gospel—if they were interested in hearing it. Then, every person would be afforded the opportunity to make their own response to the claim that the gospel makes on their lives—either to accept it or reject it. And, every person would be permitted to live with the eternal consequences of their own personal decision.

The early Baptists never sought the aid of the government to help them spread the gospel and they protested vociferously whenever they were forced to pay taxes to support the faiths of others. We believe that each congregation should call its own minister and pay for their own facilities and support their own work. In our eyes, no faith should be supported out of the public treasury. None. Period.

We expect the government to be neutral in matters of religion. The government's responsibility is to preserve the peace, secure justice, and insure a free marketplace for the exchange of ideas.

For Baptists a free marketplace for the exchange of ideas is much more important than a free market for goods and services. Whether the economy is feudal, agrarian, commercial, or industrial is not half as important as whether we are free to preach the gospel. In a free marketplace of ideas—where the truth of the gospel can compete on level ground with every conceivable religion and philosophy—we are confident that the gospel will win hearts and change lives. All the gospel needs is a free and open hearing.

What early Baptists feared most is what modern Baptists are now striving to secure—a government-sanctioned and supported monopoly in the marketplace of religious ideas. In the eighteenth century Baptists were a minority in the population. Then, it was in our best interests to have a Constitution that protected the rights of the minority and assured freedom of conscience. Today, Baptists comprise a majority. Now, most Baptists believe that it is in our best interests to grant ourselves special privileges.

To our great shame and disgrace, Baptists are proving to be as self-serving and self-interested as the Christians of centuries past. We too will use our power to suppress free thought and oppress the consciences of others. We too will flaunt our faith and force our beliefs on others.

In so doing, we discredit the deepest convictions and firmest beliefs of our spiritual ancestors. In so doing, we devalue the sacrifices of blood and sweat and tears that they shed to secure liberty of conscience. The very liberty of conscience that made this land such a fertile field for the gospel. Even worse, in so doing, we undermine the credibility of the very gospel that we have been called to proclaim.

This is not an idle concern. We read about the volatile mix of religion and politics in our newspapers and we watch it on our televisions literally every day. The most insidious examples of it are the "Charitable Choice" initiatives begun under the Clinton administration and the "Faith-Based Initiatives" that have been expanded by the Bush administration.

What could possibly trivialize genuine faith and destroy its credibility *more* than to create the impression that it can be manipulated to serve the political purposes of the highest bidder? That is precisely what is happening today in this state and every state throughout our country.

In Oklahoma, Mainstream Baptists, Americans United and the Interfaith Alliance have been monitoring the activities of Oklahoma's office of faith-based initiatives. From the very beginning and continuing to this day, there has been a consistent pattern of ignoring, disqualifying or deliberately excluding minority faith groups and, at times, interfaith groups from faith-based contracts and services. Yet, the office continues to enjoy the support of both parties for purely political reasons.

The same thing is happening all across the country.

David Kuo, who spent three years as second in command at the President's Office of Faith-Based and Community Initiatives in Washington, D.C., in his recent book *Tempting Faith* revealed that the list of grantees showed that "the initiative was purely about paying off political friends for their support" (p. 215). Kuo also described a conversation he had with a member of a peer-review panel that determined who would get government money for their faith-based non-profit. She told him: "When I saw one of those non-Christian groups in the set I was reviewing, I just stopped looking at them and gave them a zero" (216).

Such religious discrimination is similar to what our Baptist forefathers endured when the Colonies paid to support the established Congregational and Anglican churches while assessing taxes and fees and fines from dissenting groups like Baptists and Quakers. Now Baptists have become the head cheerleaders for another round of religious persecution and discrimination against minorities.

All of this modern mixing of politics and religion—with preachers endorsing candidates from the pulpit and politicians giving money to politically connected preachers to run soup kitchens—is destroying our witness. The machinations of money and the manipulations of secular politics are trivializing our faith, undermining the integrity of our witness, and destroying the credibility of the gospel of Christ.

Is there a word of hope that can be offered in the face of this alarming state of affairs?

There is hope!

There is hope if Christians who comprehend the true mission of the church will find the courage to stand up, speak out and do something to preserve the integrity of the Church's witness.

There is hope if Christian people will do something to put an end to the partisan politics within our churches.

There is hope if Christian people will speak out and make it clear that TV preachers and right-wing evangelists do not speak for them and they do not represent the best that the Christian faith has to offer.

There is hope if Christian people will stand up for religious liberty for all persons. Only then will we be able to share a gospel that is "good news" and not "bad news."

The gospel never has been the "bad news" about legislatively coerced conformity to anybody's "worldview." The gospel has never been a message about creating a Christian "culture." The gospel has always been the "good news" about the love and grace for all people that God revealed in Jesus Christ.

It's time for all Christians to stand up and start proclaiming God's love and grace again. Then, we need to demonstrate it in both word and deed.

Well?

APPENDIX VI

WHY I AM STILL A BAPTIST: A VIRGINIA PASTOR'S PERSPECTIVE

JOE LEWIS

Friends, I was born in Pensacola, Florida. I spent most of my preschool and early elementary school days in and around Pensacola. In third grade, my family moved to Escatawpa, Mississippi. And very soon after moving to Escatawpa, we moved on in to Pascagoula.

Very often, we made the trip back and forth between Pascagoula and Pensacola. Both sets of my grandparents lived in Pensacola. Between Pascagoula and Pensacola, just east of Mobile, Alabama, down around Fairhope and Loxley, many of the roads are lined with pecan trees. As a young kid I was amazed at how all those trees could grow in such straight lines.

As I understand it, on the outskirts of a small town, there was this big, old pecan tree. It just so happened to sit just inside a cemetery that was surrounded by a wrought iron fence. One day, two boys filled up a bucketful of nuts from beneath that old pecan tree, and they sat down by the tree, out of sight, and began dividing the nuts.

You could hear them. One of the little boys would say, "One for you, one for me; one for you, one for me."

Several pecans dropped and rolled down toward the fence.

Reprinted by permission of Joe Lewis. From a presentation at the National Mainstream Baptist Convocation held in Dallas, February 23–24, 2007.

Another boy came riding along the road on his bicycle. As he passed by the cemetery, he thought he heard voices. He slowed down to investigate. Sure enough, he heard, "One for you, one for me; one for you, one for me."

Immediately, he knew what it was. He jumped back on his bike and rode off into town.

Just around the bend he met an old man. Now, this old man had a difficult time walking. He used a cane, and just hobbled along.

"Come here, quick," said the boy, "you won't believe what I heard! Satan and the Lord are down at the cemetery, and they are dividing up the souls."

The man said, "Beat it kid, can't you see it's hard for me to walk."

The boy insisted that the old man come with him, and so the old man finally consented and hobbled slowly to the cemetery.

Standing by the fence they heard, "One for you, one for me; one for you, one for me."

The old man whispered, "Boy, you've been tellin' me the truth. Let's get closer and see if we can see the Lord."

Shaking with fear, they peered through the fence. They still couldn't see anything. The old man and the boy gripped the wrought iron bars of the fence tighter and tighter as they tried to get a glimpse of the Lord.

After a few moments, they heard, "One for you, one for me. That's all. Now let's go get those nuts by the fence and we'll be done."

They say the old man made it back to town a full three minutes ahead of the kid on the bicycle.

Many folk are scared to death these days of being Baptist and they run off in fear. You know what I'm talking about!

Because it's too depressing, I have stopped counting the number of my friends who have left the Baptist tradition and gone to the Episcopal Church or the United Methodist Church or the Presbyterian Church. And when I talk with folk about joining the church I serve now, Second Baptist Church in Petersburg, Virginia, the one thing the bothers me the most is hearing, "I don't want to be a Baptist—you guys are crazy." Too many folk are afraid of being Baptist.

What I want to do is to tell you why I am not afraid to be Baptist. I want to tell you why I'm glad to be a Baptist. I want to tell you why I'm still a Baptist. And the keyword in fulfilling my assigned task, to share with you why I am still a Baptist, is the word "still." Why am I still a Baptist? Why haven't I joined so many of my friends and gone some other place?

As a child, I spent most of my "growing up" days a chip and a putt away from the rear of the Naval Air Station in Pensacola, Florida. My family left Pascagoula and went back to Pensacola the summer between my fifth and sixth grade years.

I grew up listening to the roar of jets to the point that I grew used to hearing them and didn't hear them when others visiting did hear them. I grew up with the Blue Angels practicing over my house every Tuesday morning. I have vivid memories of watching them skim the top of the pine trees across from the house.

Ronnie Dale was among my closest friends. We lived nearby each other. I could walk to his house in less than 10 minutes.

As if it were last night, I remember well the evening he was devastated by the love of his life. Ronnie Dale's girlfriend was the daughter of a captain in the Navy. Ronnie Dale and I had gone out to the apartment complex on the Navy base to visit with his girlfriend. That's when he got the bad news. On the short ride back to the house, Ronnie Dale, with great pain and much sorrow, repeatedly said, "She's moving to Virginia. I can't believe it. She's moving to Virginia." On and on, shaking his head in disbelief, he said, "She's moving to Virginia. I can't believe it. She's moving to Virginia."

Trying to console my good friend, I remember saying to him, "Who in the world would want to move to Virginia? Why would anybody in their right mind want to move to Virginia?"

Remember now, I was trying to console my friend. I knew next to nothing about the landscape of Virginia. I was very satisfied with Florida, and could not imagine wanting to move any place else.

And after all these years, I'm still trying to figure out why this girl and her family moved to Danville, Virginia, not that Danville's a bad place, mind you. One of Virginia's finest colleges is in Danville: Averett University, a school that, until recently, was considered a Virginia Baptist school. Some folk got upset over something the chair of the Department of Religion wrote in the local paper in support of homosexuals, and one thing led to another, and the next thing you knew, Averett and the Baptist General Association of Virginia had an uncontested divorce. But that's another story for another day.

"Who in the world would want to move to Virginia?" That's what I said to my friend. Little did I know that in less than ten years, I, too, would move to Virginia, and I have been there now for 23 years, more than half my life.

Upon graduating from high school, I went to Cumberland College in Williamsburg, Kentucky. At the end of my junior year, my Old Testament professor, Robert Clark Dunston, encouraged me to do an honors research project my senior year and graduate as a Presidential Scholar. I agreed to do it.

I remember going up to Southern Seminary in Louisville to use the library and to have some conversation with Marvin Tate about my honors research project. Some of you know Marvin Tate. He's one of the Baptists' finest Old Testament scholars.

I remember Marvin asking me about my plans for seminary. I also remember him telling me I would be absolutely miserable at Southern. Now this was in the fall of 1983. He agreed that I should go to Union Theological Seminary in Virginia. And so I did. I must admit that next to marrying my wife and having two children, it was the best move I ever made.

"Who in the world would want to move to Virginia?" I said to my friend. After having lived there now for more than half my life, I find myself amazed that any one would want to leave Virginia.

I remember when Bill Wilson decided to leave Virginia and go to First Baptist Church, Dalton, Georgia. I said, "Bill, you gotta be crazy." And to Bill's credit he responded, "If it were not for the call of God, I would never leave Virginia."

I am happy to be a Virginia Baptist. I am so glad I don't live in Florida. Had I stayed in Florida, I probably would have joined my brother and left the Baptist tradition for something else.

Why am I still a Baptist? I am Baptist because I went to a Presbyterian seminary in Virginia. I kid you not. I learned more about being a Baptist at a Presbyterian seminary than most Baptists have learned at our Baptist seminaries.

And I have stayed in Virginia because Virginia Baptists know what it means to be Baptist. Now, I don't want to get into an argument with Charles DeWeese over the ability to define what an authentic Baptist is. While Charles will quickly tell you that you cannot define an authentic Baptist, I'm here to tell you Virginia Baptists do understand the Baptist way.

I am still a Baptist because so much of what we are about as Baptists is right. And Virginia Baptists understand that. Texas Baptists understand that. And some in some other states do, too.

With the Commonwealth of Virginia as our garden and the world as our field, we Virginia Baptists have gone on record affirming our call to live in Christ and to serve on mission for him in the context of deeply cherished historic Baptist principles like the Centrality of Christ, the Authority of Scripture, the Priesthood of All Believers, Soul Competency, the Autonomy of the Local Church, Religious Liberty and its corollary, the Separation of Church and State. I am proud to stand here and say to you that in Virginia, we have no Lord but Christ, and no creed but the Bible!

I'm still a Baptist because I believe deeply in these principles. They are right!

I'm still a Baptist because I believe in freedom. I don't want someone else to tell me what to think or do. I like to think for myself and make my own decisions. That's what my momma taught me to do!

This matter of freedom became very real for me in the summer of 1990. You remember that year. It was the year the Southern Baptist Convention met in New Orleans and it was the last year we moderates put up a candidate for the presidency of the SBC.

That year, there was an organized effort across the country to provide transportation to New Orleans for any moderate who needed it. For the first time in its 200 plus years of history, the church I served that year, Fountain

Creek Baptist Church in Emporia, sent a full contingent to the SBC. That was quite an achievement.

Up until then the only one to go the Convention, if anyone went, was the pastor. Maybe his wife would go from time to time. One or two others would go if the Convention were near by, as was the case when the Convention met in Norfolk in 1976. Never had a full contingent shown up at the Convention.

It would not have happened in 1990 had it not been for the mass effort to provide transportation. I had one lady, a senior citizen who had never been more than 25 miles away from the place she was born, go to New Orleans. I remember walking with her on Bourbon Street. I thought her eyes were going to pop out in disbelief.

Ten folk from the church met me in New Orleans. I flew down; they rode the bus. When we returned to Virginia, the very next Sunday those ten folk said, "Pastor, we don't need a bunch of city slickers telling us what to think or do."

Within a month, the congregation stopped sending its Cooperative Program gifts through the BGAV to the SBC. Fountain Creek was one of the first churches to give through the Baptist Cooperative Missions Program, which, as you know, eventually morphed into the Cooperative Baptist Fellowship.

And by the way, there is no better voice in the church for leading a church to change direction in denominational relations than the rank and file members. I didn't have to do anything, except take them and let them see for themselves what fundamentalism looks like. They saw it, and they didn't like it. It wasn't the Virginia Baptist way!

It was all because of a love for freedom. Like me, they didn't want someone else to tell them how they must think and how they must be and do church.

Freedom is at the heart of what it means to be Baptist.

The Baptist denomination was founded on freedom. John Smyth and Thomas Helwys, the two great seventeenth-century trailblazers of the Baptist tradition, began the Baptist denomination demanding freedom of conscience and the separation of church and state. And in our own country, Virginia was at the forefront of freedom, especially religious freedom, with its adoption of Thomas Jefferson's statute for religious liberty in 1786. Religious liberty and the separation of church and state have been at the heart of Virginia Baptist life since me late 1700s. Baptists are freedom-loving people!

I'm still a Baptist because I believe in freedom.

I like the idea of Bible Freedom, which is according to Buddy Shurden "the historic Baptist affirmation that the Bible, under the Lordship of Christ, must be central in the life of me individual and the church, and that Christians, with the best and most scholarly tools of inquiry, are both free and obligated to study and obey the Scriptures."[1]

I like the idea of soul freedom. Again, using the words of Buddy Shurden, "Soul freedom is the historic Baptist affirmation of the inalienable right and responsibility of every person to deal with God without the imposition of creed, the interference of clergy, or the intervention of civil government."[2]

I like the idea of church freedom. Again Buddy Shurden has defined it better than anybody else. "Church freedom is the historic Baptist affirmation that local churches are free, under the Lordship of Christ, to determine their membership and leadership, to order their worship and work, to ordain whom they perceive as gifted for ministry, male or female, and to participate in the larger Body of Christ."[3]

And yes, I like the idea of religious freedom, "the historic Baptist affirmation of freedom OF religion, freedom FOR religion, and freedom FROM religion, insisting that Caesar is not Christ and Christ is not Caesar."[4]

Buddy Shurden is right. "There is something about being Baptist, properly understood, that is both freeing and fulfilling."[5] That's why I am still a Baptist.

If you have never read Shurden's little book, *The Baptist Identity: Four Fragile Freedoms,* I encourage you to do so. If you can't afford a copy, you let me know, and I'll get you one.

I am still a Baptist because I am a lover of freedom.

I want to share with you one more reason why I am still a Baptist. And it is simply because I think these are exciting days to be a Baptist.

I believe God has good plans for Baptists. I like to look upon the denominational debacle we Baptists in the South have had to deal with in our lifetime as something similar to what happened with Joseph and his brothers. You will remember that Joseph's brothers were not very kind to him, and Joseph ended up in Egypt. One day Joseph's brothers came to him because of a great famine in the land. And Joseph said to them, "You meant bad for me, but God has taken this bad and done something good with it."[6]

I like to think God has taken the bad that Fundamentalists have done to us and is doing something good with it. I like to think that God is a new thing among us.

Hear me now! I'm not about to presume that I know the plans of God. But it is evident that what God is doing in the Baptist landscape today is exciting. I like the reawakening that is taking place in Baptist life. I like the recovery of historic Baptist values and principles that's taking place around us. I like seeing people and churches come alive as they rediscover together what it means to be Baptist.

I'm still a Baptist because I like what God is doing with Virginia Baptists and Texas Baptists. I like the networking that's going on between Virginia Baptists and Texas Baptists and CBF. Why, just this month, Virginia Baptists, Texas Baptists and CBF, in partnership with the Baptist Theological Seminary at Richmond, have produced LeaderConnect, a high tech placement service for churches and ministers.

I am still a Baptist because I like the way the Spirit of God is moving in new and energetic ways in bringing Baptists of North America together. I like this new North American Baptist Covenant. I hope you are making plans to be a part of next January's "Celebration of a New Baptist Covenant" that will take place in Atlanta. Right now, that event alone is enough to keep you Baptist! I can't wait to see what God is going to do with that event. And I want to be a part of it. I think you do, too.

Now bear with me just a moment as I get off my assignment just a little bit and share with you why I am still a part of the Mainstream Baptist Network, this body. That, too, is a fair and legitimate question to ask. Why do I believe that this organization has a reason for being? Why do I think the Mainstream Baptist Network has a viable agenda for the future? Why am I still a Mainstream Baptist Network participant?

I'll quickly share with you three reasons, and not elaborate on them. First, I am still a part of the Mainstream Baptist Network because I believe MBN is a venue for healthy denominational citizenship. MBN provides a much-needed venue for discussing and networking on compelling issues that will go a long way in preserving, promoting, and protecting precious Baptist principles.

Second, I am still a part of MBN because I believe there needs to be a watchdog group to look out for Baptist principles, even if it has to be done so in political ways.

And third, I am still a part of MBN because its agenda is not self-serving. The role of MBN is to help usher in a new day of cooperation among moderate Baptists all across America.

Now, you will be glad to know that I am going to the end of my comments. I close by telling you about a young man fresh out of college, who desperately wanted to be a star journalist. There was only one problem. He lived a small town and the opportunities with the local newspaper were not promising.

A river ran through the little town in which he lived. Just north of the town was a rather large dam in the river. One day the dam broke and the town was flooded. He said, "Here's my chance to make it big." So he got out a rowboat and started paddling around looking for just the right story.

He found an elderly lady sitting on her rooftop. He paddled over to her, tied up his boat to the chimney of her house, and told her he was looking for a story to write about the breaking of the dam.

Together they watched as various items floated by in front of them. There was a swing off someone's front porch. There was somebody's plastic thirty-two-gallon trashcan with wheels on it. There was a mailbox. On and on items passed in front of them. Every once in a while, the lady would say, "Now there's a story." The reporter would point out something and she would say, "Oh no, there's no story in that."

"Now there's a story," she would say as something else floated past them.

Finally, the reporter notices this red hat as it floats by them. All of a sudden this red hat does a 180-degree turn and goes upstream. And then it does another 180-degree turn and goes back downstream. He says, "Look at that hat. It went down stream, turned around and went upstream, and now it's headed back downstream. No, no, it's headed back upstream again. Now, there's a story." He was getting excited.

"Oh no, that's not a story," the lady said.

"What do you mean that's not a story. Just look at that hat."

"I see the hat," she said. "That's my husband Hayford. He said he was going to mow the grass today come hell or high water!"

Well, come hell or high water, I plan to stay a Baptist. For I believe in the Baptist way. I believe in Baptist principles. They are right! I believe in freedom. And I believe these are great days to be a Baptist!

APPENDIX VII

A SUMMARY HISTORY OF THE CONCEPTION, DEVELOPMENT, AND PUBLICATION OF *THE BROADMAN BIBLE COMMENTARY*

CLIFTON J. ALLEN

From the early years of the Baptist Sunday School Board, after the beginning of the publication of books, there was thought and discussion about the publication of Bible commentaries. Doubtless little of this thought visualized a commentary of definitive nature or scope. Modest ventures were undertaken in those early years. However, as the Sunday School resources increased and the needs for help in serious Bible study increased, consideration of the publication of a more serious Bible commentary developed. At least by 1950 (a memorandum is dated August 11) there was serious conversation between C. J. Allen, the editorial secretary, and W. J. Fallis, the book editor and head of the Book Editorial Department, about the possibility of producing a commentary on the New Testament to be published by Broadman Press (see no. 1). Conversations of this kind continued through the years, not restricted to the editorial secretary and the book editor.

Reprinted by permission of the Southern Baptist Historical Library and Archives, Nashville. The "Summary History" is located in the Clifton J. Allen Papers, Broadman Bible Commentary, Box 12, File 35. The numbers referred to throughout are to documents in an additional file of materials related to the projection and publication of The Broadman Bible Commentary. These materials are not included here, but the reference numbers have been left unchanged to reflect the author's intent.

On April 2, 1958, W. J. Fallis addressed a communication to the book committee as follows: "Since 1950, some of us have been dreaming about the possibility of Broadman's publishing a multivolume commentary on the Bible. Of course, we recognize that it would be a major undertaking requiring special editorial help and long-range planning and budgeting. We felt that in authorship it might be an all-Baptist affair with most of the writing coming out of the seminaries but with some being done by pastors and college professors" (see no. 2). Earlier, and subsequent to the memorandum just quoted, the editorial secretary had discussed the matter many times with James L. Sullivan, the executive secretary, whose interest and encouragement were always strong. It may be said at this point, as a matter of record, that the executive secretary, from the beginning, gave helpful counsel and responsible leadership and wholehearted support to the idea of a significant multivolume commentary.

As a result of consideration by the book committee of this matter, action was taken by the administrative staff, April 30, 1958, as follows: "Dr. Fallis was requested to work with Dr. Allen in calling a meeting of a representative group to consider the preparation and publication of a commentary. The group may also consider other major publishing projects. It is to be financed out of the appropriation for Broadman Book Publishing Expansion."

The publication of a commentary was conceived, first of all, in the context of the objective and mission of Broadman Press, the urgent need for the cultivation of our denomination in mature biblical understanding, and the deepening of biblical insight on the part of preachers and teachers. It was not conceived primarily as a commercial venture.

Under the leadership of W. J. Fallis, a conference was convened on November 28–29, 1958—invited persons being seminary professors, Bible teachers from Baptist colleges, pastors, some Sunday School Board personnel, and others—to consider the possibility of publishing a multivolume commentary on the Bible (see no. 3). The notes in the attached file identify the persons attending the conference and the nature of the discussions. The group was keenly aware of problems to be faced as to the enlistment of competent authors and particularly as to the response of the constituency of Broadman Press to an objective treatment of matters of historical criticism essential to the understanding and interpretation of the Scriptures. There was a consensus of encouragement to Broadman Press to go forward in the exploration of the matter and to seek to bring it to realization.

A follow-up conference was convened under the leadership of the book editor on March 6–7, 1959. Other persons were in attendance. The problems faced in the previous conference were again considered, including financing. The general tone of discussions by the group was enthusiastic and cooperative. The group seemed to be agreed that the editorship should be under the general direction of an editorial committee of scholars and the specific direction of an editor employed by the Board, with perhaps two editors (one for Old Testament and one for New Testament) employed on a part-time basis. The group felt that the commentary might well consist of sixteen to twenty volumes (see no. 4).

W. J. Fallis, J. F. Green, and C. J. Allen had a further conference with seminary personnel on May 30, 1961 (see no. 5).

Following conversations between the editorial secretary and the executive secretary, and on the basis of suggestions by the executive secretary, the editorial secretary prepared a recommendation, which was presented to and approved by the elected Sunday School Board at their meeting in July 1961, as follows (see no. 6):

1. That the board authorized the publication of a multivolume Bible commentary, setting as a goal completion by January 1970.
2. That the Board commit itself to providing the financial resources necessary to the production, publication, and promotion of a commentary that will reflect credit on Broadman Press and take its place along with other recognized works in this field—it being understood that as the overall plan and format for the commentary is conceived an inclusive budget will be developed and submitted to the budget committee of the Board for consideration and appropriate action.
3. That the secretary of the Broadman Books Department, the director of the Education Division, the executive secretary, and the editorial secretary select a competent person to serve as managing editor of the commentary.
4. That the managing editor and the secretary of the Broadman Books Department, in consultation with responsible Board personnel, recommend to the administrative staff and then to the board (or its executive committee) a general plan for the commentary and for implementing its publication.
5. That consideration be given to the publication of a single volume Bible commentary—designed more for Sunday School teachers, other church workers, and popular use—as a part of this larger publication venture, with the understanding that it may be initiated and produced within the framework of the program for the multivolume commentary

Appendix VII

subject to approval by the administrative staff and the Board (or its executive committee).

Because of the scope of the project which had been authorized and difficult schedules involving the responsible Board personnel, some months intervened before there could be serious initiative taken to implement the action of the Board. By that time a more negative climate related to doctrinal concern and theological study had developed in the denomination, so that the responsible leadership of Broadman Press, with approval by the executive secretary, delayed specific steps to implement the action that had been taken by the Board. There was a growing conviction on the part of the editorial secretary, however, that steps should be initiated for the projection of the commentary. Letters were addressed by him to the executive secretary on May 27, 1963, and January 15, 1964 (see nos. 7, 8), encouraging action. With the approval of the executive secretary, the editorial secretary reported to the elected Board on January 28, 1964, as follows (see no. 9).

The Sunday School Board approved (July 27, 1961) a recommendation to authorize the publication of a multivolume Bible commentary by Broadman Press, and it approved the initial steps needed to implement this action. In the light of conditions which developed, it did not seem feasible to proceed at the time with this project. The idea was not abandoned, and the matter has been reviewed recently by responsible personnel. It is now agreed that we should go forward immediately with this very major and significant publishing effort. The necessary steps are being initiated to do so. We will expect a report to the budget committee as to the budget requirements for the preparation and publication of the commentary, and we will report to the Board the plans being developed in terms of format and schedule. The publication of a worthy commentary may well turn out to be one of the major accomplishments of the Sunday School Board. It should prove to be a major dynamic for the entire publishing program of Broadman Press.

The action of the Board was the acceptance of this statement as information and that encouragement was given to those in charge of the project to proceed as indicated.

Considerable exploratory work was done by the secretary of the Broadman Books Department and his associate and the editorial secretary, but the climate in the Convention exerted a negative impact. Action by the Sunday School Board on July 28–29, 1965, laid the foundation for definite steps in projecting the publication of the commentary. This action was as follows (see no. 10).

The 1965 Southern Baptist Convention voted to request the Sunday School Board to undertake to produce a one-volume commentary written especially for and by Southern Baptists. No date was set for the completion of this project. In view of the Board's official authorization three years ago that this multivolume commentary be produced, and because the complex work would need to be produced first as a matter of procedure, we recommend that the administration continue to pursue the already authorized plan to bring out a multivolume commentary, leaving until a later date the working out of details about the one-volume edition.

As the consideration of publishing the *Commentary* had developed, the executive secretary—and the manager of the Broadman Books Department as well—had frequently expressed his thought that C. J. Allen should be asked to serve as the general editor for the *Commentary*. This, however, had never been a formal request, so that Allen, as the editorial secretary, had felt some hesitancy in taking initiative, which he would otherwise have done. The conversations had been sufficiently specific, however, to justify a letter from the editorial secretary to the executive secretary, dated September 13, 1965, to request a clarification of the matter and open the way for a definite program of action (see no. 11). The reply of the executive secretary, dated October 1, 1965, was a request that the editorial secretary serve as the general editor and that he develop a concept paper—which had been previously discussed—for consideration as the rationale and objective for the *Commentary* and the approach that should be wisely taken (see no. 12). The letter was one of inspiring encouragement as to the contribution that might be made through this assignment and the responsibility involved. A letter from W. J. Fallis to the executive secretary, dated November 15, 1965, further clarified the matter and called attention to the way in which the Broadman Books Department would need to function (see no. 13).

Early in 1966, W. J. Fallis worked out a tentative format and specifications for consideration by the responsible personnel involved. C. J. Allen began work on the development of a concept document (see no. 14 for the first state in developing this concept statement).

Definite recommendations were made by C. J. Allen and W. J. Fallis, May 16, 1966, as to an advisory editorial board, as to persons who might be invited to serve on this board, as to the enlistment of competent scholars as consulting editors, as to a tentative schedule, and as to some persons representative of those who might serve as contributing authors (see no. 15). Allen and Fallis reported to the elected Sunday School Board, July 21–21, 1966, on the development of specific plans, particularly as to the enlistment of an advisory board (see no. 16).

A cross section of seminary professors, pastors, college teachers, denominational personnel, and lay representation was enlisted to constitute an advisory board. This board met in Nashville September 9–10, 1966, with twenty-four out of the twenty-six members present and with eight Sunday School Board staff members also in attendance (see nos. 17, 18, 19, 20, 21 for a list of the personnel, for the findings of the advisory board discussions, and for related matters). The enthusiasm of the membership of the advisory board relative to the publication of the *Commentary* was outstanding. There was frankness and freedom in expression and a strong core of agreement though much diversity of opinion and viewpoint. Nothing contradicted or invalidated the general objective and concepts that had been previously developed by the general editor in consultation with other personnel. The advisory board was largely agreed that authors should be selected, assuming vital Christian faith and an affirmative and positive view about the Scriptures and their message, on the basis of scholarship and equipment for effective communication in biblical interpretation. There was consensus, without formal vote but with some disagreement, that non-Baptist authors with a definitely evangelical viewpoint should be considered. There was no agreement that the selection of authors be restricted to persons in our Southern Baptist fellowship. The discussions of the advisory board were exceedingly helpful to Sunday School Board personnel in evaluating the many factors involved and problems to be encountered in the publication of a multivolume commentary for serious Bible study.

A report of progress was presented to the elected Sunday School Board on January 24, 1967 (see no. 22). The initial draft of a concept statement was refined by the general editor, with counsel and much assistance from W. J. Fallis and J. F. Green, who were expected to serve as associate editors; and a more definitive statement was prepared and circulated April 10, 1967 (see no. 23). At that time a definite decision had not been reached as to the printing of the entire biblical text. This decision came later and was incorporated into the concept statement. It had been decided, with the approval of the executive secretary, that the Revised Standard Version would be used as the basic text in the *Commentary*. Some quotations from the concept statement are the following:

> The Commentary will be directed toward ministers and serious lay students of the Bible.
>
> The Commentary will aim at being a thoroughly competent and trustworthy resource—usable by theologically and non-theologically trained ministers and laymen and by alert young people and men and women concerned to know with certainty the message of God in the Holy Scriptures.
>
> The research of trustworthy and reverent scholarship, as this contributes to better understanding of the meaning of the Scriptures, is to be utilized.
>
> It is expected that any helpful consideration of historical and textual problems will be with integrity, with objective approach, and always in the spirit of reverent faith relative to the

nature of the Scriptures as a whole and with concern for the understanding and reactions of the reader.

The treatment of the text will combine exegesis and exposition in balance. The chief concern is to "lead out," interpret, expose the meaning—with concern for communicating the essential truth to the reader.

This Commentary will seek to be a faithful interpretation of the message of the Scriptures, based on the resources of competent and recognized scholarship and designed to serve the ends of Christian commitment, an affirmative faith, and a redemptive witness. It will seek to avoid theological labels and the sales clichés. But it is openly and completely committed to the theological assumptions of supernatural religion, the unique and inspired nature of the biblical revelation, the redemptive activity of God in Christ, and the lordship of Christ in the world, the reality of salvation from sin, and the certainty of the Christian hope.

The treatment of Baptist principles will be clear and strong wherever they spring naturally from the exposition of Bible material.

Admittedly, the treatment of biblical passages, strongly related to the doctrines of Baptists, will recognize differences of interpretation by competent scholars.

There is no *the* Baptist position. But the Commentary will seek to maintain the integrity of a faithful work in scholarship in relation to the integrity and validity and stewardship of principles cherished by the people called Baptists.

It will be kept in mind that the Commentary will seek to reach a general audience, irrespective of denominational identity and interest.

We conceive this publication to be a Bible Commentary, to interpret the truth of the historical revelation set forth in the Scriptures. It is committed to sound, honest, competent scholarship. It will be a blending of exegesis and exposition, with a primary concern to set forth the meaning of the Scriptures but always treating the meaning in relation to experience, the meaning for life, God's Word to us as we must live now. We will approach the Scriptures with reverent faith, believing them to be an inspired revelation from God, unique, authoritative, with eternal meaning. The key to the revelation is Jesus Christ and his redemptive work.

A statement was prepared by the general editor reporting to the members of the advisory board, February 2, 1967; and a further communication to the advisory board was sent March 10, 1967, as to ways in which the advisory board could continue to be of assistance in the work on the *Commentary* (see nos. 24, 25).

At the end of 1966 invitations were extended to John I. Durham of the Southeastern Baptist Theological Seminary faculty and Roy L. Honeycutt of the Midwestern Baptist Theological Seminary faculty to serve as Old Testament consulting editors, and to J. W. MacGorman of the Southwestern Baptist Theological Seminary faculty and to Frank Stagg of the Southern Baptist Theological Seminary faculty to serve as New Testament consulting editors. These persons accepted the invitation after correspondence (see no. 26 for clarification as to the responsibility of the consulting editors and the relationships which they would have with the general editor).

A conference of the consulting editors was held September 28–29, 1967. The conference was devoted chiefly to the evaluation of possible writers for the assignments of book treatments and to discussion of the approach that would most helpfully be followed in dealing with critical matters, the use of the original languages, the extent and use of documentation, ways of achieving balance between exegesis and exposition, and helpful approaches in the preparation of the introduction to a given book. Discussions clarified viewpoints and achieved a strong consensus for guidance in the exercise of editorial responsibility. A subsequent conference was held a year later, and individual conferences were held from time to time by the general editor and the consulting editors. Chiefly, however, problems calling for the exchange of viewpoints and the need for counsel were handled by correspondence.

It may be appropriately recorded here that the consulting editors gave invaluable assistance in refining the concept for the *Commentary* and in giving counsel to guide editorial personnel in a variety of matters which called for the insights, knowledge, and experience of competent scholars. They gave their time freely throughout the entire schedule of publication, one that involved arduous and time-consuming labor on the part of the consulting editors, always manifesting balance of judgment as to difficult decisions and always with keen awareness of factors necessarily of serious concern to Broadman Press. Their experienced involvement in the main stream of southern Baptist life provided a perspective for sympathetic understanding and for wise judgment. They were consulted about the selection of all contributors, and their contribution at this point was of immeasurable assistance. Their later criticism and evaluation of manuscripts provided invaluable counsel for the general editor and constructive guidance to the contributors that led to improvement in manuscripts of major proportions.

A report of progress was presented to the elected Sunday School Board by the general editor, July 26–27, 1967 (see no. 27).

A similar report of progress was presented to the elected Board on January 30, 1968 (see no. 29).

At the invitation of the executive secretary, the general editor had discussed the *Commentary* with the plans and policies committee of the elected Board, January 29, 1968. Serious concern was expressed by some of the members of the committee, arising chiefly from writers having been enlisted who were not Southern Baptists. The discussion was open and free. As a result of this discussion, the general editor immediately wrote extensive notes summarizing the discussion (see no. 28), the last paragraph of these notes being the following: "It would clearly seem to be a sound and a highly acceptable policy—wholly in keeping with our Baptist tradition that emphasizes the competence and responsibility of persons to think for themselves, to search for the truth, to be free to differ in their doctrinal interpretations and biblical understandings, to engage in open debate about the revelation of truth in the Scriptures, and to reject authoritarian and official and creedal and stereotyped formulations of the truth of the biblical revelation—to select writers widely recognized as devout Christians and competent biblical scholars, known for their reverent faith in the Scriptures, their balanced theological viewpoint, their mature experience, and their integrity in critical study, who are sympathetic with the purpose of Broadman Press in the publication of *The Broadman Bible Commentary* and who find it feasible to accept writing assignments as invited to do so. We have proceeded on this basis. We are convinced that this is the wise course to follow. We continue to receive enthusiastic support of this approach from many areas of denominational life and leadership."

In the selection of writers or contributors, seminary faculties offered the chief source from which to draw competent and experienced scholars for the responsibility involved. There was no specific plan to try to balance the number of persons drawn from the six Southern Baptist seminaries or as to enlisting persons outside the Southern Baptist fellowship. Information and knowledge by the consulting editors provided much guidance for the general editor and the associate editors in decisions as a basis for recommendation for approval by the executive secretary. The concern in the selection of writers was to find persons best qualified for given responsibilities. At the time when writers had to be chosen, a number of Southern Baptist seminary faculty personnel, particularly personnel at Southwestern Baptist Theological Seminary, were involved in other writing commitments which prevented their being available for assignments for the *Commentary*. It should be clearly stated, however, that the selection of writers was undertaken objectively, completely apart from seminary identification or loyalty and apart from any desire to achieve any geographical spread. There was an earnest desire to enlist pastors of competence in the field of biblical study and scholarship. A few were enlisted. As would be expected, seminary professors and college professors provided the best source of qualified writers. Some writers were invited to accept assignments, but had to decline because of other commitments. Some writers were enlisted from Great Britain, on the basis of their reputation and competence and long identification with Baptist life, and their recognized influence in the field of biblical scholarship. A few writers were enlisted from the fellowship of the American Baptist Convention. Two writers, having accepted assignments, later asked to be relieved of these assignments because of difficulties in schedules. In all, seventeen persons were enlisted to prepare general articles, and forty-seven persons were enlisted for book writing assignments, making a total of sixty-four contributors. A list of contributors is in the attached file (see no. 30).

As the year 1968 proceeded, the volume of work for the *Commentary* mounted steadily. This involved decisions and enlistment of writers for remaining assignments, the evaluation of initial and partial drafts of manuscripts, correspondence with consulting editors about manuscripts, and guidance to contributors as they carried forward their assignments. The general editor was confronted with an increasingly difficult schedule, due to his continuing responsibilities as editorial secretary and the necessity for absorbing all of the additional work as the general editor of the *Commentary* along with the responsibilities of his office. He had shared with the executive secretary, from the time of being requested to serve as general editor, his awareness that he could not complete the editorial assignment for the *Commentary* prior to his scheduled retirement in November 1969. In the early months of 1968 he became convinced that it would be impossible to carry forward the responsibility for the *Commentary* in addition to his responsibility as editorial secretary. He, therefore, proposed to the executive secretary that his retirement take place at the end of 1968 in order to give full time to the work on the *Commentary*. The executive secretary had proposed in conversations in 1965 that the responsibility of the general editor become a contract assignment following retirement. It was on this basis that the general editor proposed that his retirement take place eleven months before the scheduled date in order to give full time to the demanding assignment on the *Commentary*. The executive secretary approved the proposal, and the retirement of C. J. Allen as editorial secretary took place at the end of 1968.

The year 1969 brought a mounting flow of involved editorial work. In the early months of the year the editorial work on Volumes 1 and 8 was completed and the copy sent to the printers. All writing assignments had been made. Some writers had completed their assignments; others were seriously behind schedule. Volumes 1 and 8 were scheduled for release in October.

Production, advertising, and sales personnel for Broadman Press had been involved from the beginning in the consideration of the possible publication of the *Commentary* and, after publication had been approved, in the consideration of problems and decisions related to their areas of responsibility. By 1969 jacket designs had been developed and printed, and other promotional materials as well. A letter addressed to all elected Sunday School Board members from the executive secretary was sent out February 14, 1969, with examples of the jacket and other materials (see no. 31).

Howard P. Colson was elected editorial secretary by the elected Sunday School Board early in 1969. In keeping with the responsibilities of his office, he became increasingly involved for consultation and evaluation relative to the *Commentary*. His help was particularly significant in the evaluation of manuscripts.

Throughout 1969 some anxiety began to arise in certain centers of the denomination reflecting strongly conservative theological viewpoints, largely on the part of persons who had been skeptical about publishing a commentary with an approach not fully traditional. This restiveness arose in part because some few non–Southern Baptists had been enlisted for writing assignments; this restiveness reflected a strongly motivated concern for traditional and somewhat authoritarian views about the Bible, also some suspicion and prejudice related to non–Southern Baptists. Ultraconservative concerns, within and without the denomination, cultivated a somewhat negative climate even before the first volumes were published. While the administration of the Sunday School Board and the editorial personnel related to the *Commentary* anticipated diversity of reaction when the *Commentary* would begin to come from the press, they had proceeded from the beginning with sensitivity to the diversity of theological thought and viewpoint within the denomination and with wholehearted commitment, both as individuals and in keeping with the basic objective of the Sunday School Board, to a completely evangelical approach as to matters of biblical background, historical criticism, and textual interpretation. Care had been exercised from the beginning, as clearly stated in the concept statement, to avoid identifying the *Commentary* with any specific theological stance. It had been clearly stated that the *Commentary* would draw upon the resources of biblical research and the validity of historical criticism, always in the context of positive Christian faith and of reverence for the Scriptures as given by inspiration and as authentic and adequate for all matters of Christian faith and practice.

Volume 1 and Volume 8 were published in October 1969. Advance reviews had been sought from pastors and professors. In general, these were favorable reviews, but some were unfavorable (see nos. 32, 33, 34). This was, of course, to be expected. Sales measured generally up to expectations. Surprisingly, there was little editorial comment in Southern Baptist papers until the beginning of 1970. At that time some editorials appeared strongly critical, charging the *Commentary* as a production of liberal scholarship, a denial of inspiration, and a violation of the Baptist position about the Scriptures—particularly the papers of Missouri, Oklahoma, and Mississippi (see nos. 34, 36, 37). A strong editorial in defense of the *Commentary* appeared in the Kentucky paper (see no. 38); some other papers reflected a similar viewpoint. Controversy about the *Commentary* began to develop. A negative review in *Christianity Today* (see no. 34) and attacks by certain pastors (see correspondence files) kindled widespread misunderstanding, confusion, and prejudiced attacks on the *Commentary*.

At least some of the strong criticism sprang from the fact that G. Henton Davies, principal of Regent's Park College in Oxford, England, was the author of the treatment of Genesis. It was assumed by some that because he was not a Southern Baptist he would be liberal theologically. There was strong objection to his view of non-Mosaic authorship of Genesis and his support of various sources for the content of this book. Also, there was strong objection to his treatment of the Abraham-Isaac incident recorded in Genesis 22. These matters became easy topics of conversation on the part of uninformed persons and the basis of rumors that were wholly unjustified and inaccurate. It was assumed by many Southern Baptists that a non-traditional view about the authorship of books of the Bible and various matters in the field of historical criticism must necessarily be unacceptable.

The controversy referred to above continued through the months of 1970 prior to the Southern Baptist Convention in Denver. During the months immediately preceding the convention, the executive secretary had prepared articles for *Facts and Trends* about the Bible, including one for the April issue in which he quoted an extended statement by the general editor about the *Commentary*. This statement follows (see no. 39):

1. The editors and all the contributors are persons of recognized and confirmed commitment to Christ and of fidelity to the historic Baptist position. They are persons of reverent faith and fidelity to the Scriptures as the authentic revelation of God in Christ.
2. The contributors and the consulting editors are persons of recognized competence for their assignments; they are persons of recognized scholarship, some of them of international reputation and influence.
3. The commentary is based on an objective approach to the Scriptures and draws freely on the fruits of biblical scholarship. It recognizes varying viewpoints and alternative positions and the freedom of persons to accept or reject the positions set forth by the contributors. A basic presupposition is the recognition of differing views about the nature of the Bible and the interpretation of its message. The commentary is nonauthoritarian.

A Summary History of *The Broadman Bible Commentary*

4. Within the context of the clearly stated purpose and approach of the commentary, the contributors are expected to exercise responsible freedom in presenting their own understanding of the meaning of the biblical revelation. The context in which the commentary is published is characterized by the following: (1) a reverent approach to the Scriptures as the Word of God, uniquely inspired and fully authoritative; (2) the validity of objective biblical scholarship; (3) the freedom and responsibility of persons to think for themselves and to witness to their understanding of the meaning of the Scriptures; (4) the intention to help serious students of the Bible to gain a more mature understanding of the Bible and a stronger faith relevant for life and witness; (5) the recognition that there are valid and serious questions asked about how the Bible came to us, about its historical, cultural and literary elements, about how its contents are to be interpreted and made relevant to our experience, and about how its meaning and authority are to be related to the perfect revelation in Christ and to his lordship.

5. The publication by Broadman Press of a comprehensive Bible commentary must be done with integrity. It recognizes all segments of the constituency Broadman Press is expected to serve. It assumes that a commentary which simply repeats traditional interpretations and ignores the results of current biblical study would command little interest and have little value. It expects that evaluations of a multivolume commentary will be based on intelligent and objective appraisal of the entire work rather than on single volumes or on the interpretation of specific problem passages which undertake to deal with complex and crucial issues involved in God's revelation to and dealings with mankind.

At the Southern Baptist Convention in Denver, Gwin Turner of California presented the following motion, which was passed by the Convention by a vote of 5,342 (for) and 2,170 (against), as follows: "That because the new *The Broadman Bible Commentary* is out of keeping with the beliefs of the vast majority of Southern Baptist pastors and people, this convention requests the Sunday School Board to withdraw Volume 1 from further distribution and that it be rewritten with due consideration of the conservative viewpoint."

The action of the Convention was without precedent in that it called for the virtual banning of a book written by widely known and highly respected and outstandingly able Baptist authors and published in harmony with responsible denominational policies and programs; also because it made the guiding decision as to what ought to be in the *Commentary* the view of a majority of pastors, and further because it virtually implied that a commentary published by Broadman Press must be thought of as an official or prescribed view about the Scriptures and about biblical interpretation.

The action of the Convention was very likely a reflection of a climate of resentment felt by many pastors and felt in many churches toward denominational institutions, particularly toward the Sunday School Board, which climate had been further generated in the Convention sessions by negative reaction to changes in curriculum materials for use in the churches and by a controversial vote related to the Christian Life Commission. The atmosphere of the convention was, unfortunately, marked by hostile feeling, suspicion, and criticism.

Unsuccessful efforts were made in the Convention to compel seminary personnel and the personnel of some other agencies to sign doctrinal statements. Unsuccessful efforts were also made aimed at Convention action prescribing a particular view of biblical inspiration.

The action taken by the convention about Volume 1 of the *Commentary* was considered by the executive committee of the elected Sunday School Board and subsequently by the full Board in session, August 12–13, 1970, to the effect that "Volume 1 of the new *Broadman Bible Commentary* is out of harmony with the beliefs of a vast majority of Southern Baptist pastors and people and we request that this volume be withdrawn from further distribution and sale and that it be rewritten with due consideration of the conservative viewpoint. The Sunday School Board hereby instructs the staff that Volume 1 be withdrawn from distribution and sale and that a committee be appointed by the president to consider and make recommendations as to rewriting volume 1 and the effect on other volumes of the Commentary" (see no. 40). Certain members of the elected Board requested that their names be recorded as voting against the motion, and others asked that their names be recorded as voting for it. The special committee designated to consider the matter further was a combination of the Church Program and Services committee and the Plans and Policies Committee, with Allen Comish to serve as chairman.

In the meantime, the general editor had written on June 9 to the consulting editors and to all contributors a letter in reference to the action of the Southern Baptist Convention. He stated his own position, which he had stated in discussion before the Southern Baptist convention, as follows: "The *Broadman Bible Commentary* is a work of responsible and competent scholars. It is thoroughly affirmative in its approach and content. It is no sense an attack on either the inspiration or the authority of the Bible. The contributors are persons of recognized competence, reverent faith, and Christian commitment. The *Commentary* is designed to be a constructive and helpful aid to serious Bible study.... Each person is competent and free to think for himself. The Bible is an inspired revelation of truth from God and, as the Word of God, is authoritative for all matters of faith and practice. Freedom and competence assume and allow diversity of personal interpretation and viewpoint. In serious Bible study we accept the obligation to be open to all the facts bearing on an event or a teaching and to consider the fruits of objective and competent research. We do not have a perfect and complete understanding of the nature of the Bible or of the meaning of its truths and events, and we are under obligation to continue to seek deeper insight and fuller understanding" (see no. 41).

In order to be helpful to the executive secretary, the general editor had prepared various materials related to the *Commentary*, to a sound policy about publishing a commentary, and about the action of the Convention (see nos. 42, 43).

On August 31, 1970, the executive secretary sent a letter to all contributors to the *Commentary*, informing them of the action of the elected Sunday School Board (see no. 44).

The special committee constituted by the elected Sunday School Board met in Nashville on October 12. At the request of the executive secretary and of Allen Comish, chairman of the special committee, the general editor had prepared materials to be used in giving the committee adequate background for consideration of the problem and had also suggested possible courses of action (see no. 45). The executive secretary had also prepared extensive background information for use by the special committee (see no. 46).

The special committee considered with much depth the matter referred to it by the elected Sunday School Board. The general editor was invited to share in the discussion. The committee requested the general editor, in consultation with the chairman of the committee and the executive secretary, to explore with the authors of the treatments of Genesis and Exodus in Volume 1—namely, G. Henton Davies and Roy L. Honeycutt—their willingness to undertake a revision of their material to resolve as far as possible the problem arising from the action of the Southern Baptist Convention. The general editor carried out the instruction of the committee, reporting to the executive secretary and to the chairman of the committee. The response of the two authors was one of gracious cooperation and one of willingness to do all that could be done to resolve the matter. A full report was prepared by the general editor with the approval of the executive secretary and the chairman of the committee—which was approved by the committee in session prior to the meeting of the elected Sunday School Board in January, 1971, and was subsequently presented to the full Board, which report was approved (see no. 47), with a revision of the wording of the recommendation (see below).

Much care had been taken by the general editor to keep all contributors to the *Commentary* informed of the steps being taken to resolve the problem that had arisen (see letter to contributors, No. 48). The action taken by the elected Sunday School Board was as follows: "In light of the response and commitment by Drs. Davies and Honeycutt and the general editor to inquiries of the committee and staff of the Sunday School Board concerning the rewriting of the Commentary, we recommend that we ask them to accept the task of rewriting Volume 1 of the Commentary with due consideration of the conservative viewpoint, hopeful that it will be possible for this work to be done during the summer and fall of 1971 and thus make possible the publication of a revised edition of Volume 1 following the publication of the remaining volumes of the Commentary."

The general editor wrote letters to G. Henton Davies and Roy L. Honeycutt in keeping with the action of the elected Sunday School Board (see no. 49). He prepared a proposed letter to go from the executive secretary to all contributors to the *Commentary,* and this letter was mailed February 9, 1971 (see no. 50).

It was not expected that the work on a revision of the treatments of Genesis and Exodus could be undertaken immediately. However, assurance had been given to the general editor by the authors involved of their willingness to work with him in bringing a revision to consummation. The consensus of the thinking of all three was that certain passages might incorporate further emphasis on diversity of viewpoints, some clarification where the author's viewpoint did not seem to communicate adequately, and some additional emphases at especially sensitive points on more traditional interpretations. The general editor was not so visionary as to believe that all critics would be satisfied, but it was his strong conviction that a response could be made with integrity to the request of the convention, while at the same time in no way compromising the integrity of the authors involved or compromising a basic position allowing freedom in interpretation of Scripture. The willingness of the authors of the treatments of Genesis and Exodus to work with the general editor had been marked by sincere desire to try to resolve the problem in recognition of all the factors and complicating difficulties involved.

No extensive publicity was given to the exploration and plans in process because there had not been any time for the authors involved to do any work and because it was thought that premature publicity would complicate the ultimate solution of the problem and would likely result in further agitation detrimental to the ongoing publication of other volumes.

When the Southern Baptist Convention met in St. Louis in June, 1971, a motion was made by Kenneth Barnette of Oklahoma as follows: "that the

Sunday School Board be advised that the vote of the 1970 Convention regarding the rewriting of Volume 1 of *The Broadman Bible Commentary* has not been followed and that the Sunday School Board obtain another writer and proceed with the Commentary according to the vote of the 1970 Convention in Denver." After brief discussion a motion passed to cut off debate, and the motion was carried by a vote of 2,672 for the motion and 2,298 against it. This information was communicated to all contributors to the *Commentary* in a letter from the general editor dated June 17, 1971 (see no. 51).

At the meeting of the elected Sunday School Board at Ridgecrest, July 21–22, the action of the convention was the matter of major consideration. A joint committee (Plans and Policies and Broadman) had considered the matter in a serious discussion prior to the meeting of the full board. The general editor was invited to attend this committee meeting and to share in the discussion.

Following a report of the special committee and after hours of extended debate and prayerful consideration, the elected Board took the following action: "In response to the action of the Southern Baptist convention in St. Louis regarding Volume 1 of *The Broadman Bible Commentary,* we request and authorize the administration to seek to secure a new author for the Commentary on the text of Genesis, also to report to the January meeting of the Board the progress achieved and any developments or complications calling for further direction or authorization by the board" (see no. 52).

DeVaughn Woods presented the following motion, which was passed by the Board: "I move that we, as the elected trustees of the Sunday School Board, request the executive secretary to express to Dr. G. Henton Davies our very sincere and painful regret over the exceedingly unfortunate situation that has arisen in our denomination relative to Volume 1 of *The Broadman Bible Commentary* and that we assure him of our appreciation for his magnanimous spirit, of our respect for him as a Christian scholar, and of our earnest hope for further opportunities for fellowship with him in the service of our Lord—further that we record this as our official expression" (see no. 53). The executive secretary wrote to Davies, July 27, 1971, communicating to him the action taken by the board (see no. 54). Earlier, he had visited personally with Dr. Davies, who was visiting in North Carolina at the time.

The action taken by the elected Sunday School Board was communicated to all contributors to the *Commentary* by the general editor (see no. 55).

To implement the action taken by the elected Sunday School Board, the general editor recommended to the executive secretary that a conference be held with the two consulting editors—John I. Durham and Roy L. Honeycutt—to consider possible steps that might be taken to implement this action, particularly to consider what approach could be taken with integrity in a new treatment of the text of Genesis and what persons might appropriately be considered for the assignment. This conference was held on

Appendix VII

August 19. It proved exceedingly helpful as a basis for subsequent decisions (see no. 56 for a summary of the discussion and for a statement to guide in the new treatment of Genesis).

After reviewing the entire matter, the editors recommended that Clyde T. Francisco be invited to prepare the new treatment of Genesis. This was approved by the executive secretary, and a letter was addressed to Francisco relative to the assignment (see no. 57). The invitation to Francisco, of course, confronted him with a very serious problem of responsibility and relationships. His acceptance (see no. 58) included a request that the following statement be included in any press release: "My acceptance of this assignment does not imply my rejection of the previous work of G. Henton Davies, for whose doctrinal integrity I have the greatest respect, but is in response to the expressed desire of Southern Baptists for further discussion of the implications of current biblical studies for our common faith. My decision to undertake this task is based upon my confidence in the historical method of biblical study, the trustworthiness of the Bible, and the willingness of Southern Baptists to be open to truth wherever it may be found."

The general editor met with Francisco in a conference on October 1, arriving at mutual understandings as to the approach to be made and agreeing upon a schedule. At the time of the writing of this summary, Francisco has submitted a first draft of the Introduction to the treatment of Genesis and is at work on the commentary on the text.

A communication was sent to all contributors informing them of the invitation to Francisco and of his acceptance of the assignment (see no. 59).

It was, of course, hoped that the developments just recorded had opened the way for a final disposition of the problem which had arisen. However, a number of weeks prior to the Southern Baptist Convention in 1972, Gwin Turner, a pastor in California who had presented the original motion relative to Volume 1 to the Southern Baptist Convention in Denver, 1970, announced that he would offer a motion at the Southern Baptist Convention in Philadelphia, 1972, as follows: "That because a large segment of the entire set of *The Broadman Bible Commentary* (this far published) is out of harmony with the spirit and letter of 'The Baptist Faith and Message' adopted by this Convention, we request that the Sunday School Board withdraw from further sale the entire set, seek a new conservative editor, enlist a group of thoroughly conservative writers, and rewrite the entire set from a conservative viewpoint" (see no. 60). The form of the motion actually presented to the convention later was: "That because a large segment of the material of *The Broadman Bible Commentary* is out of harmony with the spirit and letter of 'The Baptist Faith and Message' adopted by this Convention, we request the Sunday School Board to withdraw from further sale the entire set, seek a new editor, and rewrite the commentary from the point of view that the Bible is 'truth, without any mixture of error.'"

This announcement precipitated extensive discussion in denominational papers and by many groups within the denomination. When the motion was presented to the Convention in Philadelphia, it was defeated by a very large majority, estimated generally as some four to one.

Summary letters were sent by the general editor to members of the Advisory Board and to all contributors on May 26, 1972 (see nos. 61, 62). These reflect an overall appraisal by the general editor of the contribution made by the contributors and by the Advisory board. A letter was also sent to the consulting editors (see no. 63) to express appreciation for their very major contribution to the publication of the *Commentary*.

Volumes 7 and 12 came from the press immediately prior to the Southern Baptist Convention in Philadelphia and were available for sale during the Convention.

EVALUATION AND SIGNIFICANCE

The *Commentary* is a balanced and responsible treatment of the background and message of the Bible in the light of the findings of historical research, the resources of biblical scholarship and theological thought, and the presupposition that the Bible is the inspired and authentic revelation of God and from God as the revelation came to fulfillment, ultimate meaning, and redemptive power in Jesus Christ. The *Commentary* reflects throughout the context in which it was conceived and produced: identification with, concern for, and full commitment (1) to reverent faith in the Scriptures as uniquely inspired and as the authority for all matters of faith and practice, and (2) to a thoroughly evangelical theological viewpoint of Christian doctrine and Christian experience.

The *Commentary* reasonably achieves the purpose stated in the concept document and the characteristics set forth in that statement. Admittedly, not all book treatments are on the same level. Not all books of the Bible are of like potential and value. The limitations of space and the demands of a publishing schedule were major factors bearing upon the work, both from the standpoint of the contributors and the editors. These factors, to a degree, affected the level of quality in achieving the ideal objective. Even so, the *Commentary* is a highly creditable piece of work in the field of biblical study. It comes short, in my judgment, more at the point of emphasis on the redemptive purpose of God and the redemptive thrust of the content of Scripture, at the point of emphasis on the intention of the scripture revelation to elicit meaningful response by Christians in terms of faith and holiness and service, and at the point of emphasis on the contemporary application to life in our time or on the fact that God is speaking to people now through the word of Scripture. This evaluation should not imply that the main thrust of the *Commentary* was intended to be on relevance rather than on meaning and interpretation.

Attention has been called to the fact that, as would be expected, the book treatments by the forty-seven different contributors are not of uniform quality. Various elements of strength and excellence apply in different treatments to: the Introduction, the organization of the material, clarity in dealing with technical matters, the balance between exegesis and exposition, attention to matters of greater significance or lesser importance, or the communication of relevance. It is not inappropriate to commend especially the contributions by the consulting editors. They had at least the advantage of involvement in the editorial process and a basis for clearer understanding of the overall objective and guiding principles. The general editor expresses the judgment that the treatment of Leviticus and the treatment of 2 Corinthians will rank among enduring commentaries on these books—and to single these out for special mention does not detract from the enduring value of all the book treatments individually and collectively that constitute the entire *Commentary*. Allowing for distinctive approaches and gifts on the part of different contributors, and the extremely diverse nature of the content of different books of the Bible, the *Commentary* is marked by general consistency in style and plan and approach to the biblical text.

The general articles are superior. While important subject areas had to be omitted due to lack of space, the articles collectively constitute a rich and fairly comprehensive coverage of material essential for introductory and background study. This material of course assumes the separate book Introductions.

The *Commentary* marks a significant advance by Broadman Press in the publication of serious books. This significance is much more than the scope of the publication in a twelve-volume series. It arises primarily from the potential of the *Commentary* as a continuing resource for serious biblical study by pastors and lay folk alike, a resource that has drawn from the wealth of modern biblical scholarship and the heritage of evangelical faith.

The *Commentary*, when it was projected, created the necessity for evaluating the resources of biblical scholarship among Southern Baptists and their competence to produce a commentary that would merit the respect of Christian scholars and, at the same time, be declarative of the genius and historic faith of Southern Baptists. I believe that the *Commentary* merits commendation in this respect. I believe that it will stand as a tribute to competent and reverent scholarship and to affirmative Christian faith.

The *Commentary* has been a medium of closer relationships between the Sunday School Board and the faculties of the six Southern Baptist seminaries, particularly the theological faculties. It has provided a medium of developing acquaintance and a growing understanding of mutual areas of responsibility and distinctive approaches and contributions to be made in the field of theological education and in the field of general Christian education for the people served by local churches. The *Commentary* has also provided a medium for a developing sense of interdependence and unity among seminary professors. They have felt their involvement in a denominational project very seriously related to the problems and concerns of biblical study and theological education.

The publication of the *Commentary,* as soon as the first two volumes came from the press, brought to the surface and into the open a widespread ultra-conservative doctrinal viewpoint in a large segment of Southern Baptist life. This viewpoint had to do primarily with a view of the nature of the Bible and principles of biblical interpretation, and arose from the widespread acceptance of traditional views about the nature of biblical inspiration. Other factors—denominational, psychological, and social—added complexity to the situation. This viewpoint manifested itself particularly among pastors. It is possible, perhaps probable, that the lay members of churches did not share the same degree of conservative viewpoint. Concern in this area found expression in the action of the Southern Baptist Convention in Denver, 1970, the facts relating to which have been recorded previously in this summary history of the *Commentary.* Thus the *Commentary,* because of the controversy that arose, became in some areas and to some degree a divisive factor in Southern Baptist fellowship. Almost certainly, the *Commentary* was not so much the occasion for a divisive spirit as it was the scapegoat of deep-rooted concerns and frustrations blending with a cultural climate, all of which created a reactionary spirit and lack of harmony.

There were, however, positive aspects of this total situation as well as negative ones. The *Commentary* has evoked widespread thought and discussion among Southern Baptists about the nature of the Bible, particularly a view of the inspiration of the Bible. This comment does not reflect a view that the fact of inspiration is held in question by Southern Baptists but that there are divergent views about the method of inspiration and what is meant by inspiration. The discussions relative to the *Commentary* also brought into focus a strong concern for freedom in one's approach to the Bible and in the matter of biblical interpretation, which freedom is of course so traditional and firmly established in Baptist life and history that one is surprised that ever authoritarian approaches could have been conceived or used as a basis of proposals for Southern Baptist Convention action. It is hoped that more recent developments in Southern Baptist life, stimulated certainly by the publication of the *Commentary*, give fresh hope for openness to truth in biblical study. It is hoped that the *Commentary* will be convincing support for the validity of the historical method in biblical study. The presupposition on which the *Commentary* was first conceived and projected and later published was the conviction that Southern Baptists are irrevocably committed to the priesthood of believers and the responsibility of individual Christians to interpret the Bible under the leadership of the Holy Spirit and in the light of all the facts that throw light on the background and the meaning of the Scriptures. It is surely hoped that the *Commentary* will have enduring value at this very point.

The *Commentary* gives promise of a deeper level of Bible study by pastors and lay folk in Southern Baptist churches. With this resource a growing number of people will come to a fuller understanding of the truth of the biblical revelation and as a result to stronger convictions about the eternal realities of the Christian faith and to a more mature commitment of devotion to Jesus Christ according to the teachings of the Scriptures.

The sales of the *Commentary* to date have not measured up to expectation, but in the light of all developments have been commendable and promising. The action of the Southern Baptist Convention in 1970, and again in 1971, a development without precedent in the life of the denomination, received attention nationwide in the press and easily lent itself to media and groups desirous to exploit the matter to attack the *Commentary* negatively. Thus, almost from the beginning, it encountered a prejudiced and hostile reception in some quarters. This closed some outlets of distribution. A by-product of this development was the psychological attitude that arose almost unconsciously on the part of advertising, promotion, and sales personnel that was negative in its impact on enthusiasm for the *Commentary*. The convention action in 1972 was not a commendation of the *Commentary* but an overwhelming refusal to sanction the effort to destroy the *Commentary*. While the controversy has encouraged some sales, the overall impact has been negative. Total sales up to June 30, 1972, were 92,134 (see no. 64 for a record of sales by volumes). With many hindrances to sales hopefully passed, with much favorable commendation by responsible reviewers, and with endorsement by many pastors and laymen as to values gained from the use of the *Commentary*, the future distribution of the *Commentary* for many years should be promising indeed.

Personal Appreciation

The general editor has written this summary story of the *Commentary* at the request of the Executive Office of the Sunday School Board. It seems appropriate to conclude the story with a statement of personal appreciation.

A Summary History of *The Broadman Bible Commentary*

The *Commentary* is the product of combined vision, concern, initiative, and work by many persons. Editors, contributors, designers, printers (Kingsport Press), Broadman Press management and personnel in many areas, and many other persons in supportive roles were the team that produced the *Commentary*. It should be recognized as a composite achievement. Special appreciation is due, however, to certain individuals:

To James L. Sullivan—for publishing vision and executive initiative, broad understanding of issues and problems theological and denominational, unfailing support of editorial personnel, unswerving commitment to the concept and goal for the *Commentary*, and courageous and wise leadership in facing unexpected and exceedingly complex problems and in seeking their solution in the total context of publishing responsibility and denominational relationships.

To William J. Fallis—for initiative and leadership in background exploration, mature judgment and keen insight related to factors involved in serious biblical study and interpretation, wise counsel in editorial decisions, and superior competence and skill in implementing the editorial process.

To Joseph F. Green—for resources of information related to literature for critical biblical study, penetrating insight related to issues to be faced in research and interpretation, leadership in developing guidance materials for contributors and copy editors, and helpful counsel in the ongoing editorial process.

To Ras B. Robinson—for concern that management functions should insure essential resources for the editorial task, loyal commitment to the purpose of the *Commentary* and the policies developed for the editorial responsibility, and encouragement to the editorial personnel during periods of negative reaction and criticism.

To Clara Odom—for patience, perseverance, awareness of involved factors in implementing a responsible printing schedule, and tireless attention to details in bringing printed volumes from the press.

To advertising and sales personnel of Broadman Press—for cooperation, expertise, and hard work to achieve favorable and widespread acceptance for the *Commentary*.

To copy editors—for long months of tedious and demanding work to insure consistent style and accuracy in references and countless details.

To many supporters—for enthusiastic commendation of this publication undertaking and prayerful support for a worthy product to assist many persons in a serious and rewarding study of the Holy Scriptures.

As the general editor, I should like to record a sense of deep appreciation for the assignment and opportunity to serve as the general editor. This has been a demanding responsibility and a richly rewarding learning experience. I have gained fuller knowledge and deeper understanding of the truth of the biblical revelation, and a greater awareness of the complexity of problems of biblical background and the factors affecting valid biblical interpretation. Withal, I have gained a stronger conviction that we have in the Scriptures the authentic word of God, given its full and final meaning in Jesus Christ, and that the Scriptures are the final authority for faith and practice under the lordship of Christ. My appreciation is for much more than a matter of personal enrichment; it is for the privilege of helping others to receive and to proclaim and to hear the word of God.

APPENDIX VIII
THE STORY BEHIND "ONE SONG"

PEPPER CHOPLIN

I had always considered myself a champion of cooperation between churches with different emphases. Choirs from our local association had worked closely during children's choir camps and other projects.

Venturing far from what I thought possible, I called a good friend to ask if he would like to combine our two choirs in a presentation of my new Easter musical, *Once Upon a Tree*. The North Carolina Symphony's new concert hall would be opening soon and I was audacious enough to want to have my work presented in the hall's early days of operation.

My friend was almost as excited as I was and agreed to check with his pastor and clear the date on his church calendar. Being encouraged by his response, I called a friend from a second church to invite his choir to join. This friend was also positive and checked with his pastor as well, responding almost immediately that their church was definitely on board.

When my first friend responded that his church was also ready to join, I told him of the good news about my second friend. All three of us were happy that we would have a sizable choir from the churches.

However, when the pastor of my first friend learned that the other church would be participating, he refused to have his church associated with the project. He emphatically instructed his Minister of Music to drop out.

Composer's notes printed by permission of Pepper Choplin. "One Song" is reprinted by permission of the publishers, Alfred Publishing Company, Inc. Sheet music is available from www.alfred.com.

It was my job to choose with which church we would participate. I immediately chose to go with the church that opted for cooperation rather than exclusion. Still, it truly pained me that fellow Baptists would refuse to cooperate with fellow Baptists because of mere association. This was not a giant mission project, it was not a theological seminar, but a very Biblical musical that would help listeners experience the story of the cross.

It seemed to be the last straw for me. My notion that intelligent and compassionate Christians of different points of view could still work together was severely challenged.

Unable to sleep that night, a simple folk-like melody came to mind. As I tiptoed downstairs to write it down, I reflected on what should comprise its text. Its thoughtful contour seemed to fit the subject that had robbed me of my sleep. And so I began to write the text for "One Song."

I have been surprised at how people from different backgrounds and denominations have felt *sure* that I had written about them or their church. Baptists do not have a monopoly on conflict. We see many dimensions of "holy war" as "brothers fight brothers in the name of the Lord." Yet as a composer and lyricist, I have not quite given up on the earthly dream and the heavenly certainty that one day we will stand before Christ, singing "One Song."

(You may visit Pepper Choplin's website at www.pepperchoplin.com to read more about him and his music. You can also hear a recording of "One Song" at www.pepperchoplin.com/onesong.ram.)

* close to "n."

* close to "n."

NOTES

FOREWORD I

1. For a popular history of the contentious dimension in Baptist life, see Walter B. Shurden, *Not a Silent People: Controversies that Have Shaped Southern Baptists* (Nashville: Broadman, 1972); rev. ed. with a new chapter on "The Fundamentalist-Moderate Controversy" (Macon, Ga.: Smyth & Helwys, 1995).

2. For an example, see Walter B. Shurden, ed., *The Struggle for the Soul of the SBC: Moderate Responses to the Fundamentalist Movement* (Macon, Ga.: Mercer Univ. Press, 1993).

3. SBC *Annual,* Southern Baptist Convention Executive Committee, Nashville, 1958, 430. The entire Branch Report, so named for committee chairman Douglas M. Branch, is found on 430–61.

4. The most conspicuous example of conflict precipitated in part by the implementation of Booz, Allen, and Hamilton recommendations at an SBC agency was the revolt of thirteen faculty members against the president of the Southern Baptist Theological Seminary in 1958. For an administrative appraisal, see A. Ronald Tonks, comp., *Duke McCall: An Oral History* (Brentwood, Tenn.: Baptist History and Heritage Society, 2001), 117, 127–30, 172–74. For a faculty attitude, see E. Glenn Hinson, "The Background of the Moderate Movement," in Shurden, *Struggle for the Soul of the SBC,* 12–14.

5. For a bristling critique of this trend in many areas of American life, with perceptive comments on the role of religion, see Christopher Lasch, *The Revolt of the Elites and the Betrayal of Democracy* (New York: W. W. Norton, 1995).

6. Martin B. Bradley, ed., "Handbook Issue," *Quarterly Review* 31, no. 3 (1971): 7.

7. "Constitution," Article 3 on membership, SBC *Annual,* Southern Baptist Convention Executive Committee, Nashville, 1979, 5.

8. William L. O'Neill, *American High: The Years of Confidence, 1945–1960* (New York: Free Press, 1986).

9. For a sweeping survey, see David Halberstam, *The Fifties* (New York: Villard Books, 1993).

10. The phrase is from Tom Shachtman, *Decade of Shocks: Dallas to Watergate, 1963–1974* (New York: Poseidon Press, 1983).

11. The "Death of God" theology was reported most conspicuously in the cover story of *Time,* Apr. 8, 1966, 82–87.

12. For a succinct account, see Jonathan Rieder, "The Rise of the 'Silent Majority,'" in *The Rise and Fall of the New Deal Order, 1930–1980,* ed. Steve Fraser and Gary Gerstle (Princeton, N.J.: Princeton Univ. Press, 1989), 243–68.

13. The literature on Falwell is now extensive, but it is insightful to study one of the earliest treatments by a sympathetic convert, Dinesh D'Souza, *Falwell Before the Millennium: A Critical Biography* (Chicago: Regnery Gateway, 1984), even though it was written when the author was only twenty-three years of age and was poorly edited by the publisher. In 2007, the year of Falwell's death, D'Souza issued an inflammatory work of radical conservatism, *The Enemy at Home: The Cultural Left and Its Responsibility for 9/11* (New York: Doubleday, 2007), that echoes a number of Falwellian themes and strategies.

14. Mark Wingfield, Associated Baptist Press news release, Aug. 16, 1994.

15. On this shift, see the many works of Earl Black and Merle Black, especially *The Rise of Southern Republicans* (Cambridge, Mass.: Belknap Press, 2002).

16. For a detailed study, see Oran P. Smith, *The Rise of Baptist Republicanism* (New York: New York Univ. Press, 1997).

17. For an analysis of this trend, see Dean R. Hoge and David A. Roozen, eds., *Understanding Church Growth and Decline: 1950–1978* (New York: Pilgrim Press, 1979).

18. The story was told from deep within the religious establishment by Dean M. Kelley, *Why Conservative Churches Are Growing* (New York: Harper & Row, 1972).

19. C. Peter Wagner, *Our Kind of People: The Ethical Dimensions of Church Growth in America* (Atlanta: John Knox Press, 1979).

20. For the presentations and responses, see *The Proceedings of the Conference on Biblical Inerrancy, 1987* (Nashville: Broadman, 1987). My comments on 61–65, 81–85 amplify on some of the matters under discussion here.

21. Arthur E. Farnsley II, "People Power: How Majorities Rule Denominations," *Christian Century,* Oct. 5, 2004, 39. This article is based on Farnsley's *Southern Baptist Politics: Authority and Power in the Restructuring of an American Denomination* (University Park: Pennsylvania State Univ. Press, 1994).

PREFACE

1. Carl L. Kell and L. Raymond Camp, *In the Name of the Father: The Rhetoric of the New Southern Baptist Convention* (Carbondale: Southern Illinois Univ. Press, 1999), 28–33.

2. Carl L. Kell, ed., *Exiled: Voices of the Southern Baptist Convention Holy War* (Knoxville: Univ. of Tennessee Press, 2006), xxxvii.

3. Charles W. Deweese, *Freedom: The Key to the Baptist Genius* (Brentwood, Tenn.: Baptist History and Heritage Society, 2006).

4. "Signs of the Times: Leonard Speaks on the Spiritual Smorgasbord of America," *Baptists Today*, Apr. 2006, 28–30.

5. Paul Pressler, *A Hill on Which to Die: One Southern Baptist's Journey* (Nashville: Broadman and Holman, 1999), x.

Chapter 1

1. Annual Church Profile, 2006, from www.sbc.net, LifeWay Christian Resources.

2. *Biblical Recorder* (North Carolina Baptist state paper), Apr. 15, 2006, 5.

3. Nancy T. Ammerman, *Baptist Battles: Social Changes and Religious Conflict in the Southern Baptist Convention* (New Brunswick, N.J.: Rutgers Univ. Press, 1990), 77–78.

4. Ibid., 78–79.

5. Ibid., 79.

6. Ibid., 134.

7. Ibid., 138–40.

8. Ibid., 148.

9. Ibid., 149.

10. Gregory Wills, "Who Are the True Baptists? The Conservative Resurgence and the Influence of Moderate Views," *Baptist Journal of Theology* 9, no. 1 (Spring 2005): 18.

11. Ibid., 18.

12. Shurden, *Struggle for the Soul of the SBC*, 19.

Chapter 2

1. Bruce McIver, *Riding the Wind of God: A Personal History of the Youth Revival* (Macon, Ga.: Smyth & Helwys, 2002), 52.

2. Ibid., 53.

3. W. F. Howard, A Word to Youth Revival Workers, June 12, 1947, photocopy of letter, in loose box, revival display, George Truett Theological Seminary, Baylor Univ., Waco, Tex.

4. Dr. Charles Wellborn, interview with author, Georgetown, Ky., Aug. 14, 2006.

5. Wellborn interview.

6. McIver, *Riding the Wind of God*, McIver interview with Justice Anderson, 224.

7. Ibid.,158.

8. Charles Wellborn, comp., *Youth Speaks: A Collection of Youth Revival Sermons* (Nashville: Broadman Press, 1949), 61–71.

9. Dr. John Wood, interview with author, Waco, Tex., Jan. 5, 2007.

10. Martin Marty, *Righteous Empire* (New York: Dial Press, 1970), 177.

CHAPTER 3

1. H. Leon McBeth, *The Baptist Heritage* (Nashville: Broadman Press, 1987), 679.

2. Ibid.

3. Roy Jennings and Ralph Elliott, "Six Years after the 'Message of Genesis,'" *Baptist Men's Journal*, Apr., May, and June 1968.

4. Roy Jennings, *Baptist Men's Journal*, Apr., May, and June 1968, 5–6, 7–8, 9–10, Clifton J. Allen Papers, Box 51-64, Southern Baptist Convention Library and Archives, Nashville (hereafter cited as Allen Papers).

5. Ralph Elliott, *The Genesis Controversy and Continuity in Southern Baptist Chaos: A Eulogy of a Great Tradition* (Macon, Ga.: Mercer Univ. Press, 2005), 7.

6. Ibid., 14.

7. Ibid., 68.

8. K. Owen White, ". . . Death in the Pot," *Baptist Standard*, Jan. 10, 1962, 6 (by reproduction from the Southern Baptist Historical Library and Archives, Nashville, July 20, 2006).

9. Elliott, *Genesis Controversy*, 70.

10. E-mail to the author, Sept. 25, 2006.

11. Ibid.

12. Letter to the author, Oct. 4, 2006.

13. Ralph Elliott, "The Pilgrimage of an Exile," Message Program #3023, http://30goodminutes.org/csec/sermon/elliott_3023.htm/.

14. *Encyclopedia of Southern Baptists*, vol. 4 (Nashville: Broadman Press, 1982), 2129–30.

15. Shurden, *Not a Silent People*, 117ff.

16. Jesse C. Fletcher, *The Southern Baptist Convention: A Sesquicentennial History* (Nashville: Broadman and Holman, 1994), 236–37.

17. James M. Wall, "Images of Southern Baptists in Contemporary America," *Baptist History and Heritage*, July 1980, 2ff., as cited in McBeth, *Baptist Heritage*, 100–101.

CHAPTER 4

1. Daniel Akin, "SBC Conservatives, Moderates Contrasted & Compared," *Pathway*, Aug. 17, 2004, http://www.mobaptist.org/thepathway/article20046.htm/.

2. William H. Stephens, "Significance of Fundamentalist Theology on Southern Baptist Convention Takeover," in *Texas Baptist Committed* online newsletter archive, May 1998, http://www.txbc.org/1998Journals/May98/May98SignificanceOfFund.htm/.

3. H. L. Turner, "Fundamentalism in the Southern Baptist Convention: The Crystallization of a Millennialist Vision" (Ph.D. diss., Univ. of Virginia, 1990), 3.

4. Morris H. Chapman, "The Fundamentals of Cooperating Conservatives," *SBC Life*, Aug. 2004, 1.

5. Ibid., 2.

6. Wills, "Who Are the True Baptists?" 18–35.

7. Ibid., 18–19.

8. Ibid., 19.

9. Ibid.

10. Cooperative Baptist Fellowship web site, www.thefellowship.info, Jan. 8, 2007.

11. *USA Today,* Jan. 23, 2007, 6D.

12. Cecil Sherman, class lecture given in 1987 at the Southwestern Baptist Theological Seminary, Fort Worth, Tex., on the "SBC Controversy," Cecil E. Sherman Papers, uncatalogued materials, Special Collections, Jack Tarver Library, Mercer Univ., Macon, Ga. (hereafter cited as Sherman Papers).

13. Ibid.

14. Bobby Ross Jr., "Baptists Still Debate Rightward Shift," *Tennessean,* June 13, 2004, 22A.

15. Larry L. McSwain, "Conservative Reform and Moderate Resistance in the SBC, 1979–89" (paper presented to the South Carolina Historical Society, Columbia, Nov. 13, 1989), 9.

16. Ibid.

17. Ibid.

18. Ibid., 10.

19. Cecil Sherman to the author, Nov. 19, 2005.

20. Ibid.

21. McSwain, "Baptists Still Debate," 13.

22. R. W. Williams, "The Role of the Peace Committee in the Southern Baptist Convention Inerrancy Controversy" (Ph.D. diss., Mid-America Baptist Theological Seminary, 2000), 66–67.

23. Ibid., 68.

CHAPTER 5

1. *Wikipedia,* the free online encyclopedia (accessed Mar. 2, 2007). This source is contributor composed, suggesting to many numerous weaknesses in trustworthiness. Recognizing the complaint, the Wikipedia staff has addressed these widespread concerns. On this site, I have found the sources accurate and well researched. I would recommend accessing the Wikipedia site on Fundamentalist Christianity and the Southern Baptist Controversy. I have accessed all of their links and found them useful and well supported.

2. Adapted from James C. Denison, "Inerrancy: Definitions and Qualifications," *Texas Baptist Committed* online newsletter archive, July 1994, http://www.txbc.org/1994Journals/July%201994/Jul94InerrancyDefinitions.htm/.

3. An excellent source for an overview of the inerrancy debate is Walter B. Shurden, *The Inerrancy Debate,* Interagency Council Forum, Jan. 2, 1980, Nashville, videotape.

4. William E. Hull, "Shall We Call the Bible Infallible?" *Baptist Program,* Dec. 1970, 5–6, 17–18.

5. John Finley, "SBC Presidents Before 1979: Just How Liberal Were They?" *Ethics Daily*, Feb. 19, 2003, http://www.ethicsdaily.com/article_detail.cfm?AID=2187/, reprinted with permission from EthicsDaily.com.

6. Clifton J. Allen, "Discussion Related to the Inerrancy of the Bible," Allen Papers, Southern Baptist Historical Library and Archives, Nashville.

7. Wills, "Who Are the True Baptists?" 30.

8. Ibid., 31.

Chapter 6

Epigraph: Thomas R. McKibbens Jr., "The Role of Preaching in Southern Baptist History," *Baptist History and Heritage Society* 15, no. 3 (July 1980): 30.

1. Ibid., 33.

2. Gerald Martin, ed., *Great Southern Baptist Doctrinal Preaching* (Grand Rapids, Mich.: Zondervan, 1969), as quoted in McKibbens, "Role of Preaching in Southern Baptist History," 35.

3. Kell, *Exiled*, xxxvii.

4. Farnsley, "People Power," 39.

5. J. L. Hensley, "Coping with Ministry in a Denomination and a Church Divided by Theological Controversy" (Ph.D. diss., Princeton Theological Seminary, 1999), 100.

Chapter 7

1. Ammerman, *Baptist Battles*, 178.

2. Paige Patterson, *Anatomy of a Reformation: The Southern Baptist Convention 1978-2004*, booklet (Fort Worth, Tex.: Southwestern Baptist Theological Seminary, Dec. 2004), 17–18.

3. Ibid., 18.

4. Ibid., 8.

5. Bill Leonard, "Unity, Diversity, or Schism: The SBC at the Crossroads," *Encyclopedia of Southern Baptists, Baptist History and Heritage* 16 (Oct. 4, 1981): 4–5.

6. Ibid., 7.

7. Cecil Sherman, "A Sense of Purpose—Text: John 17:20–23," president's address to the North Carolina Baptist Convention, Greensboro, Nov. 10, 1980, Sherman Papers.

8. Bill Wilson, "Why I Am Still a Baptist," *Baptist Heritage*, Sept. 2006, 1–2.

9. Anonymous state convention paper editor to author, May 2, 2005.

10. Leonard, "Unity, Diversity, or Schism," 2.

11. Kenneth Chafin, "Foreword," in Kell and Camp, *In the Name of the Father*.

12. Kell and Camp, *In the Name of the Father*, 128.

Appendix III

1. Reported in the 1978 *Annual* of the Southern Baptist Convention, p. 46, item 75, as Recommendation No. 13 of the Executive Committee, adopted on June 13, 1978. This action was initiated by a motion of Ray K. Hodge at the 1976 meeting in Norfolk on June 15, 1976, as reported in the 1976 *Annual*, p. 32, item 23, and p. 52, item, Southern Baptist Convention Executive Committee, Nashville.

2. Quoted by H. Wheeler Robinson, *The Life and Faith of the Baptists* (London: Kingsgate Press, 1946), 13.

3. Philip P. Bliss, "Wonderful Words of Life," in *Baptist Hymnal*, ed. Walter Hines Sims (Nashville: Convention Press, 1956), #181, refrain.

4. The basic texts of official denominational action in adopting Bold Mission Thrust are found in the 1976 SBC *Annual*, pp. 53–55, item 119; and in the 1977 SBC *Annual*, p. 37, item 57, Southern Baptist Convention Executive Committee, Nashville.

5. John Wesley wrote in his journal of June 11, 1739, "I look upon the world as my parish." John Bartlett, *Familiar Quotations*, 13th ed. (Boston: Little, Brown, 1955), 329.

6. On the 19 percent of American adults classified as "evangelical," see the 1979 Gallup Poll interpreted in *Christianity Today*, Dec. 21, 1979, 10–19. On the 47 percent of American adults classified as "conservative" ("right" of center), see the Gallup Poll of October 5–8, 1979, published as *Public's Political Philosophy* (Princeton, N.J.: American Institute of Public Opinion, Nov. 11, 1979). The most recent Gallup survey identified 17 percent, or 27 million, American adults as "evangelical." See *Emerging Trends*, Feb. 1982, p. 3.

7. The allusion is to the title of a pamphlet by J. M. Carroll published posthumously in 1931.

8. See Jesse C. Fletcher, *Bill Wallace of China* (Nashville: Broadman Press, 1963).

9. Thomas Jefferson to Dr. Benjamin Rush, Sept. 23, 1800, cited in Bartlett, *Familiar Quotations*, 374.

10. Ernest W. Shurtleff, "Lead On, O King Eternal," in *Baptist Hymnal*, ed. Walter Hines Sims (Nashville: Convention Press, 1956), #417, stanza 2.

11. Daniel W. Whittle, 'The Banner of the Cross," in *Baptist Hymnal*, ed. Walter Hines Sims (Nashville: Convention Press, 1956), #408, refrain.

Appendix VI

1. Walter B. Shurden, *The Baptist Identity: Four Fragile Freedoms* (Macon, Ga.: Smyth & Helwys, 1993), 9.

2. Ibid., 23.

3. Ibid., 33.

4. Ibid., 45.

5. Ibid., 7.

6. While this is not a direct quotation, it does capture the essence of the story of Joseph revealing his identity to his brothers found in Genesis 45:1–28.

CONTRIBUTORS

CLIFTON J. ALLEN (1901–1986) was the longtime editorial secretary for the Southern Baptist Sunday School Board in Nashville, Tennessee, and a former recording secretary of the Southern Baptist Convention. For more than twenty-five years, beginning in 1945, Allen broadcast the International Sunday School Lesson for Nashville's WSM Radio, and in later years he taught a version of the lessons for distribution to more than one hundred radio stations. Allen was a member of the Committee on the Uniform Series, International Sunday School Lessons, from 1942 until his retirement in 1968. He served as secretary of the Commission on Christian Teaching and Training for the Baptist World Alliance, and was chairman of that commission at his retirement. Allen was the author of 22 volumes of *Points of Emphasis,* a commentary on the International Sunday School Lesson, and following his retirement was general editor of the *Broadman Bible Commentary.* He received the E. Y. Mullins Denominational Service Award from Southern Baptist Theological Seminary in 1970. James L. Sullivan, retired president of the Sunday School Board and former president of the Southern Baptist Convention, called Allen "a brilliant scholar, a superb writer, and a denominational loyalist. He knew the Bible well, sought to be diligent in its teachings, and demonstrated with his life what he wrote with his pen." Allen was a graduate of Furman University in Greenville, South Carolina, and earned the Th.M. and Ph.D. degrees from the Southern Baptist Theological Seminary. In his earlier years, he served as pastor of churches in Kentucky and North Carolina before coming to Nashville in 1937 to take a position with the Baptist Sunday School Board.

LOYD ALLEN is Professor of Church History and Spiritual Formation at the McAfee School of Theology at Mercer University in Atlanta, Georgia. Allen previously was head of the Department of Christian Studies and Philosophy at Mississippi College in Clinton, Mississippi, and served as Associate Professor of Church History at The Southern Baptist Theological Seminary in Louisville, Kentucky, and as Assistant Professor in the Department of Christianity at Brewton Parker College in Mount Vernon, Georgia. Allen earned his bachelor's degree from the University of Montevallo in Montevallo, Alabama, and master of divinity and doctor of philosophy degrees from The Southern Baptist Theological Seminary. He is the author of *Crossroads in Christian Growth* and has contributed articles to numerous journals, books, and other publications, including *Christian Spirituality, Ties That Bind: Life Together in the Baptist Vision,* and *The Christian Century.* A Baptist by choice, he is executive director/treasurer of the William H. Whitsitt Baptist Heritage Society.

PEPPER CHOPLIN is Minister of Music at Greystone Baptist Church in Raleigh, North Carolina. An accomplished performing artist in voice, piano, and guitar, he is active as a studio musician and freelance composer and serves as composer/clinician at many events around the country. Choplin earned music degrees from the University of North Carolina/Greensboro and Southwestern Baptist Theological Seminary. You may visit his website at www.pepperchoplin.com to read more, and to hear a recording of *One Song* at www.pepperchoplin.com/onesong.ram

WILLIAM E. HULL is a renowned Baptist educator and author of many books on higher education and theology. A 1951 graduate of Samford University in Birmingham, Alabama, Hull is currently a Research Professor at Samford. He taught at Southern Baptist Theological Seminary from 1954 to 1975, as instructor, professor, dean and provost. From 1975 to 1987, he served as minister of First Baptist Church in Shreveport, Louisiana, before coming to Samford in 1987 to serve as provost and University Professor. Hull retired as provost in 1996, continued to teach at Samford for many years, and now serves as Minister in Residence at Mountain Brook Baptist Church. In addition to his Samford degree, Hull studied at the University of Gottingen, Germany and Harvard University, and earned a Ph.D. at Southern Baptist Theological Seminary. Hull is the author of five books on theology, chapters in 17 other books, and numerous articles in scholarly and denominational publications, and in 1999 received the Charles D. Johnson Outstanding Educator Award presented by the Association of Southern Baptist Colleges and Schools in honor of his significant contribution as author, lecturer and educator to Southern Baptist-related higher education.

BILL J. LEONARD is professor of church history at Wake Forest University Divinity School, Winston-Salem, North Carolina. He has held teaching posts at The Southern Baptist Theological Seminary, Samford University, and Seinan Gakuin University (Fukuoka, Japan). Leonard holds the B.A. from Texas Wesleyan College, the M.Div. from a Baptist seminary, and the Ph.D. from Boston University. He is the author or editor of 15 books, including *A Dictionary of Baptists in America, Christianity in Appalachia: Profiles in Regional Pluralism,* and *Baptist Ways: A History,* a survey of Baptist history from 1600 to 2000 (Judson Press 2003). His most recent book is entitled *Baptists in America,* published by Columbia University Press (2005).

JOE LEWIS is a graduate of Union Theological Seminary & Presbyterian School of Christian Education in Richmond, Virginia, where he received his M.Div degree in 1987 and his D.Min. degree in 2000. Lewis is the pastor of Second Baptist Church in Petersburg, VA, and at the time of the address served as secretary-treasurer of the Mainstream Baptist Network.

DUKE MCCALL has played an influential role among Baptists since his 1935 graduation as valedictorian at Furman University. At age twenty-five, he served as pastor of Broadway

Baptist Church in Louisville, Kentucky, and at twenty-eight became president of the Baptist Bible Institute (later New Orleans Baptist Theological Seminary). In his early 30s, he became the executive secretary of the Executive Committee of the Southern Baptist Convention. In 1951, at age thirty-seven, McCall became the president of the Southern Baptist Theological Seminary. Retiring from that position only in 1982, he served as president longer than any person in the history of that school. From 1980 to 1985, he served as president of the Baptist World Alliance. In 1990 he and several others formed the Baptist Cooperative Missions Program, an alternative channel for funding the Southern Baptist ministries, which soon transferred its resources to the Cooperative Baptist Fellowship (CBF). McCall's memoirs were released in 2002 with the title of "Duke McCall: An Oral History." That same year he was named to Mainstream Baptists' Hall of Fame for opposing the "legalism of SBC conservatism."

BRUCE PRESCOTT began his career as a police officer with the Albuquerque Police Department. After earning a B.S. in Corrections from the University of Albuquerque, he went on to earn Master of Divinity and Doctor of Philosophy degrees from Southwestern Baptist Theological Seminary. For twelve years he pastored Easthaven Baptist Church in Houston and was active in Texas Baptist affairs, serving as a member of the Executive Boards of Texas Baptists Committed and the Baptist General Convention of Texas, as well as on the Coordinating Council of the Cooperative Baptist Fellowship. Prescott presently is Executive Director of Mainstream Oklahoma Baptists in Norman, Oklahoma, and President of the Oklahoma Chapter of Americans United for Separation of Church and State. Prescott also hosts a Sunday morning radio show, "Religious Talk," and maintains the active Mainstream Baptist blog on blogger.com at mainstreambaptist.blogspot.com.

FOY VALENTINE led the Southern Baptist Convention's Christian Life Commission for nearly 30 years. A pioneering Baptist ethicist, Valentine earned a B.A. at Baylor University and an M.A. and Th.D. at Southwestern Baptist Theological Seminary, where he studied with the renowned Baptist ethicist T. B. Maston. Valentine became a forceful advocate for improved race relations and church-state separation, serving as president of Americans United for Separation of Church and State. A prolific writer on applied ethics, he founded a Christian ethics center at Baylor as well as *Christian Ethics Today,* a bimonthly magazine with a wide following. Throughout his career, Valentine was and still remains a hero to moderates because of his stands on racial integration and separation of church and state, and his fidelity to historic traditional benchmarks of Baptist principles. Valentine passed away in early January 2006 at the age of eighty-two.

DANIEL VESTAL is Coordinator of the Cooperative Baptist Fellowship headquartered in Atlanta, Georgia, the nation's largest Baptist organization outside of the Southern Baptist Convention. In 1990–91, he served as Chair of the Interim Steering Committee, the precursor to the Cooperative Baptist Fellowship. Vestal earned his B.A. and M.A. at Baylor University, and his M. Div. and Th.D. from Southwestern Baptist Theological Seminary. He served as pastor of several churches in Texas and in Atlanta, Georgia. His leadership of the developing moderate community during the conservative resurgence in the Southern Baptist Convention propelled him into the role of CBF Coordinator following the interim tenure of Cecil Sherman, and he continues in that role today.

INDEX

Abortion, xiv, xxix, 55
Abortionists, xxxiv
African American: Congregations, xxx; Pulpit, xxx
Akin, Daniel L., 180
Allen, Clifton J., 43
Allen, Loyd, 47, 111, 185
Alliance of Baptists, xxix, 53, 77, 79
Americans United, xiv, 130, 187
Ammerman, Nancy T., 3–4, 81
Anglican Puritan Separatists, 111, 131

Baker, B. O., 19
Baker, Richard O., 19
Baptist Faith and Message (1925, 1963, 2000), 4, 11, 35, 101, 158
Baptism, xx, xxviii, xxxvii, 79, 82, 84, 94, 112, 123
Baptist Press, 22, 178
Baptists: Alliance of, xxix, 53, 77, 79; Free, xxxvii; Committed, xxxix, 187; Moderate, xiv, xxx, 43, 69, 73, 77–78, 80, 84–86, 88, 139, Youth-led revivals, 24
Baylor University, xiv, 13, 15, 18–20, 23, 28, 187
Brannon, Richard, 19
Broadman Bible Commentary, 25, 42–43, 68, 141, 149, 153–54, 157–58, 185
Bush, George W., xvii
Bates, Carl, 58

Calhoun, John C., 43
Calvinism, xxviii

Camp, Ray, xxxiii, xxxiv, xl, xliv, 76, 87, 90–91
Campbell, Will, 119
Carter, Jimmy, xvi, xviii, 85, 113
Center for Biblical Studies, 67
Charismatic movement, xxviii
Choplin, Pepper, 90, 166
Christian Coalition, 126
Christian eschatology, 50
Civil Rights Act (1964), xvi, 8
Coggins, Ross, 19
Committee to Study the Total Southern Baptist Program, x
Conservative/fundamentalist, xxxiii, xl, xli, 1, 2, 10, 22, 52–53, 61–62, 73. *See also* Fundamentalist/conservative
Controversy, SBC, ix, xiv–xv, xvii–xviii, xxiii–xxix, xxxi, xxxiii, xli–xlii, xlvii, 17, 19, 23, 25, 27–31, 35–36, 42–43, 45– 69, 79, 82, 89–90, 100, 102, 152, 161–62
Cooper, Davis, 19
Cooper, Owen, 68
Cooperative Baptist Fellowship (CBF), xxix, xxxix, 47, 49, 52–53, 68, 77–78, 86–87, 119– 137, 187
Cooperative Program, xi, 59, 78, 87, 99, 137
Couch, Asa David, 19
Criswell, W.A., xiv, xvi, xxi, xxii, 43, 56, 65, 67, 100
Crumpler, Carolyn, xliv, xlvii

Davies, G. Henton, 42, 68, 152, 155–58
Dawson, J. M., xvii

Index

Dehoney, W. Wayne, 67
Denominational loyalists, 10, 12–13, 22, 57, 59–61
Democratic Party, xv, 9, 61
Dilday, Russell, 19
Dispensational premillennialism, 50
Draper, Jimmy, xvi, 81
Dunn, James, xliv, xlvii, 122
Durham, John I., 148, 157

Edward, W. Ross, 35
Elliott, Ralph, 23–25, 28, 31, 33, 36, 67
Episcopalians, xx, 8
Evangelicals, xiv, xx, 53–54, 116
Evangelism, biological, xx, xxviii, xxxiv, xxxviii, 79–80, 83, 87, 96, 99
Evelsizer, Zee, xlv
Exile, xxxvi, xxxviii, xlvii–xlviii, 17, 28–29, 36–42, 59, 76–78, 80
Exiled, voices of, xxxiv, xxxvi, xxxviii, xl, xlii, xliv–xlv, xlvii, 2, 10, 36, 74, 76, 85

Fallis, William, 31
Fanning, Buckner, 18
Farnsley, Arthur, xxvi
Faubus, Orval, 68
Freedom, xxxiv, xxxvi–xxxviii, 37, 40, 52, 61–62, 66, 70, 72, 76–77, 86, 88–89, 97, 112, 122, 127–28, 136–38, 140, 146, 152–53, 155; Academic, 32, 34, 60; Bible, xxxiv, 52, 137, 156, 161; Church, xxxiv, 53, 138; Individual, 7, 49, 51–53, 62, 73, 76, 121; Religious, xxxvii, 9, 12, 44, 51, 53, 69, 88, 137–38; Rhetoric of, xxxvi–xxxviii, 12, 22, 62, 80, 87, 90; to obey Christ, 112
Fundamentalist/conservative, 31, 51. *See also* conservative/fundamentalists

Gatlinburg Gang, 57, 59
Genesis, Book of, 23–24, 28, 31–32, 42
Genesis controversy, 23, 30–31, 35–36
Graham, Billy, xx, 113, 122
Graves, J. R., 27
Great awakening: First, 75; Second, 75
Great Commission, 99, 116
Grey, J. D., 67

Hamilton, James, Jr., xliii
Handel's *Messiah*, 93

Hays, Brooks, 68
Helwys, Thomas, 137
Hinson, Glenn, xxxix, 177
Historian, rhetorical, xliii, 81, 90
Hobbs, Herschel H., xii, 67
Holy Spirit, 1, 28, 52, 54, 70, 72, 76, 84, 100–01, 115, 162
Homiletics, xxxviii
Howard, W. F., 16–17

In the Name of the Father, xxxiv–xxxv, xl, xlii, xliv, xlvii, 11, 45, 72, 74, 85, 87, 89, 91, 100
Inerrancy, xxii–xxv, xxxv, xl, 44, 47, 50, 53, 57, 60–64, 66, 69, 72–73, 85, 89; Biblical, xxiii, xxviii, 48, 56–57, 61, 63–65, 67, 70, 72–73, 77–78; Conference on, xxiv; Scriptural, 5, 53–54, 70–71, 82
Inerrant, xxiii–xxv, xxxiv, xl, 1, 5, 9, 12, 23, 35, 43, 53, 60–62, 64–65, 71, 89, 114
Infallibility, xxxii, 27, 35, 63, 66–67
Interfaith alliance, 130
Israel, 21, 38–40, 50, 104

Jackson, Richard, 5, 57
Jehovah's Witnesses, xx
Jesus Christ, xxxv, 1, 11–12, 22–23, 25, 29, 65, 69, 72, 79, 88, 90, 103, 114–115, 118, 122–123, 128, 132, 147, 159, 162, 164
Johnson, Lyndon, xii, xvi

Kennedy, John F., xii, 45, 68

Landmarkism, 27
Langley, Ralph, 18
Lee, David, xlv
Lee, R. G., 65, 67–68
Lemay, Curtis, xiii
Leonard, Bill J., xlvii, 186
Lewis, Joe, 88, 133, 186
Lifeway Christian Resources, 2
Lindsell, Harold, xxiii
Lost Cause, 61
Luther Rice Baptist Seminary, 56

Mainstream Baptist Network, xxxix, 125, 139, 186
McAteer, Ed, 8
McCall, Duke, 67, 177, 186–87
McIver, Bruce, 15, 18

Index

McSwain, Larry, xxvii
Methodists, xx, 8
Midwestern Baptist Theological Seminary, 24, 28, 31, 35, 67, 148
Million more in '54, 23
Moderates, ix, xxvi–xxx, xxxiv, xxxviii–xxxix, xl–xlii, xlvii–xlviii, 2–3, 5–7, 9–13, 17, 36, 47–53, 56, 60–62, 67–69, 73, 75, 77–82, 84, 86, 136, 180, 187
Moody, Jess, 18
Moral majority, xiv
Mormons, xiv, xx
Myers, Phillip, xliv

Nashville, "SBC Vatican," xxi
Nazarenes, xx
New Baptist Covenant, xxx, 85, 139
Nixon, Richard M., xii
Norris, J. Frank, 27–28
North American Mission Board, 98–99
North Carolina Baptist Convention, 84

O'Brien, Bill, 18–19
O'Brien, Chester, 18
O'Brien, Dellanna, 19
Old Testament, 21, 31, 33, 50, 104, 106, 114, 135, 143, 148
One Song, 186; Sheet music, 90–91; Story of, 165–66
Ouachita Baptist College (University), xliii, 18
Owens, M. O., 43

Parks, Keith, 18
Paschall, H. Franklin, 68
Pastor's Conference, xxii, 11, 35
Patterson, Paige, xiv, xvi, xxv, 1, 10, 58, 64, 68, 82
Peace Committee (1985), 60
Pentecostalism, 50
Phelps, Ralph, 18
Pleitz, Jim, 57
Pollard, Frank, 57
Pollard, Ramsey, 67
Prescott, Bruce, 88, 125, 187
Pressler, Paul, xxv, xl, 1, 10, 56–68, 64, 67, 73

Rauschenbusch, Walter, 122
Ray, Sally J., xliv

Reagan Republicans, xviii, xix, 8
Religious Roundtable, xvi, xxix
Republican Party, 9, 61
Robertson, Pat, xvi
Rogers, Adrian, xvi, xviii, xxi, xxii, xxv, 6, 8, 56, 64, 81
Roman Catholic Church, 95, 115
Routh, Porter, 22

Seventh-Day Adventists, xx
Sherman, Bill, 19, 58
Sherman, Cecil, xliv, 5, 10, 19, 53, 57–58, 81, 84, 187
Shurden, Walter, 177
Simmons, Paul, xliv
South Carolina, xvi, xxvii, xliii, 43, 185
Southern Baptist Convention (SBC), ix, xxvii, xxx, xxxiv, xxxviii, xxxiv, xl, xlii
—Agenda, xxxiv
—Beliefs and identity in the, 4, 11
—Changes in, xxxiii, xlvii, 56
—Charter of the, 115
—Churches in the, 1–3, 79, 86, 102
—Constraints of, xxxvi
—Crisis in, 35
—Demographic/sociological measurement of, 3
—Denominational agencies of, xxxix
—Distinctive in the, 3
—Exiles of, xlviii, 2
—Fundamentalists in, 61
—Historical analysis of, xlviii
—Historical Society Library and Archives, xxxiii
—Inerrancy controversy in, 89
—Infrastructure of, 7
—Interracial aspect of, 96
—Issues confronting the, 24
—Leadership of, 2, 24, 51, 67, 98
—Loyalty to, 6
—Membership of, 61
—Message of, 22
—Moderates in the, 2, 11
—New, 56, 87, 89, 91
—Pastors Conference, xxii, 81
—Peace Committee (1985), 60
—Political party of, 61
—Programs of, 99
—Rhetorical approach/study of, xxix, 45, 57, 65, 78, 89–90

Index

Southern Baptist Convention (cont.)
—State conventions of, 96; 1960, 8; 1962, 35; 1965, 44; 1970, 42, 152–53, 158, 161, 162; 1971, 156; 1972, 158; 1979, xxii, 11, 35; 1980, xliii, 1, 78; 1981, 88
—Symbol for the, 113
—Takeback/takeover of, xl, xliv, xlvii, 62, 82, 84, 90
—Texas and Virginia, xxvii, xxix, 87
Southern Baptist Theological Seminary, 65, 97, 108, 148, 177, 185–87
Stanley, Charles, xvi, xxi, 8
Stephens, William, 47
Storer, J. W., 67
Suggs, Richard, 90
Sunday School Board, 22, 34, 42–43, 68, 141–46, 148, 151, 153–58, 161–62, 185

Tate, Marvin, 135
The Message of Genesis, 24–25, 28, 31–33, 35, 43, 67
The World Council of Churches, 94, 98

Thomas Road Baptist Church, xiv
Topoi, 77
Toy, Crawford H., 27
Truett, George W., xii, xvii

Valentine, Foy, 18–19, 21, 103, 187
Vines, Jerry, xii, xiv, xxv, 8
Voting Rights Act – 1965, xvi

W.A. Criswell Center of Biblical Studies, 56
Wall, James M., 44
Wallace, Bill, 117
Wallace, George, xv
Warren, C. C., 67
Webber, Jaroy, 67
Wesley, John, 116
White, K. Owen, 32, 35, 67
Whitsitt, William H., 27
Wills, Greg, 7, 73
Wilson, Bill, 85, 136
Wood, John, 19, 23

AGAINST THE WIND was designed and typeset on a Macintosh computer system using InDesign software. The body text is set in 10/13 Mercury and display type is set in Eurostile. This book was designed and typeset by Chad Pelton, and manufactured by Thomson-Shore, Inc.